Never Mind about the Bourgeoisie

Never Mind about the Bourgeoisie:
The Correspondence between Iris Murdoch
and Brian Medlin
1976-1995

Edited by

Gillian Dooley and Graham Nerlich

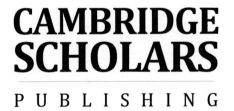

CAMBRIDGE
SCHOLARS
PUBLISHING

Never Mind about the Bourgeoisie:
The Correspondence between Iris Murdoch and Brian Medlin 1976-1995,
Edited by Gillian Dooley and Graham Nerlich

This book first published 2014

Cambridge Scholars Publishing

12 Back Chapman Street, Newcastle upon Tyne, NE6 2XX, UK

British Library Cataloguing in Publication Data
A catalogue record for this book is available from the British Library

ISBN (10): 1-4438-5544-8, ISBN (13): 978-1-4438-5544-0

CONTENTS

LIST OF ILLUSTRATIONS

Iris Murdoch and John Bayley at Cedar Lodge, Steeple Aston

Brian Medlin in the arms of the South Australian Police, 1970s

Iris Murdoch in London 1988

Iris Murdoch and John Bayley in London 1988

Facsimile: Card from Iris Murdoch to Brian Medlin [Letter 13, 1989]

Facsimile: Iris Murdoch to Brian Medlin [Letter 22, 1991]

Book launch at Flinders University, 1992.

Brian Medlin with Syd Harrex, Flinders University, 1992

Christine Vick in the Wirra in her Prospect garden

Brian Medlin with 'Truth' statuette given to him in 1970 by a supporter

The house in Hamilton Road, North Oxford, where Iris Murdoch and John Bayley lived from 1986 to 1989

Iris Murdoch and John Bayley in Japan in 1995

Brian Medlin picnicking on McKenzie Creek, Victoria.

Brian Medlin just before his death in 2004

INTRODUCTION

Iris Murdoch (1919-1999) visited Australia just once, in 1967, on a British Council trip with her husband, John Bayley. Her host in Adelaide was philosopher Brian Medlin (1927-2005), whom she had met six years earlier when he was a Research Fellow with Bayley at New College, Oxford. Recalling that trip more than forty years later, Bayley told me that their time in Adelaide with Brian was happier and more successful than their sojourns elsewhere in Australia.[1]

After that visit, they never met again. Plans for Medlin to visit England never came off, and despite all her travels, Murdoch never came so far south again. This correspondence bears witness to a friendship between them which nevertheless continued for more thirty years, until she was claimed by the "very, very bad, quiet place" that is Alzheimer's Disease.[2]

At the time of Murdoch's visit to Adelaide, Medlin had just been appointed Professor of Philosophy at the newly-founded Flinders University, ten kilometres south of the city of Adelaide, where he was to remain, more or less uneasily, until his retirement in 1988. He was impatient with bureaucracy and one of his worst terms of abuse was "vice-chancellor." During the 1970s, he had been a leader of the campaign against the war in Vietnam and a high-profile player in the radical student protests which caused much division in the University, including a lengthy occupation of the Registry building in 1974.

Murdoch was a dedicated and prolific correspondent. Many collections of her letters survive, and some are now held in the Centre for Iris Murdoch Studies at Kingston University. However, she "habitually destroyed all letters she received,"[3] so although she corresponded with dozens of people and "spent up to four hours a day writing letters,"[4] it is

---

[1] John Bayley, pers. comm., Oxford, 8 October 2010.

[2] Joanna Coles, "The Joanna Coles Interview: Duet in Perfect Harmony," *From a Tiny Corner in the House of Fiction: Conversations with Iris Murdoch* ed. Gillian Dooley (Columbia: University of South Carolina Press, 2003) p. 246.

[3] Anne Rowe, "Those Lives Observed: The Self and the 'Other' in Iris Murdoch's Letters," *Life Writing: The Spirit of the Age and the State of the Art* ed. Meg Jensen and Jane Jordan (Newcastle: Cambridge Scholars, 2009) p. 212n(3).

[4] Peter Conradi, "On Iris Murdoch's Pen-friendships," *Iris Murdoch News Letter* 19 (Autumn 2006) p. 21.

both rare and fortunate that many of Brian Medlin's letters to Iris Murdoch survive, in electronic copies that he kept. He was an early adopter of word processing and was prescient enough to save his files and maintain them so that when his papers were donated to Flinders University Library in 2008, some three years after his death, Microsoft Word files of letters written as far back as 1986 were included on CD ROM.

The earliest letters from Murdoch apparently date from 1976 and 1977 (she rarely included the year of writing on her letters, and sometimes there is no date at all). In these early letters she refers to letters from Medlin, but these do not survive. Then there is a gap of about nine years before contact is re-established. In a letter of May 1986 from Murdoch, she thanks Medlin for his letter, and in his response he reproaches himself "for having lost contact." He certainly made up for his neglect over the next six or seven years, pouring about 60,000 words into the correspondence. Some of these words were copied and pasted into the letters from elsewhere: letters to other friends and colleagues, articles, talks or reviews he wanted to share with her. But much of it was written especially for her. In particular, there is an immensely long letter of almost 28,000 words, written over the course of a year, between May 1988 and May 1989, recounting trips into the Australian bush, with explanations of Australian flora and fauna and natural history in general, quotations from bush ballads and anecdotes about his travels with his partner, Christine Vick.

For Murdoch's part, she writes with affection, but not at such length. A recurring theme in her letters is their divergent political beliefs, which she seems keen on clarifying. In the first letter in the collection, from July 1976, she notes that "we might ... differ on general principles. I am increasingly hostile to the extreme left in Europe. ... I wonder if we agree—or do you want an eastern Europe style socialist state. ... Are you a 'Marxist'? What are you, exactly, politically, if that isn't a silly question? Anarchist? Not Stalinist obviously. Maoist? Or—?" In 1986, she asks again, and in the first of his letters included here he replies, "I am a passionate, but not a bigotted socialist. Jeeze, if you ruled out people who were politically shonky, you wouldn't have any friends at all." Once again, in 1991, she asks, "How much Marxism is still with you I wonder. ... I suspect we might disagree about art ... I expect I am by your standards bourgeois." His response:

> I wouldn't be surprised if I were to find your views on art "Bourgeois." Some of the best views abroad are. And what Marxism can be made to tell us about art, in so far as it is correct, is at least woefully incomplete.

They bandy the word backwards and forwards for a while, until she says, in 1992: "My heart is with you—never mind about the bourgeoisie," and he replies, "though I *do* mind about the bourgeoisie—mind very much too—and though you are doubtless culturally and ideologically deprived in not being a child of the working class, and though you are certainly culturally intimidating to a child of the working class, my heart is with you. So there!"

They compare notes about writing. Medlin wrote stories and poems as well as philosophy, but published little. He sent some of his work to Murdoch and she was warmly encouraging, offering to show his stories, written under the name Timothy Tregonning, to her publisher. Although he agreed, nothing seems to have come of it. She also talks about her own writing, though not in any great detail. When beginning the novel that became *The Message to the Planet* she wrote,

> It's an uncomfortable time starting to invent the new one—a lot of <u>bad</u> ideas rush in, & have to [be] thrown out (indeed <u>destroyed</u>).

He, in turn, was deeply appreciative of her novels, writing an enthusiastic critique of *The Book and the Brotherhood,* and concluding,

> I have got so much from your novels, especially in recent years, that they have become, like Yeats' close companions, a portion of my life and mind, as it were. I am deeply your debtor, mate. I love you lots, Iris.

Later, during the writing of *The Green Knight,* she asks him for some guidance in writing dialogue for an Australian character. This produces one of the most amusing passages in the letters. Medlin is in his element, expounding at length the variations on the word and concept "bastard," and rounding the discussion off with, "As for 'a really good guy', the national experience is so poor in examples that we haven't developed any language to accommodate them." As I have argued elsewhere, his advice seems to have had little effect on Murdoch's depiction of Australia and Australians.[5] Despite Medlin's insistence to the contrary, she seemed content to idealise the country as an untouched wilderness, full of unique and remarkable wildlife and individuals, remote from the degenerate messiness of European politics and ideas.

---

[5] For a detailed discussion of this linguistic exchange, see Gillian Dooley, "'You are my Australia': Brian Medlin's Contribution to Iris Murdoch's Concept of Australia in *The Green Knight,*" *Antipodes* 25: 2 (December 2011) pp. 157-162.

They both loved singing. Murdoch recalls hearing Brian sing at New College, and laments that "People don't <u>sing</u> much in Oxford now. Except for the Warden of New College who is a talented pianist, and sings a lot of Cole Porter etc. if encouraged—and even if not." Medlin was not keen on Cole Porter: he loved Australian bush ballads, constantly quoting their laconic lyrics, but in the later letters complains of being unable to sing any more. In 1991 he was diagnosed with "a demyelinasing peripheral neuropathy. There! That's certainly better than ontological relativism!" The neuropathy made singing and even speaking progressively difficult, and threatened to curtail his bushwalking and the active physical life he enjoyed. Murdoch's own health was clearly failing as the correspondence draws to a close. She often complains of exhaustion, though well into the 1990s she was still travelling overseas and dutifully, if reluctantly, making speeches when asked. The final letters are heartbreakingly simple: "Dearest Brian, I wish I had written to you long ago now—how was this? I cannot feel the <u>time.</u>" This brief note, undated, has a postscript: "Also; love, mortality and the meaning of life." And with this, the correspondence is at an end.

There are more intimate and sensational letters from Iris Murdoch now available, including her wartime letters and diaries,[6] letters from the 1960s to a young friend, David Morgan,[7] both published in 2010, and other letter collections held in the Iris Murdoch Archive at Kingston University. The correspondence with Medlin is the record not of a passionate entanglement but a deeply affectionate relationship between two highly intelligent, articulate and philosophically sophisticated beings. Medlin confides in her many of the everyday woes of his work and family life, and shares with her his passion for the Australian natural world and his apprehension of the threat of its imminent destruction, for the unique culture he sees being weakened by encroaching Americanisation, for cricket, and for his friends and family. She is sympathetic and encouraging, and disarmingly modest, especially about her philosophy, but offers few personal confidences in return. The most striking proof of her regard for Medlin, perhaps, comes not in the letters so much as in the review she wrote, at his request, of his monograph *Human Nature, Human Survival* (1992). The letters written at the time show how difficult she was finding this task, and record Medlin's astonishment when she sent not the 800 words she had been asked for, but a handwritten review of 4000 words. Medlin cut it down, scrupulously

---

[6] Iris Murdoch, *A Writer at War: Letters and Diaries 1939-1945* edited and introduced by Peter J. Conradi (London: Short Books, 2010).
[7] David Morgan, *With Love and Rage: A Friendship with Iris Murdoch* (Kingston: Kingston University Press, 2010).

retaining all her disagreements with his argument, to 1000 words before it was published in the *Age* newspaper in February 1993. Her complete text, thoughtful, sympathetic but by no means uncritical, is reproduced here for the first time.

Gillian Dooley

PERSONAL REMINISCENCES
OF BRIAN MEDLIN

Brian Medlin was a philosopher, activist, poet and cultural intellectual. These letters to Iris Murdoch are written during his later life in Adelaide. He was educated here and came back to the city as Professor of Philosophy at Flinders University in 1967. He was a prominent identity in the city. He was a remarkable person of prodigious and varied abilities.

I met Brian in 1950 or thereabouts when we were students together in philosophy and English literature at the University of Adelaide. Earlier, we had been at the same secondary school (Adelaide Technical High School). He taught there briefly when I was a schoolboy; I knew of him, although we never met there. I had the good luck to be close mates with him when we were young and I was foolish. We first met each other at parties and bars.

I was 19 and he was 21 or so. Two things drew us together: philosophy and literature—ponderous as that sounds for something that was huge fun for us both. I was an amateur actor, keen on reading poetry aloud; he wrote it and went to the theatre. A bit later, theatre put me in touch with Charles Jury[1] so I joined a small circle that met to drink at the South Australian Hotel on Saturday afternoons. Brian, Charles and John Bray[2] were among them. Outside the pub, Charles was hugely hospitable to us; we revelled in it. As students we also often met walking to classes and, with others, too, deviated to the Richmond bar instead. For me it was an explosive extracurricular education. We were both invited to join the Jury "Poetry"—a more sober group, but not at all solemn. We both belonged to the Poetry when he died. I still do.

---

[1] C.R. Jury (1893-1958) poet and Jury professor of English Language and Literature, University of Adelaide. Medlin and Nerlich were among his students in the same years. He quickly saw Medlin's outstanding abilities and they became very close friends.

[2] The Hon. J.J. Bray AC, Chief Justice of the Supreme Court of South Australia, 1967-78, Deputy Lieutenant Governor of the State and Chancellor of the University of Adelaide 1968-78. He was Medlin's closest friend in the period of the letters and is mentioned in several of them.

I know Brian's early poetry best—some of it, I think, never revised or published. Sometimes I'd hear him read it with the ink barely dry on the page. I still have by heart his "Dedication"[3] and "For Margaret" about his dead sister. They were fine, contrasting poems each magical to me. I admire them as much as anything he wrote. In an early unrevised poem about himself—there may have been only handwritten copies—he wrote, partly in jest, "I, God's beloved larrikin ..." That note is often struck in the letters. It sat easily beside more distinguished themes.

He was born in Orroroo, a small country town in the mid North of the state. Some of that life appeared in his Tregonning stories. He told me that, as a child, he often used to strike out into the country alone, with a rifle and a swag to live off what he could find, for many days at a time. His experiences in the far north of the country soon after he left school—droving, horse breaking and the like—left strong, enduringly vivid impressions. That shows in the imagery of the Dedication poem. He loved the country, its toughness, challenge and beauty. The letters are full of that love.

We met often in the years to 1956 when I left Adelaide for postgraduate studies at Oxford. He followed that route in 1958, but we saw little of each other in Britain. I came back to Australia to teach at the University of Sydney in 1962 and Brian returned to Brisbane later in that decade. We swapped letters occasionally and met at conferences or passing through. I returned to Adelaide in 1974, where Brian then occupied the chair of philosophy at Flinders University. That department, as a body, had pursued a committed opposition to the war in Vietnam and remained a radical politicised group. I sympathised much with the former, far less with the latter, aim. We swapped letters and I saw him and Christine from time to time at their Prospect home and elsewhere. I last saw him at what might be called an advance wake. All of us knew he was dying but it was an evening of fun, reminiscence and celebration.

Brian saw philosophy as the deepest study aimed at moral and political thought and practice. He took a broad, generous view of its scope. He told me that the problems we got so excited about as students now seemed to him empty and trivial. I strongly disagreed while conceding that their role in practice was sometimes remote. The early days were exciting for me; the challenges to reason, both for and against it, rattled my cage, blew my mind. They still do. They were and are bedrock. They aren't for everyone,

---

[3] Published in *Meanjin* 11, no. 4 (Summer 1952), p. 352.

but for those with the philosophical gene (as David Stove[4] used to call it) they remain spellbinding and, for me, at the core. Brian thought me hide- (or perhaps ivory tower-) bound, a captive of bourgeois attitudes. I am both a sceptic and a pessimist about political theory and action. For all its grievous faults, western society is better than others that have endured. I have a deep mistrust of the upshot of revolutions and little hope about humanity's future. I feared that his students were more likely to focus on changing their world than on understanding it. I responded to his attitude to me by suggesting that he might have sold his philosopher's birthright for a pot of message. Such unkind thoughts troubled Brian not at all; his of me, somewhat. I have no doubt about the importance of what he worked on in the main period of the letters.

Brian told Murdoch that he *meant* his "Dedication" poem and he surely pursued that commitment. More than anyone else I have known he not merely lived his life but *led* it—made it an object to be considered, constantly appraised and examined, aimed at realising to the best of his abilities, what he valued most. That was the betterment of human life—its progress toward more generous, egalitarian, cultivated, considerate and caring attitudes, practices and institutions as regards both people and their environments. He was the outstanding figure here in the Moratorium protests against this country's involvement in the Vietnam War. He never sought to be its leader. Indeed he worked assiduously to promote discussion, debate and an egalitarian sharing of the direction of the movement. Perhaps his greatest achievement was himself, and the way he lived. It was a work of high moral art, done without posturing, artifice or contrivance. Donald Brook[5] once said to me "Brian tries harder than the rest of us to do what he thinks is right." That's surely true. From so formidable a trier as Donald, it's distinguished praise. He strove for what I'd call called nobility—in a sense that he might not have rubbished: he carried it with a light, ironical touch. All this shows in his letters.

I've been lucky to have many bright people as friends, but no one's company has ever bettered Brian's. So vivid, so intelligent, such wonderful style, often affectionate, often abrasive, always flying high—a distinguished larrikin, too. His talk was superbly witty, amazingly trenchant and imaginative, full of novelty and wonderful jokes. People talk, often glibly I think, of passionate commitment and concern. You couldn't miss Brian's passion. His eagerness for truth, his concentrated

---

[4] David Stove (1927-94) was a philosopher of science at the University of Sydney. He was a witty and accomplished thinker and stylist. Medlin calls him "my wonderful indispensable enemy."

[55] Donald Brook was formerly the Professor of Visual Art at Flinders University.

setting of himself to judge by what really was there in the world, independently of his own hopes and fears—that's *passionate* detachment, *passionate* objectivity. On the trail of truth he was keen as a Spartan hound, as Plato says of Socrates. None of it blinded him to its ironies. His affection could be the soul of tenderness. (See his funeral address for Bill Ivey.) The dynamics of his talk made you catch your breath. Such a range of information, analytic power and penetration at his fingertips all the time—just astonishing! I won't meet anyone like him again. It's been a privilege.

He was brave and bold. Some letters suggest more—daring and delight in dangerous challenges. He was strongly committed to non-violent civil disobedience. He was arrested in a Moratorium rally and later, briefly, jailed. A photo appeared in the *Advertiser* of Brian in the grasp of police, shouting "No violence" to his followers—daring enough. He had much to do with the police at this time, with some of whom there was mutual liking and respect.

Unsentimental love is the broad current of this correspondence, much of it impersonal. His affection and admiration for Murdoch pervades the letters. So does his love for Christine, his family and for his many mates. But the dominant, detailed and pervasive theme of the correspondence is his love of Australia, for the land, its fauna and flora, and for a main aspect of its culture, the culture of the bush and for the styles of personality and character he found there. The letters are often focussed, detailed, objective miniatures, a kind of album of Australia; that is their overarching aim and achievement. It is a celebration of all this by one who sees it as passing. He observes and records this in fine detail and with a persistent accuracy and fidelity that is surely loving. The passion lies in the objectivity, the care to set things down just as he sees them, in a truthful, generous unindulgent gaze. The correspondence is, thus, a remarkable, perhaps a unique, document of our country.

Murdoch applauded Medlin's view that "philosophy is about the texture of human life. Philosophy is about getting life right and making life right." Very few letters contain "slabs of philosophical argument" but they vividly display the texture of Medlin's life and how he lived this part of it.

Some reproachful letters late in the correspondence are addressed to, or mention, me. Candour prompts me as a co-editor of this volume to say something about two matters in them.

On Medlin's retirement I was appointed a member of The Committee of Review of the Philosophy Department and of Medlin's tenure as its Chairperson. I saw this as a review of his custodianship of the Department rather than about his capacities as a teacher and researcher. Since we disagreed about this more than I think Brian realised, I did not welcome the appointment. Had it been a review of his capacities we would have had little to disagree about. Murdoch's review of his *Human Nature, Human Survival* reflects her judgement of his abilities and of the quality of that work. It is a very perceptive account of these matters and in no way overestimates his achievement.

The Review Committee report was a painful issue for us both. Confidentiality forbids my discussing its processes. I was by no means an eager member. Experiences of politicised teaching in Sydney when I was there in 1973 convinced me that the damage done locally to universities was by no means matched by gains on the national political level, although the sorry days that have followed are not explained by it. I sometimes supported Brian's role at Flinders against internal attacks on him there. My political scepticism–pessimism had made me less than enthusiastic. I was unhappy at some achievements he was proud of. I think they eventually fostered the growth of postmodernism and what passes for its philosophy. We equally deplored its relativism and subjectivism. I was surprised and dismayed by how important the review was for him, given his rather dim view of Flinders and of academic committee processes and their values. I was grieved—still am grieved—at having played a part in his strong disappointment. Perhaps his view of my role was just. But I was never strongly sympathetic with what he saw as his achievements there.

Then there is the "slab of philosophical argument" directed at me. The theory of personal omnipotence that he ascribes to me left me bewildered at the time. He did not quote anything that I wrote. It is obviously an untenable theory and he certainly showed that it is. I am now confident that he refers to my outline of a different theory prominent in Hegel's philosophy. Since it is rather close to views held by Marx and, indeed, by Brian himself, it may be useful to sketch them.

For a time I was briefly but keenly interested in Hegel's philosophy although never a disciple of it. Crudely, Hegel was a pantheist who saw a divinity in human conscious life, in its transformation of the world through thought and action, and its progressing unity with that world. This was Spirit or God—God as immanent in human life. Spirit fully realises itself and comes to an identity with the world when it fully understands it and thereby fully controls it. Spirit as God cannot fail to complete this project and realise itself. This constitutes its omnipotence and omniscience. The process is dialectical, Spirit resolving contradictions in a series of higher syntheses although with partial success since each breeds a further contradiction. Finally History, i.e. Spirit's journey, does come to an end, arriving at the final perfect synthesis. The modern mind boggles at this but many of the details of the argument are thoroughly arresting and insightful. It is by far the most imaginative and interesting philosophy of religion. But I am no less opposed to religions than Brian was.

A famous theme in Marx springs from this. He writes: "Therefore, mankind always sets itself only such tasks as it can solve ..." The thought that humankind *can* always solve the problems it sets itself is startling. It does not follow from Marx's version that it *will* solve them. But it does state a kind of omnipotence. Of course neither of these theories states nor suggests that individuals might be omnipotent.

Brian himself states a not dissimilar view of life in one of his poems which I had not read at the time in question:

> ... for I have held,
> For half my life, hard to the faith
> That a clear mind can do something with
> Any known phenomenon,
> And everything that can be done
> Will be done, if only we're able
> To render the world intelligible.
> In this faith I have written well
> And for it lost the clumsy skill
> Of setting down upon a page
> Those inarticulate cries of rage.

The poem reminds me of a perceptive remark made by our mutual friend Charlie Martin. It was about Brian's attitude towards his enemies. "Hate was never an option for Brian. Anger would have to do."

Graham Nerlich

EDITORS' NOTE

Iris Murdoch's letters are all hand-written on unlined letter paper, aerogrammes, or occasionally greeting cards. The originals are held in the Medlin Collection, Flinders University Library. They have been transcribed by the editors. The numbers assigned to her letters were based on their physical order in the collection. This is not chronological, as few of the letters were immediately able to be dated with certainty; and by the time an approximate chronological sequence was established, this numbering system had already been used in at least one publication. It has therefore been retained for convenience.

Brian Medlin's letters were provided by his literary executor on a CD ROM as a series of Microsoft Word documents each numbered with a code beginning "MDC." These code numbers have been retained, although once again they do not reflect a chronological sequence.

Before his death, Brian Medlin made it clear to his literary executors that they should not make public any material that would disclose private affairs of close family members. This instruction has precluded publication of several passages concerning his son Bruno and his wife Christine, among others.

Murdoch's letters—and Medlin's, as edited by his executors—indicate that at times Bruno's behaviour caused Medlin considerable anguish. In spite of his and Christine's extensive efforts to counsel and assist Bruno, Medlin's anguish persisted on and off for the duration of this correspondence.

Naturally, Brian and Christine had some matters of which they spoke only, and in confidence, to intimate friends. Murdoch became privy to some such, but in accordance with Medlin's wishes passages in several letters have not been made available to the editors of this publication. These passages are indicated by ellipses in square brackets. Apart from these omissions, all the extant correspondence between Murdoch and Medlin has been included.

The letters have been lightly edited, with obvious errors silently corrected. Illegible or uncertain transcriptions have been indicated. Murdoch often made marginal notes which are difficult to reproduce in printed layout. They have been included as footnotes attached to their approximate location in the text. Occasionally Medlin jotted names, phone numbers and other brief notes on Murdoch's letters. These have not been included.

Medlin's formatting has been retained in most cases, although it has occasionally been altered either to standardise the letter headings, or for greater clarity.

ACKNOWLEDGEMENTS

The Editors are grateful to John and Audi Bayley for permission to reproduce Iris Murdoch's letters and her review of Brian Medlin's book, and to Christine Vick for permission to reproduce Medlin's letters. Thanks are also due to Peter Conradi and Ed Victor for their assistance in liaising with Murdoch's executors, and Wallace McKitrick for assistance in liaising Medlin's.

The extract from the *Adelaide Review* on page [38] is used with permission of the publisher.

THE LETTERS

Iris Murdoch to Brian Medlin
[Letter 12]

Cedar Lodge, Steeple Aston, Oxford
July 2 [1976?]

Dear Brian, thanks for your <u>super</u> letter & the broadsheets—I am very interested indeed in all you say. I wd have replied sooner only I've been obsessively trying to finish some stuff (on Plato: you wouldn't like it!)[1] and also dealing with a host of problems, my mother ill & staying here,[2] and so on. How I wish we could meet and talk. I don't often have <u>proper</u> philosophical or political discussions these days. About politics: your scene is, I think, very different from ours here, though we might also differ on general principles. I am increasingly hostile to the extreme left in Europe. I think there is an <u>irresponsible</u> drive to the left (judging from the left Labour Party here) which may land us all (one day) in the kind of regime which the Poles and Czechs now enjoy.[i] (I've visited Poland and Czechoslovakia lately—& people there watch our "lefties" with horrified amazement!) One is jolly lucky to have a parliamentary democracy: the thing is to make it <u>work</u>. Pushing <u>inside</u> it will get one a long way, actually. I wonder if we agree—or do you want an eastern Europe style socialist state? I am extremely interested by your account of your life & its changes. I'd love to see what you write, prose & poetry.[3] Tom Collins I read with the greatest pleasure before I visited Australia—he was an excellent introduction to your marvellous country.[4] Yes, I think things may be different with you in some ways. There's less <u>stuff</u> around from the past. I do wish I cd just take a 'plane & turn up! I hope I <u>may</u> be in Australia in 1978—but that's so far ahead & anything may prevent it.

   I fear you might also find me reactionary about student participation![5] (I don't teach now, so I am out of the latest dramas, here, which are not extreme, thank God.) I think students should be taught genuine objective things like history, languages, art (of course no teacher can be entirely objective, but he can try) and not led too much into "self expression"! This of course begs the question about "Marxism." Are you a "Marxist"? What are you, exactly, politically, if that isn't a silly question? Anarchist? Not Stalinist obviously. Maoist? or—? I used to be a Marxist (years in the CP)

---

[i] Marginal note: "Intellectual freedom: very very important, things rot without it."

but no more. I think Marxism is either something generally obvious or else (if it covers the whole horizon) very misleading. (Sorry, this would need to be stated at more length.) Marxist young persons tend not to learn. I learnt in spite of Marxism because I wanted to, as it happened; and was prepared to respect & obey my teachers, & to respect the institutions & authorities which confronted me. Many students now don't, & are encouraged not to. I taught art students after I left Oxford & was depressed by the numbing effect of "Marxism" upon the more aggressively opinionated ones—who were led on by similar "teachers." However I may be seeing only the dark side of a picture which has (as I see too) some good aspects!

I don't know your Leeds sociology Prof (can't read his name actually Barnam?)

I'm sorry about Pru—but these things may be inevitable. Are the children with her? Do write to me again & tell me MORE & send your book, books etc. I wish I cd see your factory & its [surrounding?] events. God bless Australia. Excuse this unclarified letter. Write. Much love Iris

Iris Murdoch to Brian Medlin
[Letter 8]

Cedar Lodge, Steeple Aston, Oxford
Nov 18 [1976?]

Dear Brian, forgive this very late rejoinder to your two stories—it was very kind of you to send them and I read them with a special pleasure and interest. The Australianness of Australia has a marvellous tang about it, and I think the <u>art</u> of your tales have got this very well—and of course they are about human nature in general, & very much so. I imagine they would be part of a series of interlocking pieces which would build up a picture of a family, a place, a society.

I liked and felt interested in both of your characters. I thought you were a bit too severe with Uncle Horrie at the end & a bit destroyed his mystery. Bruno has plenty of mystery & it persists. Creation of character is (in my view of it) much concerned with showing how contradictory, muddled, incomplete and basically <u>mysterious</u> people are. Opaque. There are all sorts of ways of doing this, actually, and it is consistent with all sorts of styles. What I liked about your stuff is a sort of lyrical sense of the funny messy mysteriousness of life. Tom Collins is very good at this. Have you written more of these pieces? They should make a book. I know you are deliberately avoiding "plot," but I feel a bit of old-fashioned plot needn't spoil the atmosphere!

How are politics now down your end of the planet? It's pretty terrible here. I hate the Labour Party almost as much as I hate the Tories. There are so few <u>human</u> <u>voices</u> in politics here. What a <u>change</u> it is when you hear one! (Shirley Williams, for instance.) Soundly sincere & rational after all the shifty rhetoric.

I do terribly fear violence—it is creeping in—meetings disrupted by shouts, fighting etc—I <u>hate</u> it. I know you feel it's part of your tradition, and maybe that it's unavoidable. I fear the extreme left here. They are so irrational and <u>stupidly</u> impatient. The violence in Ireland is so <u>deeply</u> damaging and awful, the result of abstract politics & impatience as well as sheer callous lack of humanity. As things stand now there isn't even any point in a united Ireland!

Do write again & let us keep in touch. Let me know if I can do anything helpful for you up here (or down here) such as sending a book.

I've finished my stuff on Plato, thank God. (Just an extended essay.)[6] Look after yourself! <u>Thanks</u> for sending those pieces. With love, Iris.

Iris Murdoch to Brian Medlin
[Letter 10]

Steeple Aston Oxford
June 3 [1977]

Brian, so sorry not to have replied sooner to your interesting letter. Life, generally too much to do, has rather overwhelmed me lately. (Too many letters, no secretary, and the house & garden which somehow have to be "done" in spare moments!) Here, it's the Jubilee. I fear you wd be, if present, a "stuff the jubilee" man! I am rather monarchist. After all, we have to have a head of state, and this lot are fairly picturesque—though I deplore their barbarism, lack of interest in art, failure to marry black men etc. The political scene continues gloomy. Indeed, as you say, there are "too many Trots about" here. There's a sort of lunatic purely destructive left whose idea of "changing capitalism" is just to smash the nearest thing they see. Such people are on the way to terrorism. Endless mean-minded unofficial strikes are a symptom. Genuine Marxists are more rational—or seem so—and yet what can they be aiming for? A miserable unjust autocratic state like Russia or Czechoslovakia? I begin to think that sort of "socialism" is an illusion. (It's "national socialism" in the end.) The only real socialism is the stupid old muddled Old Labour party. A depressing conclusion in some ways. I wish I cd write some political plays expressing just what I think, perhaps finding out in the process![7] I don't think I cd do it in a novel. I hope you are continuing with your post-Tom-Collins work? I liked that. And what happened about the swimming pool? And what news of your now numerous family? We may conceivably be in [remainder missing]

Iris Murdoch to Brian Medlin
[Letter 17]

68 Hamilton Road
Oxford OX2 7QA[i]
May 12 [1986]

Dear Brian,

I'm delighted to hear from you. I was thinking about you lately. I'm so sorry to hear of the road accidents and injury. It sounds as if you are now well put together and walking. I wonder if you made friends with the PhD in chemistry lady? I'm glad you're out of the tunnel. I hope the spoggies have gone (whatever they are): what a nice language, and I do like your story which has also arrived. Sorry the hip hurts. Philosophy again good—I keep on with it—mug's game over thinking half the time, <u>too</u> difficult for humans. As you see, we've left Steeple Aston (house too large, therefore cold, garden too large, therefore covered in nettles) and now live in Summertown (warm house, small garden, city conveniences). I wish you'd come to England, we cd sing a few songs together.

About the stories—have you got a book full? I cd show this one, if you'd like, to my publisher, an <u>Australian</u> (Irish mother, Lebanese Christian father) called Carmen (after the opera) Callil. I like the tone, vocabulary, content and moral sensibility of your story. Are they all very various or similar? Let me know if you want me to try that one on Carmen.

I am working away as usual, have a novel to write[8] and am also writing some philosophy which may be hopelessly bad. It is an addiction. How are things at Flinders? I imagine your politics are much the same—mine have moved a bit to the right. It wd be good to have a talk. Please keep in touch now. Reply requested.

With love—Iris.

---

[i] Marginal note: "Note new <u>address</u>"

Brian Medlin to Iris Murdoch
[Letter MDC1]

69 Albert Street
Prospect, 5082
31.V.86

Dear Iris

Delighted to get your letter and also delighted that you were delighted to get mine. I reproach myself for having lost contact.

I must reproach you, though. I say, "Come to Australia" and you reply, "Come to England." What sort of a bloody answer is that. England!

At the moment Christine and I are camped on a beautiful lake with a beautiful name—Mournpoul—in the Murray Mallee. We are camped amongst ragged old black box, surrounded by river reds. Black box is a rough-barked eucalypt that grows near water and on flood plains. It tends to take over from the red gums as you move to higher, dryer ground; though, like them, it needs flood conditions to germinate. It gives the landscape an austere, muted, undisciplined, tough quality. The red gum is the smooth-barked large tree that gives watercourses all over Australia, their Australian feel. They vary amazingly from tree to tree, yet they're instantly recognizable—except that most people mix them up with *eucalyptus leucoxylon*, the South Australian blue gum, a dry land tree. The red gum is without doubt, to any objective judge, the most beautiful tree in the world. They also provide fire-wood in the bush and rough building materials. Not quite the best fire-wood in the world. That would have to be Napunya, another Eucalypt that grows on the Cooper and the Paroo. Or maybe, the weeping myall, *acacia pendula*. (That reminds me of a by the way, but I'll save it till the next paragraph—if I ever finish this one.) The redgum, as I was about to say is dignified, noble and yet bizarre. (Why "yet," for God's sake. To a sense of history, "noble" *means* "bizarre.") You must never camp under red-gums, though, when you come to Australia. They're likely to drop up to ten tons of wood on you without notice. That's why they're such generous providers of fuel. You don't have to cut the bastards down.

By the way, do you know the poems of John O'Brien? He was a Mick[i]

---

[i] i.e. Catholic.

priest in country towns for many years during the last of the ballading days. He published a book, "Round the Boree Log," boree being *acacia pendula*. It has sold in bundles because it so beautifully hits off the humane side of Australian Mickery. Do yourself a favour before the holocaust and get hold of it. It's bound to be in some English library. Read especially, "Said Hanrahan." Yeats lied. He didn't create the *real* Hanrahan. O'Brien did. If you can't get hold of it, let me know.

Iris your hand-writing is awful. Worse than mine even and I've got an arthritic thumb these days. Did you too break your thumb crossing Mambray creek in flood? There is still one obdurate bit that I haven't worked out. The bit after the spoggies.

I've come to use a computer for everything except cheques. You can plug it, and the little printer, into a gum tree. (In fact the charger of the car.) We were going to spend the first week here working and the second back-packing across to the Murray botanizing and ornathologizing a bit on the way. The lakes are fed, when they are, by a sort of anabranch of the Murray, Chalka Creek. It runs through sand-dunes, mostly mallee, The country itself is pretty arid—though not really dry by Australian standards. Most of the water comes from elsewhere, the High Country of Victoria and New South Wales. We're above the confluence with the Darling, so we don't get anything from Queensland here. That means that it's still drinkable, not having been fouled by Bjelke-Jo's shit.[9] We're below the Murumbidgee (*sic*) so we get stuff from Central New South Wales.

This letter seems to have been taken over by the gabby Timothy Tregonning.[10]

And that reminds me, water from the Lachlan does, do you know Banjo Paterson's poem "Hay, Hell and Booligal"?

> Oh send us to our just reward
> In Hay or Hell, but Gracious Lord
> Deliver us from Booligal.

One of these days I must tell you how Christine was delivered from Booligal by a party of pigshooters. That will have to wait until I'm not in the grip of the garrulous Tim. He'd quite intolerable if he got hold of that story. She was doing this big solo motor-bike trip, you see, on the roundabout way to teeming up with me at Yanga Lake in the Balranald area. And there's a story about Yanga Lake too and the white-breasted sea-eagle there. Yanga Lake is mostly enclosed by Yanga, which—along with 20 or 30 other places in New South—is the biggest freehold property in the Southern Hemisphere. Now the manager's wife at Yanga was ... Enough!

Those Tregonnings are terrible gas-bags all of them. Bloody rat-bags with it. Can't believe a word they say. Except the Old Man. He's not a bad poor bastard. Though how he ever puts up with that missus of his beats me.

I was trying to talk about the Murray. It's a wonderful old river with a character all its own. But where it brings tears into my eyes is at Wellington on the ferry, just above Lake Alexandrina. Here it is, just about the mouth of a river just about as long as the Nile (if you count the Darling), a system that drains almost a quarter of the continent, an area comparable with that of the Amazon Basin, and do you know, it's not much bigger than the Thames at Oxford. It's a bit like having a lad who was a good cricketer at school grow up to be a rock drummer.

But I was really telling you about Christine and her mate Brian on Lake Mournpoul. We have been crook as dogs with AIDS-sized wogs for the past week. Utterly incapable of doing anything useful or pleasant. Thank God the camp's pleasant—it could have been a motel room. Now that we're on the mend there's no work done and we're too weak for back-packing anyhow. So maybe a quick car trip to the Murray.

A pity. Because of the mixture of habitats, you get a lot of birds here and a lot of variety. In a week last year, we recorded 81 distinct species. This year, we wanted to find emu wrens and mallee fowl. For that you need either luck or patience and hard work. It doesn't look as though any of those is going to be available this time round.

Then at the end of next week, back to rotten old Flinders.[11] Rotten old Flinders is rotten. One day I shall tell you, not all about it, but some. There are things that keep me going there, but I don't know whether I'm wise to stay. I'm sure it's a major cause of my depression. That and constant pain. But another time.

Yes, politically, I remain much the same. I've been forced to take longer views and that's damned hard in today's world. Long views on the brink of universal catastrophe seem a bit out of place. There is no left in Australia any more. The best one can do is do what one can here and there and hang on. In some ways it's a relief. For the most part, I prefer to work with people who aren't doctrinaire ignoramuses. *Lefter than thou* is a game I tired of years ago. I'm surprised to hear that you've moved a bit to the right. I wouldn't have thought that there was much room to the right of some of the letters I got from you a few years back. Still, I suppose that Mad Maggie is a bit worse than Shirley Williams. We probably put the divisions in different places. For me, the questions are whether you take a conscious class stand, and whether you are objectively pro-working class. The answers can be "No" and "Yes" in that order, which is better than the other way round. I think we would argue. Or possibly choose not to.

I am a passionate, but not a bigotted socialist. Jeeze, if you ruled out people who were politically shonky, you wouldn't have any friends at all. Singing songs sounds a good idea. I know millions of sounds. Bloody beauties too. I've been trying for years, but I haven't yet worked out a way of accompanying myself on the Baroque flute.

Used to play and sing a lot in pubs, till I got fed up with other people's fags and egoes. Still do a bit with Christine in country pubs. Not that the fags are fewer, but the egoes are smaller.

Of course philosophy is too hard for human beings. It is after all the rag-and-bone collection of unsolvable problems and unusable ideas. As soon as we sort something out from the heap, it's lost to the profession. Fortunately it begins immediately to generate more philosophy. Logic becomes a science, unlike thinking, and gives rise to the philosophy of logic. Some of the Questions are, of their nature, unanswerable, in spite of Big Tom.[12] "Why is there something?" "Does the universe have a beginning in time?" I mean unanswerable even by God. Then there will be some that we can't answer just because we don't have the ability. I am sure that we'll never have a science that is complete in principle. And even if we did have that we did (*sic*) would be something that not even God could know. Then there are other problems, like the problem of free-will and the various kinds of radical scepticism.—From an intellectual point of view, these are contemptibly easy to solve. Yet historically and biographically, they just won't go. I think it's possible, though not easy, to say why they won't. But that still doesn't drive them away. Whether it is possible for us to change our material conditions so that they do go away, is a question that we may some day know the answer to (but only if the answer is "Yes"). Whether that would have to be as a result of a serious impoverishment of our social or intellectual life is a different question, of course also currently unanswerable, and not by any means as clear. Does this make any sense to you. It's not new.

"Yes" please do show that story to your publisher. I suppose I've got a book full. Not one that would satisfy me, though. The time is approaching when I must start thinking seriously about publication. Not yet, but soon. Overseas publication has a lot to be said for it. A few years back I wouldn't have considered it. Now I'd prefer it.

I don't know whether to say that the stories are similar or different. They all concern the Tregonnings and they are all narrated by Tim. They differ in mood and content, I think, but they deal in a single set of overlapping themes. I'll send you a couple more and you can judge for yourself. Everything you will have seen will be pretty different from the stuff I am working on and projecting now. Much of this concerns the young Bruno in the Northern Territory. Then there's a lot of stuff to come about a young woman a generation younger than Bruno. She's a humdinger that one. Don't know what I'll call her yet.

I've just made out another bit of your letter. Of course I made friends with the PhD. in chemistry! I pick up most of my women that way. It's an old bikies' trick. Not on your life, mate. She was in fact the dullest dreariest lump of human tissue you'd fear to meet outside the morgue. Having failed to kill me on the road, she had a determined go at boring me to death in hospital. There I was sitting with a traction pin through my shin try to get a bit of a listen to a bit of Bach and there was Dr. W[...] K[...] with a face like the bottom of a dried up dam shaking her head by the yard and hour and telling me how terrible I felt. Right she was too. In the end I told her that my lawyer would be happy to hear from her in court how terrible I felt, but that I wasn't interested. Never saw her again.

What is the novel—or don't you want to talk about it. Never managed to get you to talk about your books in the past. God, how many is that? You make me ashamed of my utter unproductivity.

I remember Steeple Aston as a pretty place, but damp, like so many villages. Rode my bike there once. Do you miss it? Obviously you're enjoying things about your present place. I have a beaut little 100 year old cottage in Prospect. I've converted the garden to a patch of bushland. There's a painting of the two boys on the stobie pole[13] outside. They spend a good deal of time there and we cook mostly in camp ovens outside. I spend much time sitting under a tree or in the sun with a book on the end of my nose or my computer in my lap. I used to sleep outside a lot once, but the traffic has got a bit much in the last year or so. No wife or lover or landlord can tell me to bugger off. The neighbours on each side and at the back are great. Some of the others are pretty awful, but the worst of them are mad as cut snakes so life's not dull.

How is John? Please give him my love. If it hadn't been for the rare human being like him at New College, I'd have gone bonkers. Tell him that I've seen a bit and corresponded a bit with Stephen Rose over the years. And Hilary. We've got a fair bit in common, though I could wish that Stephen would slow down for twelve months and acquire some philosophical sophistication.[14] I used to correspond a bit with Croix. I think his big book on class in the ancient world is superb. But I haven't heard of him now for years and don't even know whether he is alive.[15]

Iris, my friend. This must stop. Resist Timothy Tregonning's reactionary line of verbosism, ramblism, trivialism. Hold high the great red banner of concisism, relevantism and importantism.

With much love

Iris Murdoch to Brian Medlin
[Letter 21]

68 Hamilton Rd
OX2 7QA
Aug 2 [1986]

Dear Brian,

Thank you very much for your letter. I am so sorry to hear of your father's death. I don't know how you got on with him, but in every case it's an awful shock and absence—one never really expects people to die. I'm very sorry. Maybe you can tell me a little about him.

I'm glad you think of coming to England—please do that. It's not a bad place, in spite of its government. In fact, in my view, where else can one live? certainly not USA. Italy & Spain? No, when one thinks it out in detail. France, yes, actually, & that's where I'd go if I had to leave here. This is a civilized country and in numerous ways a jolly nice place to live. Australia wd certainly also be such a place, only it has <u>one</u> drawback, too far from Europe.

I am impressed by your computer. I cannot even bring myself to touch a typewriter. Sorry if my writing is sometimes illegible! I'm sorry about Flinders. Yes, do come to England. This is just a letter about your Dad and to send love

    I.

Brian Medlin to Iris Murdoch
[Letter MDC2]

69 Albert Street, Prospect 5082, Australia—Where else?
5.XII.1986

Iris my friend,

Thank you for your letter of 2 August. So long ago? And for your words about my old Dad. The grief has been greater than I expected. It's not just a personal matter, but the death of an era and of a way of life that was distinctively our own. They've all gone now those tough sentimental men and women. Small expectations, big achievements. Laconic eloquence. Now it's all discos and dope and cricket played badly in fancy dress. Can you imagine Don Bradman in a canary suit?

(Bradman, by the way is a real man and not just a bit of folklore. He lives right at the back of my brother's place.[16] I detect in myself a belief that he's immortal. But I thought the same about Bertrand Russell, my other early hero.)

I have finished teaching, though not work, for the year. I am staying with some friends at Casterton on the Glenelg River. They are very interesting, vital people, though in many ways very reactionary. They drive me bloody crazy at times. They run beef cattle and breed thorough-breds and shetlands and arabs (and arab mules). They have extensive aviaries and breed birds, mostly native, but some exotics.

They have recently bred a t.b.[i] colt called Wait-a-While, the most exciting little horse, I've ever seen. Superbly muscled, with a glorious head and trustworthy eye. Very affectionate, like his Mum. The pair of them will trot up to nuzzle you from a couple of hundred yards off. He'll stand in the paddock while you go all over him, pick up his feet. I'd dearly love to get him off Bob and Ivy, but nothing doing.

I'm recording some bird-song while I'm down here. One superb stretch of a jacky winter which is a little grey robin with a very robust voice. At this very moment I'm recording a grey shrike thrush family while the baby is preparing to leave the nest.

I am working my way through the volumes so far out in the Teldec set of complete Bach cantatas. I have a portable disk player, so I can sit in the

---

[i] i.e. thoroughbred.

scrub and listen to Bach and play my flute.

I have read a book about the siege of Malta and another about the Paris Commune. The Knights of St. John get a much better press than the Communards. And yet they really were a bloody awful lot.

I came down here to work, as I often do, but found myself so exhausted that I've decided to give myself a brief holiday instead. I'll pitch in for a week or so when I get back. Then Christine and I are putting in nine or ten days bushwalking in the High Country. Then I'll bring my two youngest boys down into this country for a week or so camping and getting firewood. By then I ought to be fit for another year.

I'll almost certainly be in England in the foreseeable future. I'll either come on study leave in 1988 or retire at the end of '87 and come at my own expense in '89. The second is the more likely, I think. I've got too much work to do to go on working much longer. Now that my hip hurts all the time, I have to consider carefully how best to use my energies.

How are you, anyhow?

Love,

Iris Murdoch to Brian Medlin
[Letter 20]

68 Hamilton Road
Oxford
OX2 7QA[i]

Dec 18 [1986]

Brian dear, so glad to hear from you, I had been thinking about you. I can imagine that your father's departure was deeply disturbing and full of grief for you. I'm so sorry. One does miss parents. I miss my wonderful father & mother. My father died in 1962, my mother last year.

I like your account of your holiday, before your work, leading the good Australian life—very enviable—doing such lovely good things, being with trees & animals. I especially liked the account of the little horse. I see you as a horseman, your friends there sound a good lot too in spite of their political views. How splendid about the birds, & Bach, & your flute. Best news of all that you'll be in England, tho' I note, looking at the dates, not so very soon. Will you write a lot of philosophy when you retire—or other things? Poetry of course. I wish that your hip might be getting better. I am trying to start a novel—I think I told you I'd just finished one, out next September.[17] It's an uncomfortable time starting to invent the new one—a lot of <u>bad</u> ideas rush in, & have to [be] thrown out (indeed <u>destroyed</u>). I hope the bushwalking (with Christine) and the camping (with the boys) has been (is, will be) very good—sounds good. I have no very clear picture of Christine—and none at all of your children. Perhaps you cd tell me a little sometime. Also more about your political feelings, actions.

My chief activity at present, in fact, is CHRISTMAS, which perhaps you ignore, and which constitutes a continuous operation here from Dec 15 to Jan 3. I rather like it actually—but it does disturb one's work. I like the things, like Christmas cards, Christmas tree ornaments, holly, etc. etc. Keep in touch. Au revoir & all best Christmas & New Year wishes & love
    Iris

---

[i] Marginal note: "Note the address to be written <u>thus</u>. Your rendering was a bit different."

Iris Murdoch to Brian Medlin
[Letter 14]

Professor Brian Medlin,
Philosophy Dept.,
The Flinders University of South Australia
Bedford Park, South Australia, 5042.

68 Hamilton Rd
Oxford

[no date]

Brian, thanks so much for lovely inspiring photo. I wonder if you are always bearded now. I await further news. I hope you survive the desert. Be careful, don't run out of water. I wish you were over here. I'm still sorry I never heard you read your poetry at the Mermaid Theatre. With love

Iris[i]

[Written on Royal Mail aerogramme.]

---

[i] Date on postmark illegible. Notes in Medlin's writing re slow combustion stoves, hot water, phone numbers and prices etc.

Brian Medlin to Iris Murdoch
Letter MDC41

69 Albert Street
Prospect
South Australia, 5082

20(?).iii.1988

Dear Iris

{12.v.88: Gosh this is gunna be long. I hope you find some of it interesting.}

Bugger! I had been writing to you for most of the morning. Contrary to my usual practice, I hadn't saved my work. Then up I got, kicked out the plug without noticing and lost the bloody lot. Well here goes for anothery.

I'm sitting in my back yard. It's a mild sunny march day. There's a bit of a wind rummaging through the trees showing their tones and colours. I'm watching them grow. There are exactly fifty-nine trees planted, mostly eucalypts, that will grow to fifteen metres or more. Of these more than half will grow to some thirty metres and of those a few will eventually top forty metres. Not quite two hundred feet to the first branch like the original mountain ash stands, providently removed by our heroic forefathers, but not bad for a suburban block. And not a cluttered block either.

I've just had lunch. The billy's on the fire, but I've settled for a small bottle of Cooper's Adelaide Bitter, The Best Beer in the World. Also on the fire is tea for my mate Mary, a neighbour who's coming over later on. We'll drink a half bottle of red (not the best in the world), listen to Bach and Monteverdi in the garden. We'll watch Venus and Jupiter set over the rainwater tank—an awesome sight at present. We'll watch Sirius and Canopus appear and perhaps even worship

Yesterday my colleague Dene Barnett and I worked all day in the garden. We set up a white-board and paced about all day. A wonderful blend of leisure and excitement. Jack Smart and I used to work in my garden more than thirty years ago. But I didn't own that garden, had no control over it and certainly hadn't created it. This garden is as much part of me as anything I have ever done. I include any thing I have ever written.

I think you will never have seen a garden like it. Nor has anyone else who hasn't seen this one. Red piles of red-gum fire-wood, from Casterton, newly cut. Weathered red-gum slab seats and logs, leaden grey and bright silver. Huge sections of South Australian blue-gum, *Eucalyptus leucoxylon*, right here one supporting this computer, another my beer, another my current reading—Thea Astley's <u>A Boat Load of Home Folk</u>, Mary White's <u>The Greening of Gondwana</u>. Camp-ovens on the iron-frame range, black and rusty (a disgraceful condition). Billy-cans and tripods. The cooking fire-place a simple bordering and paving of brick. Other fire places to sit around, one with five-foot logs prepared in it. *[89: This last changed since then to burn more economically. Greenhouse!]*

5.iv.88

Bugger again!
The phone rang, a couple of weeks back was it?, and I've only just got back to you. In Christine's garden now. Another beaut place, though smaller as befits her lowlier station. *[89; Now demolished, along with the house, by the local authority to make a car park.]*

The main excitement in mine at present is that the dingy swallowtails are active. The dingy swallowtail is a butterfly, not at all dingy, that likes citrus trees. Consequently, it is much persecuted by commercial growers. Not by me, however. If you pick the right time and place in my garden and stand still in both for an hour or so, you will see a butterfly lay one white, sticky egg on the edge of a leaf about six inches from your eyes. The grub that hatches out in a few days will be black and yellow to black and orange. In a week or ten days or a fortnight or so it will grow from a millimeter or so in length to 5 cm. or so, having consumed during the process a tonne or so of foliage. Two days ago the first grub hung itself up by its girdle in my valencia and yesterday it pupated. The pupa is camouflaged to blend in with the chomped and chewed citrus stems. Interesting, because both the grug ("grub" I meant, but "grug" is nice) and the butterfly are strikingly marked and, I suppose, mildly toxic.

The other striking butterfly in our gardens—the most striking—is the Wanderer. You will know it in England. The Wanderer chrysalid also is well camouflaged, though both the grub and the fly also are highly visible. The Wanderer is toxic, of course, the grub taking aboard alkaloids with its tucker. The Wanderer is an exotic here having been blown across from South Africa by the Roaring Forties. (Some authorities say it arrived from the United States. Very hard to choose between two theories each so repulsive to national pride.) Since White settlement and the introduction of the Swan Bush, and plants of the same genus, it has been able to establish itself. The grub eats only the Swan Bush and near relatives. Hence the Wanderer has never become a pest. Christine and I both grow the Cottonweed bush for Wanderers, a trick we learnt from her Mum, Dulcie.

Talking of Christine. Yes I agree. A stunner. She started a Science degree last year. She had no science background at all. A major in psych. at Flinders more than fifteen years ago constituted a large part of her scientific ignorance. Her maths was what you'd expect from someone who'd attended a girls "technical" school—and it still amazes me at times. One result of this flying start in the wrong direction is that she topped her year.

Iris, part of this letter overlaps with material in a letter to Roy Edgley. Do you know Roy? I had occasion to talk to him about my mate Bill Ivey. I'll send you the valedictory address that I delivered for Bill some time back. Bill, Albert Facey,[18] my dad. They were of a breed now vanished.

- -

BILL IVEY
a valedictory address

Friends, and especially
Jess,
Margaret, Richard, Catherine, Helen,
Peter, Maria, George, Peter,
Peter-Boris, Pauli, Anna, Mimi, Alex, Tom, John,
Alistair, Anita, Lara -
dear friends:

Bill Ivey was a beautiful bloke, a truly lovely man. A good mate. A staunch comrade. And we all loved him.

I met Bill only twenty years ago, in the high times of the anti-war movement, days of activity and optimism for all progressive people. Some of you have known him longer and indeed much better than I. I'll talk to you, though, about my old cobber Bill as I knew him.

Thinking about those days now, one thing really strikes me. Bill was always right. Right enough, at any rate, and nearly always, anyhow. If sometimes he wasn't effective, that was usually because others were determined to be wrong. Most of us, looking back to the part we played then, will give some thought to the plentiful mistakes we made. Or so I hope. But Bill was different, always on the right track. I can remember times when he led me back to the track—led me in his own tough, gentle way that could look a bit like following if you weren't awake-up to just how subtle a really plain man can be.

It wasn't mere fluke that his judgment was so spot on. There was good reason for it. Bill was entirely without personal ambition or self-concern.

He was no aspiring M.P. with his nose pressed to the Cabinet room window, no respectable public figure with a reputation for grovelling to preserve. He was no fiery activist, lefter-than-thou and desperate to inflame a following. No book-bound intellectual, keen to prove his point though the world should perish for it. And, strikingly, he was no self-indulgent sentimentalist doing good by feeling bad. He was a toiler—radical, militant and judicious—a wise and simple man, an old Broken Hill-ite, a tough-minded bushy, an embattled miner, a free fossicker, of and for the working class. He saw the issues and he saw nothing else. And so he saw them clearly.

And yet he was no fanatic either, no heartless zealot for an abstract cause or builder of mere systems. Politics was a passion for Bill, a passion that sprang from generous love. Tears came easily to him, tears of pity, tears of joy. He hated oppression, not for the sake of the hatred, not so that he could ride on it to some personal glory. He hated oppression because he loved people. He was a kind, affectionate, humorous man. He hated the factionalism that plagues the Left and fought hard against it. Hated it, not only for its destructiveness, but for its lack of love.

Bill's humanity was always there, always visible. Shot through with his humour, it cropped out in the numberless yarns he had to tell. (Jess can tell a pretty good yarn too, by the way.) His were big yarns often enough, but always there was a host of little ones. Like the one about Richard when he was a tiny tacker out in the bush with his dad. On dinner camp, confident, expansive: "This is the life!" On night camp, nervous and clinging: "Dad ... Will heagles heatcher?'

For all its ugliness, Bill relished the beauty of life. He put a lot into life and he got a lot out. His needs and tastes were simple. The last time I saw him, we talked about going bush together. With his age in mind, I remarked that I could run a fridge off the generator. "Oh blow that! Give me a drink of water and a bit of shade under a tree. That'll do me." As Jess once said, "No mod cons with Bill Ivey.,"

Altogether, Bill was an extraordinary man—the ordinary bloke, but on an heroic scale.

Nobody gets to be like that, nobody stays like that, just by their own effort. It takes good mates. And Bill had good mates, friends of all kinds. But Jess particularly, and also his kids, their wives and husbands, and his grandchildren. I've seen a little of how much joy and strength they gave Bill. They were lucky to have him, but by golly he was lucky to have them. And he knew it.

For my own part, I'll always regret that I never got to go bush with Bill. Brewing up. Swapping yarns. Spuds in the red-gum coals. Our spirits aloft with the heagles. Our bodies luxuriously earthbound, laid back in the bend saying, "This is the life!" It would have been a great time. As I've told you, we talked about it a bit a while back. I realize now that Bill knew when we did talk that it was unlikely to happen. He knew then that he didn't have much longer. I'm sure that Bill would have loved to have taken off into the donga one last time. But I'm sure too that, while we were talking, he was savouring the irony of that situation. He was, after all, a man who could joke on his death-bed.

All the same, I'll always be sorry that it didn't happen, that we never went bush together. But a life well-lived is like that. It always leaves things to regret. It promises more than it can ever give. It promises so much, because it gives so much. If we have cause to grieve for Bill, that's because he was so good for us all, and gave us something we shall never get again. Something to rejoice in and draw upon for the rest of our lives.

That last talk I had with him, he said, "There's a good time coming." Knowing that he was soon to die, he said, "There's a good time coming." His face was radiant as he said it. The good time that's coming—the just, kindly world that Bill dreamed of and struggled for all his life—that will be his best memorial. But the memorial has yet to be built. Built, as he knew, in this life—built here and not in any hereafter. Built here or nowhere at all. Built by us, by people like us, today and tomorrow. Built by us and them or by nobody at all.

Our best remembrance of Bill, the one he would have wished for, is to continue building where he left off. Let's make sure that we do continue, not only with Bill's vigour and passion, but also with the good humour, the benign toleration, the humane kindness and the abundant love with which he has so remarkably enriched our lives.

Bill, our marvellous comrade, our beautiful old mate ... There is a good time coming.

{89: While I'm sending you stuff, I'll send a copy of a review I did of Barnett's new book—I think it's quite important (the book) though I don't know that it'd be your cuppa. Do I remember sending you a copy of this before with the remark, "I bet you didn't think I knew anything about this stuff now, did you?"? Now there's a classy bit of punctuation.}

The Art of Gesture: (etc.)
by Dene Barnett with the assistance of Jeanette Massy-Westropp,
Carl Winter Universitatsverlag, Heidleberg, 1987

This is a remarkable book. Robert D. Hume, a distinguished theatre historian, has just described it for *Studies in English Literature* as "Dene Barnett's revolutionary account of eighteenth century acting," as "a truly seminal piece of research." He concludes,

Mark these words: a century from hence this book will be viewed as one of the principal twentieth-century contributions to the history of acting.

On this witness, then, a notable achievement; one to which, declares Barnett, a "major contribution" has been made by his research assistant, Jeanette Massy-Westropp.

Barnett is a remarkable man. In the late forties he founded an ensemble of leading professional musicians to pioneer authentic performance of Baroque music. He built the first harpsichord constructed in Australia. He published a series of essays on Baroque performance practice, said by A.D. McCredie, in 1979, to have "constituted a watershed" for Australian performance.

Simultaneously, he was conducting philosophical and logical research—down the lonely years when modern mathematical logic was otherwise unknown here. Having published one paper of quite fundamental importance, he is two up on most philosophers.

Barnett's passion to reconstruct performance practice for Baroque theatre grew in parallel with his musicological studies. I first heard of this undertaking in 1970. My immediate opinion, almost immediately revised, was that the job would prove impossible. I couldn't easily believe that the material existed. Otherwise, one would have expected to encounter similar material in Joseph's study of Elizabethan acting, published in 1951.

The material exists alright, but deeply buried. Barnett has gouged it out from the libraries and languages of Europe. From it he has constructed the first systematic, detailed study in print of Eighteenth Century tragic acting. He has set this in the context of widespread Eighteenth Century aesthetic theory. His sources include prompt copies and treatises by actors, teachers of acting, rhetoricians. Barnett's book is densely illustrated with contemporary drawings and also with photographs of modern demonstration. These are set carefully against the spoken text. The result is a fine-grained picture of Baroque technique: the appropriate gestures are resolved down to the very phrase, the very word, sometimes even to the syllable.

Barnett's approach is rigorously empirical. No significant claim goes unsupported. No speculation floats away from the evidence. Conforming to this approach, he has, throughout the investigation, directed larger and smaller productions in Australia and overseas—in major universities and in cultural centres such as Covent Garden. These have often been associated with formal academic teaching. They have involved such performers as Marie Leonhardt, Emma Kirkby, Beatrice Cramois, Max van Egmond, Judith Nelson ... They were intended to illustrate the reconstructed craft, but also to test it for aesthetic viability.

Barnett's work early claimed the attention and support of scholars like H. Kinderman, Director of the Theatre Institute of Vienna University. It excited professionals in related fields—Gustav Leonhardt, for example, and Frans Brueggen.

For all its empirical rigour, Barnett's work is exciting. It is imaginative. Yet he can hold down the big ideas from ballooning away because of his philosophical strength. There is never the least danger of his indulging in the highfalutin twaddle that increasingly disgraces academic publication and of which I cite this single example:

The academic ideology which dominates modern theories of Rhetoric, and modern discussions of Renaissance rhetoric, is radical Nominalism, whose fundamental postulate is the total disjunction between language and reality, words and things.

This book is subtle as well as rigorous and exciting. An unsubtle reading of it might perhaps produce the impression that Baroque acting, being highly formal, was therefore somewhat rigid and wooden. The text, however, supports a contrary conclusion: namely, that what may strike us, reared as we are on so-called naturalism, what may strike us as a style rigidly formal, in fact provided, by its very formality, ground for delicate variation.

And all this, hooray, in good, sweet, candid English; spectacular in its plainness, with no taint of looney learnedness.

If Barnett's work comes to be challenged by future authorities, these will have been called into existence by his very labours. Indeed, for the near future, the most useful response to his work may be, not so much challenge, as the experimental attempt to discover what it can yield in today's theatre. For he has left little doubt, where Joseph left much, that we are looking at pervasive practice in the theatre of the past. And indeed, if the Eighteenth Century could, as Barnett demonstrates, be proud to profit from Quintillian, it is conceivable that we might have something to learn from our much closer predecessors and might not be too proud to learn it.

Brian Medlin

■ ■ ■ ■ ■ ■ ■ ■ ■ ■ ■ ■ ■ ■ ■ ■

Iris, skip as much as you like (unnecessary advice) but I'll also send you my note on Brian Matthews. It may persuade you to read *Louisa.* Better than anything by Derrida. Both it and the Barnett review appeared in *The Sydney Review.* [19]

BRIAN MATTHEWS
a note on the recent work
**(*Louisa,* McPhee Gribble, 1987; *Quickening and Other Stories,*
McPhee Gribble/Penguin, 1989)**
Brian Medlin

Brian Matthews had a dazzling 1988. *Louisa* carried off four major prizes. Now his volume of stories, *Quickening and Other Stories,* just appearing promises to stir up 1989.

This collection constitutes a disquieting study of modern life. One pervasive theme is the estrangement of sexual lovers, and especially their bewildered perceptions of the sundering. Matthews' characters are, or come to be, cruelly cut off from one another's inner lives. Often these inner lives will be hidden from narrator and reader as well ("Crested Pigeons').

Paradoxically, this is largely because changed attitudes are seen as coming solely from within. We perceive the inner life of others in their behaviour and ultimately behaviour involves response to external circumstance. Hence, where the inner life dominates the causes of action, it seems to disappear; the person becomes a mere opaque non-reflective surface. In one character, it *has* disappeared, drowned out by *itself* ("Going Deaf").

Often enough, Matthews central "characters" aren't characters at all. They have no readable faces; they change but don't develop; they act without interacting, without *re*acting in any way. One—at the literal level anyhow—starts turning into a fish! ("Moroccan Man").

In this respect, Matthews' characterization differs from that of Henry Lawson, of which he has been a notable student (*The Receding Wave,* MUP, 1972). In the great Joe Wilson series Lawson, too, examines estrangement. But to Lawson, as to Joe, the estrangement is intelligible, as are the personal changes that flow in and out of it. Intelligible, because visibly the result of external pressures. These pressures make up and are represented by The Bush, which comes pretty close to being an allegorical Presence.

Our times are a long way from Lawson's. Lawson dealt in readily identifiable hardship. For us, characteristically the human spirit is formed and eroded by undetected *soft*ship, by factors invisible in virtue of their omnipresence. Mostly we have full, even obese, bellies. But we've grown used to musak in public as we shall also to the canned corn that now oozes everywhere from the private earpiece. To the extent that we are blind to outside influences, our response to them will seem purely autonomous. We will be opaque, not only to one another, but also to ourselves.

Don't think that Matthews writes by formula—this or any other. To Maguire in "Songs out of Season" the invisible minutiae composing our unlived life become unbearably visible. His response is to get out of sync by some months with the rest of the world. In this way he escapes it. But notice: *first* that this change is completely unintelligible to all about him; *second* that (if indeed it occurs) it is not a development of character. It is a lucky internal wiring defect.

There are characters presented more or less "from the inside." Yet of these at least two are quite opaque to themselves. For Jeremy Randall, unintrospective yet self consumed, the *outside* world becomes terrifyingly incomprehensible as it begins to manifest what he can't see *in himself.* The woman in "The Dark, the Cold" vividly perceives her own inner life. But again externally, not as hers. It holds no meaning for her, only pain and terror.

We see, as well, the private experience of the woman in "Quickening." Her husband, however, is confronted with a baffling estrangement. And baffling it must be, since it proceeds, not from their lives together, but solely from her inner world.

There is one character, viewed from the inside who is fully self-aware—the wife in "At the Picasso Exhibition." Significantly, her self-awareness contains the estranging knowledge that her Ocker husband could come no closer than contempt towards understanding her passionate responses to the paintings. In this realization, she determinedly conceals her real self from him—hides those responses together with the affirming sexuality involved in them. Her shut-offness is intelligible to us just because it is a response to the external world.

All very different from *Louisa* and yet all springing from the same root.

Louisa is a full, objective study of a real person; an attempt to reveal what is knowable about her; to guess what is guessable; to distinguish each from each and both from what can't be known or guessed at either; along the way to indicate degrees of plausibility. An attempt, too, rationally to evaluate Louisa's life; to ponder all those perplexing equally (or unequally) legitimate emotional or evaluative attitudes; to distinguish these from judgment and speculation concerning matters of fact; to enquire how attitude and judgment interact.

All this, and no less, is required to achieve objective history. And *Louisa* is that—objective, not merely "notionally objective" (p.7). *Louisa* is no post-modernist essay in radical scepticism and nihilism. It is a successful attempt at history in the face of well-known *realistic* epistemological problems. To people like the characters of *Quickening*, these problems are insoluble—for deep social reasons. To Matthews, the historian, they are partly soluble in practice—and largely solved.

Such problems could receive another kind of solution—judiciousness in discursive form, as exemplified by John Bray's "Gallienus" (*Satura*, The Wakefield Press, 1988).[20]

But one particular problem compels the form adopted by Matthews—compels so strongly that it's a wonder nobody's done it before. Yet the form is original and, generated as it is by the problems, solves them brilliantly. Not without its own problems, though. (It took me three reads to get into this damn book.)

The particular problem is that the effort to understand and assess sometimes "fragments the self" (p. 204). This is not a matter of simple indecision, of cautious agnosticism, but of strongly held *incompatible* judgments and attitudes, of irresolvable contradictions. It is a common enough phenomenon analogous to, doubtless related to, but usually distinct from, multiple personality.

The "selves" of Matthew's *Louisa* are fictional characters. Not one of them can be identified with the author, Matthews. Contrary to the *Advertiser* (14.xi.87), *Louisa* is not "the Life of Brian," but in a sense a work of fiction. The fiction concerns the construction, by fictional characters, of a doubtless merely "notionally objective" biography. And yet, by means of this fiction, a *really* objective biography is constructed *in fact*.

This is a striking achievement. It is made possible by a "plot," a developing interaction, both internally amongst the fictional characters and also externally with their real subject. It can be argued (and will be elsewhere) that this plot, for all its difference in kind, is comparable in ironical complexity with that of Tom Collins' *Such is Life*.

- -

**Headings Cliff
in the Murto Forest
near Renmark**

28.iv.88

Bugger again! ... Now on the Murray. My tall son Jake wanted to do some fishing in his school holidays. So I brought him away with the boat—a 16 foot flat-backed Canadian. We slap a 2hp outboard onto the aluminium transom and poke around the winding creeks and back-waters. Disgrace, I know, but my back isn't up to paddling canoes and Jake isn't purist about such matters. The Murray flows mostly through very flat country, so pretty often it can't make up its mind just where it's going or through which channel. The maps and charts are sometimes a bit inventive and in any case can go out of date pretty quickly. The river reds drop massive falls of timber or get torn out in floods, so there are under-water snags everywhere. The main river is kept fairly clear, but no-one bothers with the creeks, thank god. That means you can get away from the hired house-boats and the speed maniacs. It also means you could disembowel your craft or tear off your motor if you don't know what you're about.

Jake's learnt plenty. He does learn these days. During the twelve months before last Christmas, he transformed himself from a five-foot high indefatigable pain in the arse into a beaut bloke 6' 2-or-3" in his socks. Plenty about boating, but not about camp cooking. He's just served up a quite nicely flavoured plate of river sand—an offence for which a drovers' cook would have had his ears boxed with hobble chains by some leathery gourmet called Splinter or Tragedy or Warrigal Bob.[21]

Not about fishing either. In three days so far, he's caught one carp! We've seen plenty of red-fin jump, but they haven't made themselves available. The Murray system is pretty well stuffed as a fishery, I'm afraid. When I was a kid, people were still catching 90lb Murray cod in the rivers. (No-one has any idea how long it takes such a fish to grow and now no-one's likely to find out.)

After the WWII, some idiot released carp into the system—for what purpose I've forgotten. Oh yes, I seem to remember that they were washed out of dams during flood time. The carp in this country has proved the aquatic equivalent of the rabbit, a main cause of the dramatic deterioration of a system of fisheries that drains the main basin of the continent. Fortunately, the Cooper system—the Cooper flows into Lake Eyre, when it gets there—is still free of the bastards, but it's only a matter of time before somebody lets a goldfish go in the reach at Longreach, say.

{89: I've learnt since I wrote that. Fish of 110 kg. and 1.8 m. are still being caught. Nonetheless the Cod is headed for extinction unless extreme steps are taken to rescue it—and a number of other Murray species. The main trouble is the flood control from the many weirs. The Cod needs the warmer waters of the flood plains to reproduce.}

Well fishing. I hate fishing. I can sit on the bank and watch the water, but throw in a line and I get impatient. I don't like impaling worms either. So I've come here to renew my reading of Christopher Hill.[22] That marvellous historian. I find him a good corrective to my dogmatic tendencies. I wish he were widely read by Marxists. By and large, the comrades would do well to trade in some of their knowledge for a bit of learning. And a bit of their learned speech (sorry, *discourse*) for a little plain talk. Jake at present has no interest in such matters. He's a bright enough kid, but not so far very intellectual. Not a goon,—though he does smoke and listens to AC-DC, for Chrissake—but progressive by instinct, sensitive, thoughtful. At present, he's rejoicing in his new-found stature and strength and is intensely physical. I've done some serious bushwalking with him twice now and each time been bloody proud of him.

Once in the Lower Flinders and once, very strenuously, in the High Country of Victoria.

And by the way, if ever you get the chance and can bear to sit through a ridiculously bad flick, have a look at The Man from Snowy River II. The country is superb. It's the country we often walk in. Graeme Stoney, one of the local crack riders for the film, built Bluff Hut, much visited by us. The Lovicks work from Lovick's Hut, another of our haunts. (The huts are bush-built cattlemen's refuges, but open to travellers in the mountains.) Mt. Speculation and the Crosscut figure a lot. The opening shot is of Mt. Koonika, the destination of our next walk. *[89: Wrong! Mt. Cobbler.]*

There's a bit of politics behind the film. There's a strong conservationist lobby trying to push the cattlemen out of the mountains. Playing upon the traditional ALP[23] hatred of everything rural, it has come very close to succeeding a couple of times. As a result, the cattlemen have organized themselves into an effective force in Victorian State politics. The research on which the conservationist case is based, is very shonky, I reckon. My natural sympathies are with the cattlemen. I admire their skills and their character. I believe, as they do, that their traditional way of life actually cherished the mountains.

Unfortunately the matter is a lot more complicated than that. To start with, the two Man from Snowy River films show the cattlemen charging about the mountains day in day out in a way no mortal horse- or man-flesh could endure. They are shown knocking the mountains about in a way that would rapidly reduce them to the Western Plains. And that can't be doing their case much good. Why, I can't imagine. Film makers are film makers, we know, and about as deeply committed to veracity and verisimilitude as journalists. But this one is a bit of a High Country cattleman himself. And the cattlemen, particularly the Lovicks and the Stoneys, were heavily involved as riders, organizers, advisers. Worse than that, though, is the effect the films are having on tourism. The mountains are filling up with tourists on horse-back. Every parklands cowboy in New York and Melbourne wants to tear divots out of the High Country. Five years ago, only cattlemen working cattle, and bushwalkers got onto the tops. Tracks that were then compacted and stable are now knee-deep. Two years ago the northern side of King Billy carried a single steep track a foot wide. In January this year, it had been worn into a lattice of trails fifty yards wide, some of them three feet deep. Jake and I very nearly got into a punch-up with some mounted morons at MacAlister's Springs near the Crosscut. When Christine's part of our party first came upon them, they were lost! No maps, no compass! ("What's that you've got? Maybe it'd be an idea for us to have one of those.") Cattlemen don't carry maps and compasses

either, but then they don't get lost. When Jake and I encountered this
bunch, they'd been without water all day. This was just too much for them
all, man woman and beast. Soft riders have soft horses. We directed them
to the Springs—they were in fact on the track there anyhow. When we
arrived we found that they'd ridden their bloody nags into the water—
twenty of the bastards. The spring is small and, though the flow is reliable,
the stream is small and the basin very fragile. It's suitable only for
walkers. Bushmen would have watered their horses out of their hats,
however long it took. Without any idea what it was, they'd trampled the
metal filler out of shape. Jake and I remonstrated quite politely.
Whereupon some of them began to go berserk. One pocket Rambo offered
to beat us up, but got himself laughed off. A couple of them were a bit
apologetic and we managed to talk to them about it. They seemed to listen
when I told them what I thought the issues were. Even when I suggested
that next time they went bush they should go with a bushman instead of
the fat and fancy riding school dude who'd got them lost. The dude wasn't
too rapt in this. And I reckon most of them learnt bugger all from it. It was
convenient for them to see it in ready-made terms. The conflict was that
between horsemen, cattlemen (them!) and romantic, arrogant citified
greenies (us).

(I remind myself that I'd intended to write to Jack Lovick about this
incident and some other matters.)

Talking about horsemen.—I got thrown by a mare recently. At 12.30
pm. on February 21st, to be precise. On Tolka at Casterton. I was teaching
Christine to ride! She never got up. Bob had yarded her horse, a big old
quiet gelding of about 100 hands. When we passed the yards on the way to
get my mare in the bottom paddock, Christine said, "He's very big, isn't
he?" "Don't worry. When you're up, you're always bigger than they are."
I shan't tell the shameful story of my downfall. Not in shameful detail. But
all she did was pig-root. If she hadn't been quiet and I consequently
complacent, I hope I'd have stuck to her. As it was, it was my worst fall
ever. The only one where I haven't been able to get straight back up again.
Sixty miles in an ambulance. Overnight in the Mt. Gambier Hospital (Inc.)
I had to drive myself back to Adelaide a week later hanging onto the wheel
so that my back didn't touch the upholstery. In the end, I had a litre and a
half of blood evacuated from a whacking great haematoma in the small of
my back. I was bruised a deep and—except for the area of the
haematoma—uninterrupted purple from low on my buttocks to well above
my waist. I was thinking of taking up a new career in the baboon business,
but eventually decided against the accommodation. I am still stiff and sore.
There's a lot of intricate scar tissue to be stretched daily. Don't get the

wrong idea. I can still touch my toes and, better, put my palms flat on the ground beside my ankles. It just hurts like hell. I now have a new kind of bad back to keep flexible.

I tell this story because it interests me and so I assume that it's interesting. One thing that interests me is the clucking, chookish reaction of so many of my friends. "You're not going to get on horses / ride bikes / climb rocks / ... / ... / cross the street / get out of bed / *breathe* again are you?" They seem not to realise that you ride horses precisely because you *do* come off the buggers. Christine is a striking and marvellous exception. I *could* love her for herself alone and not her red hair. (Happily, I don't have to.) Her very own special unique once-off and superlative beauty consists in her understanding these things and living her life by her understanding. Bob and Ivy, being horse-(wo)men understand them—for horses, anyhow. "We all come off 'em." Barnett had come down to Casterton to do some work with me and has been an intolerable bloody gobbling turkey ever since. He keeps on trying to nobble Christine to nobble me. She'll say something like, "Dene, I wouldn't do that. I don't believe you have the right to do that to people." Whereupon, to her fury, he'll make some such reply as "What Brian really needs is someone as fiery as himself." Sooner or later he'll find out I've got what he reckons I need. If he gets Christine's wild up, he'll know all about it. Bloody harpsichordist, that's what he is! And the recorder! I've been forced to re-bethink me of a poem I wrote when I was a young fellow and just down from the donga. It's called.

A dedication
I have not come so far that I remember
No country but my own, nor hand but mine
Under the nail. November means more than
Thirty days on the wall and home holds
More in my hope than fear, not a haven,
A homely fire or my private sun in the yard.
I who have known the summer ascend that sun
And shatter the basalt plain, lay fire in the year's
Dust, breaking the river, lay death in the
Water-hole, beast in the water, shall not come home
To death indoors, but follow the hand of fire
Pointing my blood and the sun to the same home.

I meant it then, by God!, and by God! I still mean it now.

Brian Medlin to Iris Murdoch
[Letter MDC42]

Billiatt,
North of Lameroo,
S.A.
8.v.88

And bugger yet again!

Now camped with Christine in burnt-out mallee. Billiatt is a
conservation park of perhaps 330 sq. k. It's mostly untouched mallee and
contains some of the most beautiful scrub in the state. Lacks water and big
features so it isn't at all touristy, thank God. In fact, we have never seen
another person in the park. A fire took out practically the whole park in
January. Jake and I camped here a couple of weeks back on our way to the
Murray. Christine and I have camped here pretty often in a spot she found
on a big solo motor bike trip in 1982. Now we're back again. The idea is
to make a monthly survey of the regeneration. (It'll probably turn out to be
three-monthly.) There mightn't be much regeneration in parts. Just over
the road about 1 mile from here, they have huge scarifiers at work and are
ripping out all the burnt scrub. Bloody idiotic. Most Australian botanical
species are well adapted to fire. But not to having shit ripped out of the
country—here all wind-blown dunes and so very fragile. Mallee, for
example, has a ligno-tuber, an underground trunk, the famous mallee-root.
These sprout again after fire. They find that difficult to do, however, if
they've been torn out by a scarifier. (It's an ill wind, but. ... Mallee roots
are superb fire wood and I'll load a tonne or so onto the trailer this arvo.)
Next week I'll go into the Department and see if I can discover what
they're up to. It would be wrong to assume straight off that they're up to
anything conscious, that there ever have been any intentions or reasons.
There's a slim chance of getting the work stopped. We're both afraid that
they may be going to work over the whole park. It would be a disaster if
they started on this side of the road. Our camp is in a superb and unique
patch of mallee. In the centre of a basin it contains only eucalypts and
shortish ground cover so that it makes up a structured space. Now that it's
burnt out it is still unique and superb. White branches, straightish,
radiating out of the ground. The bases of the trees are about 8-10 feet
apart, but many of the branches meet overhead. They used to form a light
low canopy, but now the trees are leafless. Black strips of bark hang from

the upper branches. Even without foliage, the scrub is thick—you can only see into it for about 50 yards. The base of each tree is aflame with new foliage, varying in colour and texture according to species. There are at least four of these.

We camp on the lip of an excavation—Highways Department, probably—20 feet deep, and 50 by 100 yards. This usually holds a bit of water much used by emus and kangaroos, but very boggy to get at. The whole area is rich in plants of the semi-arid persuasion—of which we too are members. And so there are plenty of birds.

These are much reduced in the burnt-out areas of course. But there are plenty of fresh emu and kangaroo tracks still. Yesterday we saw some extensive echidna digs. (Oh, by the way, did you know that the platypus has electro-sensors in its bill? If not I'll tell you about it.) There are still white-backed magpies around and galahs and ravens and pied currawongs. These are birds with a fair range. More surprisingly, we have seen thorn-bills, probably striated, and willie-wagtails. I don't know how much these names will mean to you. The willy is a fantail, *Rhipidura leucophrys*, of the family *Muscicapidae*. The pied currawong, *Stepera graculina*, is of the family *Cracticidae*, as are the Australian (i.e. real) magpies and butcher birds. The galah is a beautiful pink and grey cocky. We have heard a honey-eater of some kind calling, but haven't been able to identify it.

{89: But of course you know the galah. Do you remember seeing a very exciting flock of them when we went up to the Barossa Valley?

{You may remember too Cyril Henscke, the wine-maker. How he kept very civilly offering to sell us wine (then illegal on a Sunday). Poor Cyril is now dead, shot by his wife many years ago. She poor girl had had a very bad car crash and had sustained serious head injuries. She was hallucinating at the time and was eventually acquitted. What a life!}

And most exciting of all. Yesterday, in an unburnt patch, we saw a mallee heath wren. A pair, indeed, but on that Christine and I differ. No doubt, however, about the one about which there's no doubt. A very presentable bouncing twitching little wren-like bird. Of the family *Acanthizidae*, like the thornbills, it is in fact a scrubwren *Sericornis cautus*. *{89: This patch of scrub has now gone. Scarified to make an Ocker holiday—or swimming pool or Merc.}*

(See Pizzey, *A Field Guide to the Birds of Australia*, Collins, 1983; and especially, Cameron, *Bird Families of the World*, Elsevier Phaidon, 1978, subsequently Peerage, undated.)

Don't be surprised at all if this arrives decorated with flies, ants and jumping spiders. They are being so persistent and intrusive as I type this that I'm sure some of them will get themselves on file.

Christine's place
13.v.88 (the day after Christine's birthday)
Well, as it turned out, the area being scarified is private land under the management of one Ivo Yancovich. And he has the right to scarify. A mere nine or ten phone calls on Monday produced the information. Fortunately, I had already taken off a load of mallee roots under the impression that it was conservation park—not that that's legal either. Mr. Yancovich won't miss them. He was taking steps to burn them on the site.

Charlie Martin has come and gone, reviving old memories. Do you know (of) Charlie? Reading some good papers, some not so good, perhaps. All of them bloody difficult. And made more so by Charlie's elliptical, gnomic pronouncements in discussion. Also by his tendency to interrupt in order to tell you what you are saying so as not to waste his time and yours before he tells you what's wrong with it. "I'm not really interrupting." "No, Charlie, but it's an illusion to which we are frequently subject in your presence." Still, it was good to see the mad old bastard again. And he's certainly a better philosopher than most.[24]

Couple of days ago I took him to Strathalbyn, a beautiful town in the Adelaide Hills, built by the Poms[i]—in spite of its name—before they had become Australians. It's more like a good English village than any other Australian town I know, and not yet buggered up by either brutish prosperity or chic tourism. I had one particular house to show him, a beautiful colonial house with an extra room tacked onto the symmetry, transforming it from a merely beautiful building with no surprises into something breathtaking. The corner of the block at which this room stands is somewhat less than a right angle. One wall of the room stands right on the boundary and extends into the stone wall that runs down the lane for perhaps 150 feet. The front of the house is buried in trees.

While we were hanging around suspiciously, out came a large betweeded, square-built 70-ish woman with a solid leg in each corner like a sturdy, two-legged table. I explained that I had brought my friend, a visitor from Canada, to admire her house. Her first words, very English, were, "Oh dear! What can I give you." She hadn't time to give us lunch, because she had to be at the school. And she didn't have any biscuits. We were very happy to have nothing. But she took us into her house. On the table in the hall were volumes by Kath Walker (an aboriginal poet) and Dorothy Wordsworth. There were books everywhere and a wonderful smell that meant fifty years of living by wood fires. I've only ever smelt

---

[i] "Pom", or "pommy", is a colloquial term for an English person, especially an immigrant to Australia.

that smell in the Hills and then hardly ever since I was a boy. They'd lost their farm during the Depression and had moved into this house, then derelict.

She took us out the back and showed us her trays where she was germinating native trees. "And are you a member of Trees for Life?" "Oh, yes, indeed." "Then perhaps you know my neighbour in Prospect, Mary Minigall?" (Mentioned above.) "Oh dear Mary and dear little Liam!" At this point we were away at top speed. I then introduced myself and Charlie. Astonishment! "Oh! Medlin! I know that name! Professor Medlin! I never thought I'd have you in this house!" I think that she expected long orange fangs and instant mayhem.

But she was lovely. She took us into Hoot Hall, the added room. It had originally been a butcher's shop but was now full of owls, ceramic wooden, cloth, and two-dimensional ones as well as solid figures. The collection (all gifts) had been started years ago when she had been Matron at a "boys" boarding school. (Prince Alfred's College, I learnt later. That explained a lot. PAC is one of our poshest. In days gone by, it attempted to teach an English accent, but Ian Chapel[25] must have broken their heart. *{89: Wrong! St. Peters. Bob Hawkes' son, John, was under her care. The difference between Methos and C-of-Es would matter little to my misinformant Mary.}*) The first gift had been a picture of a stern old bird that the kids found to be like her. For years, they used to put it up in her absence and consult it about what they might or might not do. Mostly it responded, "Certainly not!" Eventually, they presented it to her with an account of their use of it, "Stimulated, I think, by a little grape juice." And from then on the owls rolled in, drunk or sober, at all hours of the day and night, till now there are hundreds of the buggers and I'm looking for one myself.

She turned out to be the cousin of one Michael Taylor, now and for many years past professor of physiology and a pro-Vice Chancellor at Sydney University. Taylor is now a very august and elevated personage, but in happier times almost forty years ago, we were young poets together, convinced that we were the ant's pants. And probably only half wrong. I think the full conviction, translated into more dignified language, has remained with Michael. Charlie knew him in Adelaide in the fifties when Taylor was not yet a big stiff and then later when Charlie had a chair in philosophy at Sydney and was, as he says and I know, "drunk and mad."

All the time, "I never thought that I'd have you in my house." And all the time casting about for something to give us. In the end, Charlie settled for some huge, sculpted gum-nuts off her Illy-arrie. Dumb bastard broke the branch getting them.

When I told Mary, she recalled a story of Betty (her name) and Liam. Liam, looking at pictures: "Ooo! Red-backed spiders. You kill them, don't you!"—squashing the image with the ball of his hand. "Well, I suppose that's all right if Mummy says so. But I always say that there's room in my house for my spiders and me." Then last night I was telling this story to people at Christine's little party. There was an ex-student of mine there whom I hadn't seen for 12 years or more. I'd only just started telling the story and Bill said, "Is this a big woman that walks with a staff?" And he knew her too. She talks to the Fleurieu Peninsula Nature Society about trees.

I'm in process of retiring, I hope. Have I told you? It doesn't seem easy to get off the payroll at Flinders, but I think I'll manage this time. I have too much to do to keep on working. Too much philosophy, fiction etc. Even too much nothing to waste any more of my life on the optimistic no-hopers that swarm over us these days. I should be out by the middle of the year. *{89: And was.}* I'll keep on with some post-graduate supervision. I think, though, that I'll go to the U of Adelaide seminars, rather than ours. I'm fed up with being the one that takes responsibility for ensuring a discussion. I've had twenty bloody years of that.

The Butterfly House
Murray Bridge
15.v.1988

Well here we go again. Tomorrow's Adelaide Cup day and, would you believe it?, a public holiday. So I've brought Bruno and a rather nongish mate up the river till tomorrow morning. We've had a look at the butterflies. The proprietor, as I discovered the first time I came, used to "march behind" me in the "good old days." He's a bloke that sweated for years as an accountant till he got sick of "helping greedy people get richer." Now breeds butterflies and has a nice little place on the freeway to show them in. Graham M[...]. Not Marsh, as I thought till today. The same name as the golfer. A huge man who, when he isn't smoking, eats lamingtons—stalish ones I suspect, left over from the tea room stock. Graham has given me a gold pass. (A yellow ticket actually.) It will admit me for life. I hope that means for the life of the <u>ticket</u>. The boys have gone to Puzzle Park, an adjoining commercial playground. That is their real interest in the district. Bruno's got a red swallowtail chrysalid to take home and wants to come back after Puzzle Park. Luke is a bit bored, I think. Then to Tailem Town, an assembled, but authenticish pioneer settlement outside Tailem Bend. ("Tailem Bend" is pidgin for the big bend in the Murray a few miles upstream from the Lakes.) Just been interrupted by Erica, Graham's eleven year old daughter, a real charmer. I expect that bits of our conversation will find their way into this letter yes indeed that is my fourwheeldrivewiththeboatontop. I discover that the lamingtons etc. are being taken out to customers—so the weight must be booze. I am installed in Graham's office. I set myself up in the tea-rooms, but then two coachloads of big game hunters arrived to chase the butterflies around and Graham set me up in here. Only trouble is it stinks of fags and I'm afraid I don't know whether your brother would mind if you used his calligraphy pen no I wouldn't want to know your brother if you say so.[i]

---

[i] This appears to be continued in the next "letter": that is, they make one continuous letter sent all at once.

Brian Medlin to Iris Murdoch
[Letter MDC3]

Monte Collina Bore
The Cobbler
Strzelecki Track
26.v.88

Bloody Beauty!

Monte Collina is an old artesian bore, now disused. It was installed to service the Strzelecki stock route down Strzelecki Creek, now disused, but in its time one of the toughest in Australia. There are some permanent holes in the Creek, but most of the time they are salter than the sea. (You may remember that Old Wally used to take stock down The Track.)

You probably don't know that Burke and Wills and King[26] tried first to get down Strzelecki Creek to Mt. Hopeless when they found themselves abandoned on the Cooper. The gap between the lakes had been found by Gregory about a year earlier, but they couldn't manage it. Mt. Hopeless was then a police station and is now a sheep station about 40 kilometres South of here. It is named after the last sizeable hill of the Northern Flinders Ranges. The hill in turn was named by Edward John Eyre in honour of the country he saw from it—mostly dry salt lake.

The two main lakes to the north of Mt. Hopeless are Blanche and Callabona. Lakes! Huge evaporation basins, seldom full, always boggy. Blanche, the Western Lake is fed, when it is, by creeks from the northern Flinders, notably The MacDonnell, of which later, but also occasionally by the Strzelecki, an overflow channel of the Cooper. A bend of The Strzelecki brings it to within less than 2 kilometres of the bore on a bearing of about 300 degrees. After a few meanderings it "flows" into Lake Blanche about 15 k. almost due west of us. I've never seen the Strzelecki at this point and I may do so on this trip. There may well be water in it here, especially after the rains, but I would expect it to be at least as salt as the sea. The Strzelecki can run fresh when the Cooper overflows into it, but that requires 24 feet over the Innaminka crossing. The latest flood has produced only 22 feet!

Callabona too is fed by creeks from the Northern Flinders and particularly by the Hamilton. The jewel of the Hamilton is Terrapinna Waterhole, perhaps the finest hole in the Ranges. Callabona is also fed through Monte Collina Channel from Blanche. Blanche is 0.1 m. above mean sea level and Callabonna about the same depth below. You may have heard of Callabona. It is a vast field of fossilized diprotodon skeletons. The poor buggers kept bogging down there when the country was drying up. I'm making the figure up out of my general knowledge, but that should have been about 100,000 years ago. Certainly that was the time when the eucalypts were becoming dominant and that was associated with the drying up of the continent and with the appearance of widespread fire. (Christine's cousin used to manage Skeleton Station on Callabona, but you would hardly have heard of that. The name was doubtless a reference to the condition of the stock turned off annually.)

Eucalypts: God, it's hard saying anything that's just right. First, the eucalypts are fairly old: the earliest known pollen fossils are from 30 million years ago. Next, the continent has been drying up for much longer than 100,000 years, though I don't know for how long. And I suppose that the eucalypts have been taking over from the original rain-forest throughout that time. Next, Christine tells me that ash began to appear plentifully in the record about 120,000 years ago. (My figure of 100,000 years above is a rounding off of that more accurate figure.) That was probably because the continent was now dry enough for bush-fire to occur naturally. The eucalypt devices for coping with aridity—dormant buds under the bark, ligno-tubers, hard seed cases—also fitted them to survive fire. So that would have put them at an advantage. Next, the first people probably came about 50,000 years ago. They used fire as a standard technique both for hunting and for promoting new growth. This gave the eucalypts an added fillip. The aboriginals certainly changed the landscape. Whether they also changed the climate, I don't know and rather doubt.

The continent was once entirely rainforest. Now the greater part of it is divided into deserts, sclerophyll woodland and savanna—or was so divided before we arrived. (I call desert what some regard and use, disastrously, as pastoral country—it is important to realise that we don't have droughts in Australia. The whole concept of drought is a misrepresentation of the true state of affairs. We live in an arid continent where there are occasional rains and, from time to time, anomalous good seasons. A recognition of that simple fact might lead to less destructive land management.) The eucalypts are now the most successful trees. Yet large areas are covered with acacias and particularly mulga. (See Arthur Upfield, *Boney and the Mouse*, Pan Books. Upfield really knew the bush.) The mulga is well-adapted to aridity. It's worth noting that acacias and eucalypts are both of the myrtle family.

(I'm told, by the way, that in California they believe that Uncle Sam invented the Eucalypt. "What part of Austrlia do you come from? New

Zealand?")

To complicate all this, the drying has proceeded unevenly with damp spells along the way. The last two were from 4,000 to 3,000 BC and from 500 BC to 500 AD. These changed mainly the distribution of eucalypts themselves, since there are now eucalypts adapted to almost all Australian conditions. There is even one, recently discovered, *E. recurva*, that has to be germinated in the fridge.

(Only one stand of *recurva* is known. It is 5 metres across and contains five small trees. It was discovered in a search for specimens of another rare eucalypt, *E. gregsonii*. The search was mounted because a stand of *gregsonii* is under threat from a car park development *in a national park*. I suppose that we can now expect the newly discovered stand of *recurva* to be bull-dozed to make room for a toilet block.)

Well, having spelled all that out, I have to say that I don't know, and must discover, exactly when Lake Callabona and company went dry on us.

The Cobbler is a dune of compacted sand forty miles across. It is humped and hummocked with tussocky, clumpy little hills from two to twenty feet high and arranged utterly without pattern. The hummocks are much eroded by water. My guess is that this is probably a consequence of white settlement and of over-grazing by stock and rabbits, the latter are plentiful at present after exceptional rains. The rabbits have also quarried the dunes quite badly, as is their wont, the rotten cows. Great country to get bushed in. Monte Collina is the only permanent useful water on the Cobbler. As far as I know! There may be an old usable well on Monte Collina Station, now abandoned, about 12 k. west of us. I'd like to walk over and check it out one of these days. It would be useful to find something since the water here is strictly stock only stuff.

Innaminka, on the Cooper is about 300 k. north of here and these days Moomba, on the Western side of the Strzelecki Creek, about 200. Moomba is the centre of the Cooper Basin gas fields. It is only a matter of time, I fear before the bitumen runs all the way to Moomba. The old track runs up on the Eastern side of the Creek. We are some 800 k. north of Adelaide.

The Cobbler is so-named because it was the worst stretch of the route to the Northern shearing sheds of the Cooper region. The cobbler is the worst sheep in the pen (or the day's tally, or the shed's, or the season's). "Cobbler," then, is short, for "dirty, stinken, rotten, lousy, bastard."

Christine and I are camped here because on 21st May we set out for Coongie Lakes. Coongie is way up in the North of the state, the terminus of the North-west Branch of the Cooper. Unlike the more southerly lakes that receive channels of the Cooper, the Coongie waters are permanent and fresh. According to report, the Coongie area is a promised land. More promise than fulfilment for us: We've been trying to get there for years. This time the rains came the night before we set out and cut the roads over much of the state. The bitumen comes only as far as Lyndhurst a dumpy town over 200 k south of here. The road out of Lyndhurst to Moomba was opened only hours before we took it.

(Lyndhurst is a place of some interest. To give you an idea.—A couple of years back the publican there died, the justly famous hard case, Allan Dunn ("Dunny"), aged 31 years, weighing 31 stone. The funeral service was conducted in the bar of his hotel by the local C-of-E bloke Trev the Rev. Packed out it was for the free piss. The Lord subsequently destroyed the pub by fire. That was early this year. The locals, no children of Rechab, had a new pub functioning in the Community Hall, before the fire was properly out. The landlord was still grieving his way through the hot cinders when they came for him ceremonially to broach the first keg. The pub at Leigh Creek South, next town down the road, hearing of this greatest of all disasters that could befall such a town as Lyndhust, had rushed up emergency supplies.)

On the first day we came just to Mambray Creek in the Southern Flinders. This is only three hours good driving from Adelaide, but we knew we weren't in a hurry and took all day. Mambray Creek is in Mt. Remarkable National Park a large and rugged area, heavily timbered. In January, it burnt out. We spent Sunday walking in it. Awesome! Some of the big old red gums are burnt right into the ground. In some cases the holes are 10 feet across and I reckon one is ten feet deep. Mostly they're spectacular enough, but not that spectacular. Over the years the trees collect at the base large quantities of litter, leaf and twig. In a region of regular fire, most trees of any age are burnt hollow. They fill up and so are in danger of getting burnt off at the roots. That does for them. Otherwise, however, they are almost certain to survive, even if burnt black. Most of the old fellows at Mambray Creek are now struggling back to life. Australian flora is mostly well-adapted to fire and a walk like this one is always inspiring.

Our camp site at Mambray Creek was much visited by emus, particularly by a family of eight half-grown chicks with fluffy top-knots religiously attended by Dad. (Feminism hit the emus early in their evolution.) The Mambray Creek area is especially precious to us. We have an illegal overnight camp there (not used this time) presided over by The Third Best Tree in the World. The fire didn't reach it, thank God, or it would have been a goner, no worries. The hollow base of it straddles a swirl in the creek. When the creek runs, it dumps fuel into this swirl, so that for most of the year the tree encloses a tonne or so of first-rate fuel.

This is one of the many things that makes the camp-site superb. The tree is many hundreds of years old and has burnt and broken many times. In its various parts, inside and out, it bears every possible colour and texture available to a red-gum. Its roots and trunk carry great boulders lifted clean out of the ground and now exposed by old fires. (A crow has just taken the bone we left out for the fork-tailed kites.) It has to go in a fire some time, but I hope not in mine.

Next day to Bunyeroo Creek in the Middle Flinders just where it comes out onto the Western Plain. Jeeze! I hate change. Time was you could camp anywhere in this country. You were welcome to knock off a rabbit or a kid for the camp oven. Now the joint is cluttered with four-wheel drives full of pot-bellied he-men and their she-women with chain saws, heavy artillery, beer bottles, san-pads, disposable nappies, black plastic, white plastic, red plastic ... Result: Fences and signs everywhere. Keep out! No camping! No shooting! No breathing! It is forbidden to exist! And for half these useless bastards, fair enough too.

Next day, 14th, Christine showed me Sliding Rock, a huge tapering curved cliff above Sliding Rock Creek. There is an old abandoned mine and smelters with graves going back to the Eighteen-seventies. I showed her Kanyaka, the ruins of a station founded by one Hugh Proby 120-odd years ago. The buildings are all of local stone and must have been amongst the most impressive in the colony. Even the woolshed is a most imposing piece of architecture. Bare ruined choirs now, but with the sweet birds still singing in them—spiny-cheeked honey-eaters. Down the creek is Kanyaka Waterhole and the Death Rock. The water-hole is a lovely intricate intimate, rocky system of linked permanent ponds, in a landscape of obviously waterless hills. There couldn't be water there! Over it all towers the Death Rock, perhaps not twenty feet high, but in the context huge and brooding. The blacks, who knew their stuff when it came to such matters, used to leave their dying mates to die in its shade. They'd bring them a bit of food and water once a day and wait around some distance off for the event. As Christine said, that was doing them proud. It is, of all the places I've ever seen, *the* place to die.

Latish that day we got here and here we have stuck and are likely to for a few days. We know now that we could get to within twelve miles of Innaminka and probably all the way there. But we *could* get stuck and that could be stuck for weeks even so close to the town. Town! Six inhabitants! There's no reliable information to be had, but we do know that the Cooper's in flood. The Cooper in flood can inundate an area about twice the size of Southern England. Put our boat into it and we're likely to finish up half way to Lake Eyre! The whole point of Innaminka on this occasion is to get to Coongie another 100 k. further on. The Coongie road is out—as usual—and will probably stay out for weeks. Even to get onto it you have to cross the Cooper at Innaminka. All the places we'd like to camp on *this* side of the river are underwater. (I remember Christine years ago taking me to see her old campsite at Pooncarie on the Darling. You'd have needed to have been Jacques Cousteau.[27]) So we've pretty well decided to stay here till our water runs short.

—Whacko the diddlo! Since the last paragraph. I've found fresh water less than two miles from the camp. This means that we can stay here for a few extra days. The old trick for finding puddles is to look from a rise towards a sloping light—in this case the planet Venus. Sometimes you can see a puddle five miles off. The water is little better than mud but it's good and sweet—unlike the bore water—and a pinch of epsom salts should clear it. In any case it's drinkable.—

To resume: There are worse fates than hanging around here, five seconds with a Flinders undergraduate being one of them, five milliseconds with a vice-chancellor being another. We've always meant to sit down awhile on Monte Collina. It's Christine's first visit. A wonderful mysterious place. It's on the Artesian basin and puts out a steady flow of beautifully hot water. Years back a road crew diverted their earth-moving equipment and did the world a good turn by constructing an earth tank. Ever since you've been able to take a warm swim in the cold desert mornings. I was here briefly with Bruno last year. It took ten minutes to get him into the water and three hours to get him out again. The water is slightly sulphurous and harsh to taste. But beautifully soft on the skin, in fact quite silky and slinky, even without soap. Especially after Adelaide water which is used for cutting glass. The overflow has made a nice little swamp. No fish, but stacks of birds. They don't seem to have dispersed much with the rains either. In this particular stretch of country even after heavy rains, the water wouldn't lie around long. I won't give you the catalogue, but this morning we saw different kinds of falcon in the same sky and all interacting—brown falcons and a nankeen kestrel. Yesterday a tiny nankeen kestrel frog-marched a huge brown falcon off the premises. There are dingoes about in plenty and plenty of rabbits for them to dine off. They howl with great enthusiasm every night. On the way in on Tuesday night, there was one standing on a dune right in the headlights. A beautiful yellow dog, well-coated, and obviously practising his poses for a Parks and Wildlife poster. (Don't believe, by the way, that a dingo wouldn't come into a tent and snaffle a baby.[28] One of these days, if you're interested, I'll tell you the story of Squinny Bill when I was well-boring with him outside the Alice in 1949.) There are tracks around our camp, made since the rain, but none since we arrived.

There are few visitors. Two cars yesterday, none today. The Moomba semies[i] go raging past, lit up like cities, out of the night into the night. We are only a hundred yards from the road.

Few or many visitors, over the years they've left a swag of litter. When he was here Bruno thought he saw a fork-tailed kite drop a feather and wanted to retrieve it. We started from where it might have fallen and beat around in ever-increasing circles over an area twenty yards or so in radius. No feather. But a long list of artefacts—some thirty kinds of object. But given the rate of accumulation, it's beaten down into an acceptable historical residue. In a clump of hard-bitten acacia about a quarter of a mile off there is, for example, an abandoned dunny home-made out of petrol drums.

Bloody moths clogging up the key-board!

Well, we're having a ding-dong bludge. Christine reading around, walking a bit, running a bit, doing a bit of a plant survey. Me having my ten-yearly re-read of Damon Runyan. Tomorrow, I suppose, I must start working again on the paper for the Charlie Martin Fesstsschrrifftt. But not too long, not too hard.

We are eating like drovers. Great mounds of meat. You mustn't count the fresh vegies and fruit. And particularly not the King Island double cream. King Island is a tempest-tossed Island in Bass Strait. It is the only remaining source of real cream, that is cream that tastes and smells like cream used to when it tasted and smelled like cows and milking sheds and green grass and chewed cud and not like plastic as does the emulsified muck you get these days. And like *cattle* drovers, I mean. Sheep men eat crap such as mutton.

There's no real wood here, but we carried some just in case. Including some Billiatt mallee roots. I can cook a roast in the camp-oven on three or four smallish sticks of good firewood. And the little twiggy bits of desert wood lying about do very well to boil the billy. Both these operations rely heavily on an instrument called a mini-quicker, a small hand bellows originally designed as a pump for air mattresses. We have gas, if needed, but perish the thought! In fact we are beautifully geared up and life is a bowl of cherries.

Not like it was for the poor bastards who wheeled their loaded bikes (with pedals removed) to the northern sheds. There were no made roads for them and the tracks would blow away from season to season. God only knows what they did for water. Perished a lot of them, you can bet. When

---

[i] Semi-trailers, i.e. large trucks/lorries.

some earl's son, like Hugh Proby drowns in the Willochra, he gets into the history books. (Not for shooting blacks of course, or sweating and starving his station hands.) But these poor bastards mostly don't even have marked graves.[29]

27.v.88
Well that was handy! A couple of self-styled desert rats from the gas fields called in for a swim. They had a billy with us and filled up our canteens with beautiful clean sweet water. Also left us a bit of firewood.

Also told us about a splendid camp nearby—about 50 kilometres south. (It's on the MacDonnell, whose waterholes, Blanchewater and St. Mary Pool, get into the history books—of that later.) They obviously thought we were a bit nuts to be camped in the desert when we could be on permanent fresh water with fish and yabbies and firewood. The thing that makes it most interesting to us is that they reckoned that they'd found big fossils there. Pretty obviously not diprotodon. They described a big "tail" set in a boulder. Since they also described the boulders as "volcanic," I think we may well doubt whether what they saw was a fossil at all. Certainly, it would hardly have been set in igneous rock. And amongst the much that I don't know is anything about traces of volcanism in the MacDonnell. Probably what they saw was sedimentary rock from the Adelaide Geosyncline, water-worn to look like solidified lava-flow.

Notwithstanding my scepticism, they have left us with more decisions. We'd almost decided that when, we left here, we'd find Mulligan's Springs in the desert on the edge of Callabona.

These are mound springs. Mound springs rise from the artesian basin, by a process I can describe if ever you are interested. They form little oases over a very large area of central Australia—without date palms and Peter O'Toole and Omar Sherrif (*sic*), I'm afraid. A matter of some concern at present is whether the mound springs are being destroyed and will eventually run dry along with the artesian bores. There is a huge uranium and what-else-you-name-it mine at Roxby Downs near Andamooka in South Australia. It was brought into existence by the customary perfidy of ALP politicians. (Vague, but just. Any account I could give in a hurry would be over-simplified to the point of inaccuracy.) It was also approved with inadequate environmental studies, particularly with regard to the effect on the Artesian Basin. The mine uses about 500 million litres of water per milli-second. The pastoralists round about believe that their springs and bores are drying up in consequence. One lot is even suing Western Mining. I suspect that the real state of affairs is unknowable at present. At anyrate, I don't know it. But certainly I want to get a good look at some of these springs in the next two rather than in the next ten years.

Another thing we wanted to do was to walk into the northern ranges from Terrapinna Waterhole for a few days. That's pretty wild country unused except by yellow-footed rock wallabies and, of course, bloody great goats. The last of the inland explorers, Warren Bonython, has walked through there, but I don't know of anyone else.[30] (I think that Eyre took the Western side of the Ranges to Mt Hopeless, but I don't have any means of checking that here. But yes he did, because he crossed MacDonnell Creek without naming it.[31]) There'd have been a mob of prospectors in the last century, you can be sure, and I bet we'd find plenty of traces of them for the looking. But nobody ever mentions them. They were often enough the first in, prospectors for pastoral country as well as for minerals, but they don't count as "explorers." Fair enough, I suppose. Certainly, they weren't interested in enlarging the sum of human knowledge. Indeed, they were inclined to keep any useful discoveries—pretty rare in this country—very much to themselves.

Well, we don't have time for everything. It's not just that life is too bloody short. It isn't thick enough either.

Acupuncture! I have acquired, on the strength of a mate's claims for it, a machine called (regrettably) an Acuhealth. It's a little gadget developed and marketed by a South Autralian medico for administering acupuncture to yourself. It delivers a highly localized electric shock, so you don't need needles. It comes with a sensible book of instructions—sensible if you ignore the theoretical rubbish. And, bugger me, within less than a week it began to produce detectable results. I was actually free of pain, for the first time since 1977, and for four whole days. That alone was worth the two hundred and fifty bucks. It didn't last, of course. Travelling and camping soon brought me back to earth. All the same, this trip has been apples and roses compared with any other I can remember. What pisses me off, though, is that I just don't believe in it. It's like having to acknowledge the efficacy of prayer. I find I can have it both ways a bit. When I don't hurt, or not much, I can hug myself with both arms. When I do, I can say, "Bloody told you so!"

[…] I was having a drink in a pub with Bray after the funeral of a mate of ours. I was telling him that I was knocking off the piss. He reminded me of a mate of his, now long dead of the booze, one Shep. Shep was a very stupid and ignorant man, salt of the earth perhaps. He once announced that when he was in grade six he did a test in which he got 3 out of ten for mental and none for menstruation. Well. Bray reminded me of the time he'd advised Shep to join Alcoholics Anonymous. "Not on your life! Why should I get pissed with a mob of bastards I've never even met before!"

I shall leave you, *pro tem,* with a profound question. The bend in the river is justly celebrated in Australian song.

> ... .
> Oh isn't it nice and cosy to be whalin" in the bend
> ... ...
> ... .
> And now that the season is over
> And the shearing is all at an end,
> It's there you will see the flash shearers
> Making Johnny-cakes down in the bend.
> ... ...
>
> And so on ... .[32]

The hot bores have not done so well by long shot. In fact, I can think off-hand of only one reference to them –

> And I've sweated too on Ondaroo
> Bogged down in the great bore drains.[33]

I can't account for this disparity. This injustice, one might even call it. People got bogged in rivers too, for Christ's sake. Even drowned in rivers and I've yet to hear of anybody getting drowned in a bore. Though I'm sure some newchum Pom[i] managed it somewhere. Anyhow the question, and one that relates nearly to the meaning of life and the purpose of the universe, is this.

> Whether a hot bore bludge might not be in some ways superior to whaling in the bend?

(And that reminds me ...) Such a question, touching as it does on the intimate and ultimate fabric of things, should doubtless be answerable out of purely *a priori* considerations. Otherwise, or course, there'd be no point in putting it to Pommy new-chums.

What it reminds me of is two stories. One about Bertrand Russell, interviewed on the BBC, which you may well know. "But in that case, Lord Russell, what could be the purpose of the universe?" "I do not believe the universe hes a purpose. Or if it hes, I believe it to be ay ttrivial

---

[i] "new-chum", colloquial expression for an immigrant, usually from Britain.

wunn." (You know how he spoke. You can't really spell it.)

The other about two swaggies sitting under an inch-high salt-bush for shade, all around them bare gibber plain to the four horizons. The sun hammering down, the flies clambering over them in red-hot hob-nail boots. "Eh, Bert." (You'll understand a five-minute pause between utterances.) "Yes, Fred." "Eh, Bert. Which would you rather have?" "What of Fred?" "Eh Bert. Which would you rather have? A good fuck? Or a wet dream?" "That's an interesting question, Fred." "Eh, Bert. Which would you rather have?" "Well, I dunno, Fred ... Well, I reckon I'd rather have a wet dream." "That's an interesting answer, Bert. ... Eh, Bert, why do you say that, Bert. "Well, I dunno, Fred ... I reckon you meet a nicer type of girl."

One of the saddest stories I know.

29.v.88

Well that's not the end you'll be dismayed to hear. Can't post this here and doubt I have enough paper to print it out, so why finish it?

Yesterday, we took a most marvellous walk into The Cobbler. The original intention was to case out a possible short-cut to the mound springs. The oil and gas pipe-lines cut the road at Monte Collina. They had to be built, so I'd hoped that the tracks alongside them would still be passable. They go to within a few mile of the springs. But this is pretty shifting country. A couple of hundred yards into the desert and you lose all trace of track *and* pipelines. If that's all that's left of the track, then the only way we could get through by that route would be to take a compass bearing straight across the desert. I'm sure we'd make it, but I'm sure also that we'd use more fuel and take longer than by going around three times as far. But the main concern is damage. Plants in this country are precious and we'd churn up one hell of a mess. But there's got to be a maintenance track. There's a turn-off on the eastern side of the road a few K.s south of here and I bet that's it. Decisions!

(There are two huge chestnut-breasted shell-duck feeding in the water. They've been here all the time while we have. The two Moomba rats the other day showed signs of wanting to put them in the pot, but were easily discouraged.)

We discovered two superb little red coolabahs, *Eucalyptus microtheca*. These are best known as a river tree. On the Cooper, they are the dominant tree (not the red-gum) and they grow into huge specimens. Twisted, gnarled, rough old trunks and lower branches, sombre grey. The upper branches smooth, silvery, sometimes blue-ish. Burke, showing good sense for once in his life, died under a real beauty. We'd been surprised on earlier trips to find them in the desert. Here they are quite a small tree, gnarled and twisted. We'd been very unsure of our identification then, not finding buds or fruits, but since then, I'd identified them on the hard stony uplands around Broken Hill, Wilcannia, Cobar. There they grow into a medium-sized tree, quite straightish. There is now no doubt about these two buggers. They are grown trees, one of them hundreds of years old and astonishingly convoluted and fretted at the base. The massive roots have been much exposed by erosion of the dune. Both of them in their sunday best; they stand out across the hummocks as very healthy trees. But neither more than fifteen feet high.

While we were looking at a weeping pittosporum nearby to these trees, a brown falcon, male, of the light phase flew, crying its falcon cry, to the top of one of them—probably from the other, say two hundred yards away. That description should call up a picture of the prettiest bird God ever made (after the nankeen kestrel). It perched there while we walked to within feet of it. It seemed very content to be admired, even making a small exhibition flight before returning to the same top twig. It was being mobbed by a couple of (?) crows but seemed not much worried. We walked over to the second coolabah, the very special one. It held two twig nests, one of them very large, and hence, since it wasn't an eagles' nest, very ancient. It was within seven feet of the ground, so there was no sweat about seeing into it. Just a flat platform across the top. It would have been a ravens' nest or a crows', but falcons also take over these nests. So it would be worth a walk in from the road any time they might be breeding. Like now after the rains—though there's no action so far.

By the time we were walking back to the first tree, the crows had got up a real gang of a dozen or more and the falcon was showing some concern. They had managed to get it into the air, and while it could fly the pants off the whole mob of them together, they wouldn't let it settle anywhere. And there were only half a dozen of perches worthy of a falcon in the area.

(It seems especially easy to mob birds of prey in such an area. A day or so back, we saw a boobook owl—mopoke—getting badly hammered by a pair of willy-wagtails and a pair of singing honey eaters.)

Suddenly, while all this was going on a nankeen kestrel came blistering across the sky, she too crying a falcon cry, straight at the crows, throwing them into confusion. (*She* because she was too large for a male, though still much smaller than the brown falcon.) The Kestrel is the smallest falcon and she was pocket-sized to the crows, but she scattered them like Jove's thunder. Before they had time to think such thoughts as are available to crows, a flight of at least four, and maybe more, fork-tailed kites arrived on the scene and began flying nonchalantly with the crows. By flying I mean sailing, of course, and I tell you, the fork-tailed kite is the best nonchalant flyer in the world.

Then appeared on the scene a *Square*-tailed kite. This is an animal much like the fork-tailed kite, but a heavier flier. (Trust me: I know the differences. So, in spite of the doubts of the manager of Moolawatana Station, does Bruno.) This bird seemed mainly interested in us, as had been the original brown falcon, and not at all in the above-mentioned transactions. Quite strikingly, it perched low sometimes on a small sand hill 3 feet high—even though a bush growing on the top of the same hummock would have given it another four or six feet. Often enough, it would perch only half way up such a hill. It would allow us to approach to within about 15 yards and then lumber off, circling us low to perch again, and again low, about 15 yards off. Soon another bird got involved with this one, a fork-tailed kite. We would have sworn from their behaviour that they were a pair, if they hadn't been clearly of different species and surely more clearly to themselves than to us. Soon enough the inevitable crow began to hassle them. At one stage the three of them were perched, each within two feet of the other, about fifty yards from us. By the time they had taken themselves off, so had all the other birds.

What was all that about? Something surely. Even if somebody knows what such things mean, there'll be something just as mysterious just around the next corner. I'm impressed with the huge edifice of human knowledge, but more than that with the desarts of vast eternity, the endless reaches of human ignorance. As a kid I wondered about the origin and extent, in space and time, of the universe. Nobody knows, or *can* know, more about these things than I did then. I'm fed up with hearing that the universe originated in a big bang 15,000b.+ years ago. Originated, mind you. How could anybody know that? (I've even seen a diagrammatised history of the universe in which the big bang is shown coming out of a black cube labelled "VOID"!) Or that the furthest objects that we can detect are getting towards the very fringes of the universe and that we see them as they were not long after the beginning of time. We do know plenty, of course. One cc. of a pulsar weighs as much as the QE2. In the late Seventeenth Century the small brown rat crossed the English Channel and pretty well wiped out the big black rat, thus ending the epidemics of plague. For years I wondered why hakeas expend so much energy developing heavy wooden seed-pods to protect just two winged seeds. Now I know. (But I bet you don't. Our collective knowledge, may be imposing enough, but our individual knowledge is a mere sand castle confronting a king tide.) These are the kinds of thing we can know. Up with science and down with scientism! Up with science and down with relativism. Up with science and down with absolutism.

Since that little bit of sloganising, we've done a brief reccy. As a result we have an all-day walk planned tomorrow. We've pushed into the Cobbler South of here on the Western side of the road investigating lines of coolabahs. It's obvious that they're related to water even here, though the odd one seems not to be. Tomorrow we'll walk straight to the Strzlecki and search for the ruins of Monte Collina Station. If we find it in time, we'll strike straight across the desert where the creek turns south and pick it up again where it enters Lake Blanche. That will be a minimum of 30 k. No great problem in itself, but I doubt we'll make it. The dunes between the Southern bend of the creek and the lake will run North-south straight across our course. The ruins will be invisible till you fall down the well and there will be much to see. We make marvellous discoveries (for us) every time we move. Christine is industriously recording the latest right now. Today's best was a pair of very very old emu bushes, *Erimophila longifolia*.

Before leaving here we must walk back to that wonderful coolabah on the eastern side and boil a billy under it. It deserves some such mark of respect.

Now we'll turn off the lights and watch Scorpio sprawling across the sky exhausted by yet another losing battle with the waxing moon. I think often how the sting of Scorpio never rises over England. Who are you blokes trying to kid! The country of the Oxford don and Maggie Thatcher!

31.v

Well, the ruins were hard to find and there was indeed much to see and we didn't make Blanche. On the way we were waylaid, no enticed, by orange chats. The orange chat is a somewhat elusive bird of arid regions and, despite its vividness quite hard to observe. And blue-wing wrens. The male, very shy and cunning, occasionally burning like an iridescent coal in the heart of a sombre bush. The blue-wing is everywhere on The Cobbler, but the male rarely shows himself well. Then the ruins! Monte Collina Station now consists of a small pile of brick rubble that would be hard enough to find in a suburban back-yard. That, some broken glass, one water worn stone in a country of sand, and one rusty sardine can. The last of these disintegrated when I dropped it back on the ground.

All this on the most appalling site for a building, a harshly eroded, depressed sandy slope, clearly a torrent in wet weather. Nobody in their right mind would have built in such a place. So it looks as though the degradation of the immediate area has occurred since European settlement.

And this suggests that the degradation of the whole region is the result of European settlement and particularly of the attentions of our accursed sheep and trebly accursed rabbits.

Other things suggest the same. When we crossed the creek to look for the ruins we were struck, by what seemed a new kind of eucalypt. No real surprise: there are hundreds of different eucalypts. They are often very hard to identify and their taxonomy is constantly being revised. A new classification soon to appear proposes to break up the old genus altogether. What helped to confuse us was the appearance of red-gum for the first time on the Cobbler—three trees, one of fair size and multi-stemmed on the flat between the river bed and the dunes. River dunes, that is, between channels. (This is an area of harsh salt. Some river-reds are highly tolerant of salt and can endure water salter than the sea.) On the very tops of these dunes, with hummocks building up about them, were clusters of eucalypts, smooth-barked like red-gum, but of markedly different habit. About twelve feet high at the highest, with slim wandering trunks and blueish foliage slightly coarser than red-gum leaves. At first we could find no fruits or buds to help us out. (The red-gums were heavily in bud.) An interesting question was: *How could such trees get established in the first place?*. Their roots would be in water now, but there would be no water in the dunes for the seedlings—not for more than a few days at any one time.

Finally, the solution hit us. These weren't clumps of small individual trees. Each clump was one quite large coolabah, most of it buried. We could now see that, far from the trees growing in the dunes, the dunes had grown around the trees. The dunes were, in fact, one dune, extending upstream for at least a mile. And following exactly a line of coolabah that was in turn following the creek. My guess is that the sand is being cut out of the Cobbler by water, carried into or towards the creek and then, before it gets compacted again dumped by wind against the trees.

There are many other signs of degradation, one of them being the prevalence of dillon bush, which, Christine tells me, tends to take over when more useful plants are over-grazed.

We'd taken time, too, looking at mistletoe birds and variegated wrens in the acacias of the dunes between channels. The mistletoe bird is a very presentable little fellow. Minute. Active. Dense blueish black-backed. Intense scarlet on the breast and bum. (The female, of course, is somewhat more demurely turned out.) This bird is the main propagator of mistletoes in Australia. There is a close relationship between bird and plant. The bird excretes other faeces in the ordinary way, but mistletoe berries come out in a long sticky chain which is attached to the host plant. They take only about thirty minutes to pass through the bird, the berries by-passing the stomach in which tougher matter, like insects gets pulverised. (30/03/00 Note.—When passing mistletoe seeds, the bird sits along the branch; but sits across it when passing other matter.)

The variegated wren was exciting. First-off because it's an exciting bird. But secondly, and mostly, because I saw one bird, a female, a male in eclipse, a juvenile, who knows?, with a whitish surround to the eye from the beak. This is a characteristic of the race (of) and *dulcis* is found only in the top end of the Northern Territory. Here we are in the range of the nominate race which extends over most of the continent. Pizzey's distribution map shows a distinct break between the ranges of the various races, but I bet that is more than anybody knows, especially as the vacant bands are shown as being very narrow. The old problem of the negative existential. And it is worth remarking that, at last count, nobody knew even whether the males of the <u>races</u> <u>dulcis</u> and <u>amabilis</u> have an eclipse phase. The observation was quite certain, though of one bird and once only. The bird was observed for some minutes, with glasses, within less than ten yards for most of the time and down-light. For much of the time, a bird, also plain but with red eye surround was feeding in the same branch, sometimes within inches of the subject.

If this observation is OK—and I would bet both eyes on it—then it suggests an interesting little hypothesis. I would suppose that the whitish marking of the race *dulcis* came about as a result of selection operating upon a spontaneously mutating gene. That the races remain distinct, and more or less invariable with respect to this characteristic, suggests in turn one of two things. Either the mutation rate is very low, in which case it is hard to see how the characteristic could have yielded a useful mark of differentiation. Or the mutation is still being selected out in the nominate race (and its "converse" mutation in *dulcis*) in which case there would seem to be some reason for preserving it as a mark of differentiation. In which case the ranges probably do overlap after all.

This is home-made genetics, as you will recognize, There are some pretty shaky assumptions involved, some of which I can spot for myself. But it's at least as good as the mass-produced steam-driven genetics of the professor of genetics who last year told Christine's Biology class at Adelaide that mathematical ability is hereditable. You can guess the argument on which this socially useful doctrine is based. If you can't and if you wish, I can supply it. You may then like to amuse yourself applying it to characteristics like *living at number 6*.

From the rise above the ruins, just where the Creek swept south, we could see our route westward to Blanche. See it to the first big dune, with a tiny tree almost dead on our bearing. Here we were past lunch time, with

five of our day's thirty-odd kilometres walked, though some of them
walked many times. With wonderful trees all about us, fire-wood and
birds, and ahead the transverse dunes. No choice at all! Brewing up, of
course, and yet another easy day.

I had a bit of a read of Moravia who always makes me wild.

> Blow the bloody bugle!
> Beat the bloody drum!
> Blow the bloody bourgeoisie
> To kingdom bloody come.

Especially the lumpen bourgeoisie. And, along with them, especially
Moravia. He is so systematically concerned with the mere phenomena
rather than with the systems of decadence. So devoted to anatomising its
manifestation in bizarre individuals. So psychological. So unpolitical. So
politically reactionary. So inhumanely humanist.

So that was the day. Except for the wonderful walk back. And, saved
up till last (if you're lucky), the first sight of the Strzlecki. Rivers have a
character of their own, sometimes maintained over hundreds of miles and
this was the old Strzlecki alright. A long, broad, shallow, curving sweep.
Noble and brutal (to split a hair). Soft pretty reaches of clear water, miles
long, Salt as Lot's wife. The clarity indicating the saltness—a fresh would
bring in mud. Hard and harsh. Soft and delicate. (I can't approve your
dislike of harsh landscape, by the way. Only in hard country, can you find
real subtlety. Where everything is pretty, nothing is. Where every prospect
pleases, as Alexander Selkirk said, it gives you the shits. I go off green
very quickly in Oxfordshire and only get to be able to tolerate it again on
the moors and in the Highlands.) And then from the high dunes, looking
south across The Creek and way out over the Cobbler, the Northern
Flinders. Blue. A mere bulking out of the sky at the horizon. More of a
mere emotion than a mountain range.

While I was looking at them some lines of Flexmore Hudson kept
coming into my mind. (It must be 30 years since I read them and I won't
have them right.)

> And I stay a long time trying to distinguish
> The purple plain from the purple ranges,
>
> The purple ranges from the purple sky.[34]

*{Back in Adelaide: "ranges" should be "mountains," "sky" should be
"clouds."}*

Wilf (i.e. Flexmore) is much present to me at the moment. I went to his cremation ceremony the day before I came on this trip. I've known him since 1944 when I was an ignorant, gauche schoolboy and he was an "established" poet of thirty or so. He was also editor of a magazine called "Poetry". He'd carved this with his bare hands out of Australian indifference and philistinism. It became in time, one of the "leading" literary magazines in English. The British Government eventually put him out of business with their ban on the import into England of Australian magazines. *After* the collapse of "Poetry," and because of it, Commonwealth Literary Fund policy changed and private magazines became eligible for grants. He was a country school-teacher when he started the publication. I went and stayed with him and his wife, Merle Desmond, at Lucindale where Wilf ran a one-teacher school. Till then I'd had no idea that there could be anything but cold war between teachers and students. Wilf actually used to wrestle with his kids on the school-room floor! My intellectual life really began with my friendship with Hudson. He introduced me to authors like Bertrand Russell, Freud, Ingersoll,[35] Aldous Huxley. My first five minutes with Russell's essay "The Value of Scepticism" have left their mark on my mind to this day. Later, their son Rory was a philosophy student at Flinders. He was fairly able but, wisely, is now a lawyer in the public service. Nice lad, but the kind of student who drives you barmy by talking religiously about "so-called physical objects." In spite of my immense debt to him and my large respect, I found Wilf a somewhat difficult, touchy character and we didn't see all that much of one another, in later years. Merle suicided in 1979 and Wilf spent the next couple of years blowing his brains out with booze. He cracked up entirely and had to be put into a nursing home about five years ago. His short stories, written over many years, were published last year. A few years back he was granted a Commonwealth Literary pension. But the recognition, such as it was, came too late. Bray and I used to get him out to my place for lunch and play him Vivaldi in the garden, but he didn't have too much idea of what was going on. Bray spoke at the service, well and movingly. There was also a disgusting bit of grandstanding by another bloke. Hardly any of Adelaide's self-acclaimed literati were there. A poet, a small publisher, a few drinking mates. I don't know.

Christine's place
6.vi.88

Bugger and bugger and bugger it!
   Recently in a shop I saw a notice saying

   To err is human.

To really stuff things up takes a computer.
My correspondence disk has a bug and won't release any of the info on it. The back-up disk didn't have the last part of my letter to you—i.e. most of what follows. It was some 18,000 characters. But I'm not going to be beaten by the 20th fucking Century. I'm gunna do the whole friggin' lot again as though it were first time round. Even down to the spontaneous expressions of immediacy. Here goes then:

<<<<<<<<<<<<<<<<<<<<<<<<<< ... ...

St. Mary Pool
MacDonnell Creek
Strzlecki Track
3.vi.88

Look! I've got to tell you about our billy that we boiled under that little old coolabah. We walked over on the day before we left the bore to do homage. On the way over we discovered some brown falcon pellets. (I can tell you why they were probably brown falcon pellets and in the first version I did.) Two of them were pretty much like ordinary owl pellets. Fibrous, furry, small bones. One of these two had a tiny feather sticking out and, woven into the fibre, numerous little beetle skeletons. A multitude of minute tragedies! The other two pellets were the interesting ones, however. They consisted entirely of conglommerated seeds. Unidentified, but very like ruby salt-bush. This is fruiting heavily at present. I like ruby salt-bush berries. So do emus. So, as I found out last night, do white-plumed honey-eaters. But falcons?
        And next!
        Next after we'd had our billy and I was reading bloody Moravia with increasing impatience and Christine was absorbing the ambience, two dingoes came padding towards us through the hummocks. Right up to us! I measured the tracks afterwards. Twenty-five feet. By the time Christine had got me aware of them and I'd got my thick head up to look, they'd tumbled to us and turned back. One of them turned again almost immediately and stared at us. Seconds only or maybe even only parts of a second, but it seemed forever. It seemed to use up all the time in the universe. A golden, lucent animal! The life glowed from inside it. Its gaze was intense, brilliantly young, but ancient. Not old. Ancient. The inhabitant of every desert ever. Then it turned and became mere dog again. The two of them threaded the hummocks. Just at a trot, but probably faster than I could run these days—if I *could* run with this rotten hip. Not even bothering to lope. At the top of the ridge, the second animal turned briefly

to look. Gloriously beautiful, but all the same just a dog.

Experiences like that have their roots deep in the ineffable. (I mean something quite naturalistic and sayable by that.) Try to utter the ineffable and you start talking bullshit.

Dingoes were always present on The Cobbler. Their voices held the night together, thrown out in long looping cries from every quarter of the desert. But mostly it was an absent presence. I'd seen them often enough in the bush, in zoos, conservation parks. But this was *seeing*.

There are dingoes here too and this morning one was going about its leisurely business just over the creek from us. So the move here isn't a come-down to rock bottom. Though certainly it is to rock. This is big boot country. So Christine can't do her 12k run here without risk of injury. We've been kicking around the donga together now for eight years man and boy and this time at the bore was the first time we've set about conscientiously to have a massive bludge. (Not that we left home with that in mind, but the idea soon developed.) All the same, Christine had to do her run each day.

I was right. On the way south from the bore, we found that the turn-off to the pipe-line track is just 6 k. down The Track. And opposite the turn-off is a system of clay-pans, Wilf's Crossing. We'd walked a bit in a bit of it a few days earlier. The pans support small coolabahs at their edges. In a country with few trees and many birds, as this is after rain, every tree carries at least one nest, sometimes many. The whole area was thronged with a frenzy of breeding birds. Willy-wagtails, crested pigeons, peaceful doves, singing honey-eaters, crows, probably ravens, falcons, nankeen kestrels, fork-tailed kites, black-shouldered kites, letter-winged kites. All hassling for a nest, a living, a place in the sun. A surprising absence was wedge-tail eagles. There were certainly nests of their size there and we saw some flying high.

(The letter-winged (*Elanus scriptus)* and black-shouldered (*E. notatus*) kites, by the way, are two small hawks, somewhat bigger than a kestrel of the family *Accipitridae* and the subfamily—damn, I've forgotten. Both are snowy beneath and silvery grey above. Much more pure and luminous, though, than gulls or terns. Each has characteristic black markings both above and below. You are unlikely to need the details to get through your day, so I'll say merely that *scriptus* has the letter L clearly defined under its wings. It has a somewhat larger head than the *notatus*—though if Hollands[36] is right this is an illusion—larger eyes, too, and a large black mask about them. These make it a bit owl-like. There is an opinion which links these features to a supposedly more crepuscular life-style. Hollands, as I remember, describes *Scriptus* as "entirely nocturnal" and his observations support this. *Notatus* is the more successful and wide-spread and common of the two. It has penetrated towns and, to some extent, cities. This is attributed to more versatile feeding. *Scriptus* is quite rare and yet can build up rapidly to very large numbers when the going is good, as it is now. This is followed by a massive dying when things get tough again, as they always do in this country. In late 1976, there began a large migration of Letterwings into the settled areas as the Inland dried up after a succession of unusual good seasons. This resulted in some strong but temporary colonies, one even in Port Melbourne. By next summer the colonies had disappeared.)

(Both birds deliver dainty, precise flight full of soft hoverings and sharp, banking turns to leave you quick as a blink with an empty sky. There are differences in flight that seem quite striking, but my perceptions of these are still mostly at the gestalt stage. One notable difference, though, is the high-winged flight of *scriptus*. The wings are held up at an angle of about 60 degrees to the horizontal, the very tips vibrating rapidly. This was observed by Hollands. No evidence from our observations that this is a special pair bonding display flight. It was observed several times and as often as not in the absence of the partner. Doubtless it is used in pair bonding flight, as observed by him. This may be merely because it can yield a very slow flight, near enough to hovering. Or indeed it may be because of the visual aspects of this kind of flight.)

(The fork-tail is the good old cosmopolitan black kite, *Milvus migrans*.)

First thing we saw walking up to the pan, a male brown falcon hunted four crows out of a nearby tree, and perched himself near its nest. As we were approaching him, a female flew cackling to a tree right by us. As we were approaching *her*, she began cackling in earnest mantling over a nest about two feet below her. She kept this up for as long as we stayed near her. A fork-tail flew from a huge nest in a largish tree about 50 yards off. One of a pair, it hung round this tree with its mate. And then a letter-wing flew overhead uttering a scratching croak that developed into a scratching, croaking, rattling scold when it seemed to need one.

It tended to hover over a nest in yet another nearby tree or to perch in a tree alongside it. Then suddenly, like thought, it had leapt large lengths of miles a quarter of a mile or so down the pan. We seemed to see it flying there with a similar bird. Then two letter-wings were back. Suddenly, without coming, there they were overhead. One of them took on one of the fork-tails, repeatedly buzzing it and scolding while the big bird repeatedly rolled presenting its talons. Then the two little kites flew to yet another nearby tree where one of them settled down briefly on a nest. This was the first time we had seen letter-wing kites. Anyone who sees even one in a life-time is lucky and we got to see two pairs in one eyeful and three pairs altogether.

And so on and so on ... and so on ...

In the end, after about an hour we had to leave. We couldn't take in any more. All of this in a walk of less than a mile from and back to the car.

St. Mary Pool is a fairly conventional Australian water-hole, one of five permanent holes that form a chain up MacDonnell Creek. Good wood, sweet water, reasons why most people would prefer it to Monte Collina bore. And a vibrant bird-life of the kind common on water holes. A good reason for preferring the bore—I'm coming to abominate corellas. Here too is the rufous song-lark. Camping with rufous song-larks is like living in a house full of other people's children. Fish. Big bastards of some kind and always jumping. But bugger them. There are yabbies too, I think. The area is a bit cramped for camping space, at any rate on the water, but there's plenty of room for one party of our size. Flies and mossies in millions standing twelve-hour shifts.

Much left to do at the bore, but we were running out of wood and water. Another time, if we wanted a long stint at the bore, I'd bring a trailer and load up from here. We came straight here from the bore, because Christine was keen to look for the fossils.

Fossils! Well, right again, wasn't I! Christine looked yesterday without success, in spite of the fact that they are "everywhere." The "volcanic" rock turns out to be a long, sloping cascade of sandstone just above the hole. A superb formation. The boulders have been wonderfully worn by water so that they look like pumice magnified perhaps 100 times. (There are indeed some fragments of quartz in the creek-bed debris and out on the gibber, but these have obviously been carried down from elsewhere. No trace of anything like that in the bed-rock.) This morning I found a boulder with a formation in it that you could take for a dinosaur's tail-bone. Just! That is, if you were the sort of person who could mistake these for volcanic rocks, who could expect a dinosaur to survive a roasting in molten rock, who had never noticed that in most skeletons the vertebrae tend to resemble one another. If you were the sort of person who could mistake pictures in the fire for the real thing.

There is an interesting story about MacDonnell Creek. (I'm sure that Edward John Eyre would have called it Illusion Creek, though he wouldn't have been taken in by either of the illusions in question, the one above or the one below.) It's told by Hans Minchan *the* historian of the Ranges,[37] but I'll have to do it from memory—now memory within memory. You'll recognize the story as amongst Bruno's sources, though his Inland Sea was

Lake Eyre.

In 1857, W.G. Goyder led an expedition into this area. Goyder was Deputy Surveyor General of the Colony of South Australia, a man of some ability, though at that time obviously a newchum Pom. He followed the creek from St. Mary Pool past another hole, another, another and then Blanchewater, out onto the plain and further to where the channel becomes about four miles wide near its entrance into Lake Blanche. The season had obviously been good because there was an expanse of water spilled over from the creek. This was real enough, right at Goyder's feet. But he also saw a large stretch of water stretching away to the north east. And this was pretty certainly mirage. In it there were islands at great distances and presenting towering cliffs.

Goyder was naturally excited by this new fresh-water lake. He "galloped" into Adelaide with the news and a proposal that a boat should be "placed upon its waters" to explore its full extent. The announcement embarrassed the government with a rush to take up pastoral leases in the area.

Later that year, an expedition returned to the area led by one Captain Freeling, Surveyor General to the Colony. This party lugged a dirty great boat up through the Ranges, a task that would be difficult enough even today by their route and by their conveyances. (There was no properly watered route on the western plains at this time.) With much effort, they got the boat to the margin of the water. They were unable to launch it. They couldn't even launch a small dinghy. Empty, what's more! It took six men to manhandle it through the mud and three miles out the water was only six inches deep. The towering islands turned out to be mere nearby heaps about a foot high.

Freeling reported on this with some restraint. He too saw Goyder's cliffs and promontories, but remarked that "a careful observer" would hardly attribute "too much reality" to them. The boat was "abandoned to its fate" by the "fast vanishing waters."

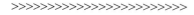

I have a good compressive memory. It's reduced the above by over a third.

I know what it is now. I'd told you some of the Wanaaring stories. Can't remember now how they came up and I forgot them second time round. I must indeed tell you the Wanaaring stories. (Wanaaring is a town, of 21 souls, black and white but all indifferently damned, on the "parched Paroo/Where the water's scarce and the houses few." The publican claimed it to be "The parched Paroo where churches are few/ and men of religion are scanty." The claim was accurate enough, but Banjo Paterson's lines were actually written of the Outer Barcoo. The Barcoo is part of the Cooper system, while the Paroo flows into the Darling at Wilcannia. I actually know a bloke, in fact it is Bob Hawkes, who has actually seen Daniel Magee's shanty on the Outer Barcoo.[38] Strong on scholarship at Wanaaring they are not. I stayed in the pub for one glorious week in 1985 after being knocked off my bike by a feral pig. Christine drove up with her Mum and Dad to retrieve me. Then I was back again with Bruno to pick up the bike much out of my road hooray on my way home from the Sydney conference. I once asked the general storekeeper how to find the dump. "Well you just drive around till the rubbish seems thickest and you're there." Bruno loved the joint.) Yes, I must tell you the Wanaaring stories. But another time now.

Oh, and another thing I managed to overlook—a pair of black-breasted buzzards, *Hamilostra melanosternum*. Twice on consecutive days. Hacking back and forth very rapidly over the ground across the river. This bird is a very large hawk. Very rare. Peculiar to Australia. These were of the dark phase, very black and white against the light, very characteristic. Not a buzzard. Perhaps related to the snake eagles of Africa. A reptile-eater and a nest-robber. These birds have been known to raise Kestrel eyasses, pretty clearly first taken as prey. In one case, there were no buzzard eyasses, but *seven* kestrels in the nest. (Hollands, D. *Eagles, Hawks and Falcons of Australia*, Nelson, Melbourne, 1984.)

Something, I've forgotten what, reminds me of a story about my mate John Bray, an eminent poet. (Of course, you met him.) He was chief Justice of South Australia for a decade or so, appointed directly from the bar to become, according to those who know such things, the Great Judge of his generation in the English speaking world. John used to booze a bit in those days and was, implausibly, a life member of the Amateur Sports Club. (The Adelaide Club, haunt of the posh, had black-balled him when he was originally appointed to the Bench, and he had subsequently declined their invitation to join.) In the days of his High Office, Hurtle Square where he lived was a hang out for abos and they used to sit around on the grass in a circle day and night. Three am. on a Sunday morning and Bray would be walking home from the club ... "Hey mate. You godda ssthigarette?" Bray would produce a packet from which every fag would vanish almost before it could be opened. "Feel like a wrrink mate?" And the Chief Justice of South Australia would sit down on the grass at three in the morning and demolish a flagon with a bunch of abo piss-pots. At eight in the morning, he'd have begun on his Sunday reading, some three or ten books to be remembered in fine grain till hell freezes over. I used to have a flat at the back of his Mum's house in the fifties and we used to do our Sunday reading together on the back lawn. It was terrifying to watch him demolish books. I have to content myself with being brighter than Bray, because I'm sure as God not more learned.

Talking about Hell freezing over ... Charlie Martin once sought treatment from a traditional Chinese medico (not, however, a Chinese traditional medico) for a crook back that was driving him crazy. The bloke held a burning stick near his back telling him to sing out when he couldn't stand it any longer. Charlie being Charlie, the medico gave in first and Charlie had to seek treatment from the orthodox Occidental profession for a barbecued back. He didn't want to get his traditional Chinese mate in the shit, and the doctor was very puzzled at Charlie's explanation. "You think you must have pressed up against something hot. You *think*! My dear man, you have a blister eighteen feet across!" (Or however big.)

Tolka
Casterton,
Victoria
1.viii.1988

Esurientes implevit bones et divites dimissit inanes.
So reckons the counter-tenor chipping in with his threepennorth towards J.S. Bach's *Magnificat*. Well, I've got news for him! And suppose he had, same difference, ain't it?

I'm in the livingroom with half a redgum burning in the grate. Bob and Ivy have gone to Queensland and I'm baby-sitting the joint. Pretty busy actually, trying to write a paper that won't come—I'm a bit unsettled at present. Retirement, probably, and no booze, perhaps, though I'm not conscious of deprivation in either case. But there are two exciting things here, at present.

One is Anderson, a splendid thoroughbred stallion. Coal black. *Brown* coal black. Big powerful bastard, but lithe as a kitten. Every morning he comes thundering across the yard as I get through the fence by his feed stall. It's about fifty yards across so he can get up a fair gallop. He'll brake to a halt just before he knocks you flying then throw himself straight up on his hind legs and strike vigorously at the air above your head. As if that's not alarming enough, he'll then throw himself onto his front feet, spinning though 180 degrees in the same motion and lash out with both feet over your head. The first time he charged up, I hunted him off with severe words and illustrated by emphatic gestures. But the old boy doesn't mean any real harm, I'm sure, though I still make sure to keep well in the open. He's just making clear that he's in the stallion business. No other bastard's going to get a mouthful of his lucerne hay. And that includes me that's bringing it to him.

The other is Careless Talk. A mare. Due to foal while I'm here. She has a transmitter rigged to her halter. The receiver is in my room to sound an alarm as soon as she lies down. I've never seen a mare foal before, let alone delivered one. My job should amount to no more than brewing up cups of tea in the paddock, reading a book—by lamplight if necessary—huddling over a gas heater if it's cold, timing the developments and ringing the vet if necessary.

(Bob just rang from Queensland. Anderson is 17 years old!)

Another possible source of excitement is the river. But by it, perhaps I prefer to be bored. The Glenelg runs along the southern border of Tolka. There have been good rains. The river was high under the bridges when I came down four days ago. All the billabongs are full.

(There is a fine horseshoe billabong immediately below the house.) It's fallen a foot or so in the last twenty-four hours. But a quick three or four inches anywhere between here and its source in the Grampians—no, not those Grampians, these Grampians—would be interesting. There's a bend in New Billabong Paddock, just a bit west of here. The river chokes at that point and the banks dip. If the water comes over it sweeps past the homestead, obliterating the billabong, then along the whole length of the property. The best part of Tolka is chocolate-loam river flat and it can go under water very smartly. So one has to get the cattle and horses out in time. Fortunately, there is stringybark scrub on high ground backing the flats all the way along. But it could be a bit tricky not getting bogged. The property is long and narrow and cattle dense as jarrah. The last flood here, five years ago (?), floated an old red-gum log five feet in diameter and maybe twenty feet long clean over the top of a fence. So blow that.

Down to Meath—no up(stream) today to say hullo to Shekel, The Arab stallion. He's running with the cattle there. A poem in horseflesh. He always trots straight across the paddock for a yarn and to strike a few Mr. Universe poses. Also to look at my camp there. Beautiful and full of memories, but it's not a good winter camp in this country, being inside the curve of the boomerang.

Bob and Ivy have been swept off their feet by David Suzuki and now are convinced that expanding economies are out. Suzuki has been in Australia this year and has been broadcasting a lot. He's been saying the things that I've been telling undergraduates and trying to tell Bob for the last 5 years. I'll refrain from saying, "I told you so." I hope Suzuki is as effective elsewhere. One criticism I have of him is that he seems completely untainted by the Marxist tradition. But this same deficiency probably makes him more accessible to a lot of people. The trouble is, though, it also means that anyone he does convince about how things are is likely to sink into despair. Our present behaviour is going to seem the inevitable result of "human nature." Along with this, Suzuki's pretty strong on the genetic determinants, the "reptile brain" especially. If he's right on that one, then he might as well not bother.

Brolgas! I've seen brolgas often enough now. They come to Tolka fairly often, but mainly to Kangaroo down the Eastern end. They used to visit Meath regularly when I was camped there. But now I've seen them dancing for the first time ever. The North Killara Bridge is out and I was making an unnecessarily roundabout trip into Casterton. Suddenly two brolgas flew across the track in front of me. The brolga is a beautiful grey crane, <u>Gurus rubicund,</u> with red colour to the head. These two swooped low across the track, then planed up over the fence, their extended legs just clearing. They landed after several "attempts" in a sheet of water lying just up over the grass. One of them stabbed into the water quickly a couple of times then turned to face its mate with two or three long pieces of grass hanging down from each side of its bill. It approached the other bird shaking this vigorously and jumping into the air from tip-toe with every other step. The second bird was bowing deeply with wings extended out and back. From this bow it would move into an upright position, stretching on tip-toe with head and beak erect. The wings would be held out at the sides, fingers parted. Then bowing, then stretching. When the two birds came together they began stabbing energetically with their bills, alternately on one side then the other of each others heads. At the same time they would leap into the air from their toes, gently moving their extended wings so that they seemed to float up and down. Bursting with life like Anderson, but gentle, gentle, gentle. Awkward and graceful. (The most graceful things I ever see build their grace on awkwardness. That is why Fonteyn always left me cold and why, generally, a good batsman who has to make the best of what's on offer, whose movements can't be choreographed, leaves any classical ballet dancer for dead.) Next, the "first" bird turned away and walked off bowing deeply as it went. Then at ten yards, it dropped its piece of grass and they were both birds again.

One interesting thing was that this all happened within about thirty yards of me and I'd got out of the car to watch it. In the past brolgas have never let me approach them closely, always melting away quite accidentally into the landscape. Or flying off if I put them under pressure. The nearest I'd ever got (out of a car) was in Kangaroo once with Bob.

The birds flew then when we got to about fifty yards of them. They circled overhead. But on that occasion, they had a chick planted in the scrub.

Another interesting thing. ... On the same trip today, a flock of about a hundred black cockatoos in a pine forest. (These birds love pine nuts.) <u>White</u>-tailed black cockies. The nearest white-tailed cockies should be in south-western Western Australia 2,000 miles away. I didn't have glasses, but the light was excellent and the nearest only a bit more than a cricket pitch away. They <u>had</u> to be yellow-tails. But they bloody well weren't. I searched for a dropped feather, but there was none. Caution: watch your eyes. Reminder: ask Bob.

A couple of years back I saw a yellow-tail perched in a tree in Lucerne. Its head and shoulders were gold instead of black. That was not an illusion. Bob and Ivy had both seen it too.

Bob is going to farm ostriches for leather. He'd prefer to farm emus and that would make more sense, but the conservationist lobby would go out of its brain at the suggestion. So it's got to be an exotic animal. Conservationists are about as rigid in their thinking as lefties. (They're not alone, of course, but I don't so much mind other people making fools of themselves.) There are very good reasons for farming kangaroos for meat and hides in Australia. But there's no possibility of that being allowed in the foreseeable future. So we go on letting sheep and cattle tear the joint to bits and pug up the waters.

14.v.89

For the conclusion of all these unfinished narratives you'll have to come to Australia.

Iris, my dear friend you keep on saying you wish I was there and I'd love to be. Not in England particularly, but having a jar (of orange juice) and swapping songs and lies with you. But that's further off than it was. […] Plenty of time, of course. I'm only sixty-one so I count on at least another forty good working years. Eventually I'll make it. But in the meantime youa have to leg it out here. Worth your while. I bet you'd learn more from Australia than I'd learn from Britain. Not simply on account of the superiority of this end over that, but also because of your greater educability. But you'd need to be able to get at the place. So this time you wouldn't want to be tied to anything like the British Council. Not all the time anyhow.

Till then, much love me old china,
Much love
Brian

Iris Murdoch to Brian Medlin
[Letter 9]

[Aerogramme postmarked 21 Nov 1988]

Professor Brian Medlin
School of Humanities
The Flinders University of South Australia
Bedford Park
South Australia 5042

68 Hamilton Road
Oxford

Nov 20 [1988]

Brian, I'm so glad to hear from you, and thank you for sending your very interesting and stirring article. Powerful stuff.

I hope you are also writing poems and songs. I wish you would come over here and we could have a jar and sing a song or two and discuss all sorts of matters. I do hope you are well and very OK.

I've sent the letter you mention. I am OK, finished a novel; but am overwhelmed by jobs, tasks, obligations of a tiresome kind. Do write.

with love & best wishes,
ever
Iris

Iris Murdoch to Brian Medlin
[Letter 19]

68 Hamilton Road
Oxford OX2 7QA

June 4 [1989]

Brian, thank you so much for your long scroll letter (word processed?) and for the <u>delightful</u> enclosures. I loved Bruno's splendid adventures and your Birds of Meath. What a country, what chaps. And what nice pictures of Christine, & her lovely hair, and her lovely daughter, and you, and Mount Speculation.

I'm very interested in (Giordano) Bruno. I expect he'll be a writer, but also something else, something surprising. I like the sound of all the people you mention. It also gives me a sense of the far-awayness of Australia. I'm glad I've been there. It's hard to imagine it unless you've seen it. I wish it could be towed up to somewhere near North Africa. (No I don't—that would be <u>impossible.</u>) You ask about my parents. My father was born in New Zealand. His people were sheep farmers (protestant settlers of course) in County Down, but his father set off for NZ & my father was born there—but when my father was aged about one they all sailed back to County Down, I suspect because the elder brother who owned the farm there had died, and my grandfather inherited it. I never met my grandfather—my grandmother went on wishing herself back in New Zealand. My mother, also protestant of course, came of an old Anglo-Irish squirearchy family, settled in Tyrone about 1610 (about when my father's family, presumably from Galloway, were settling in C. Down.)[39] I was born in Dublin, but my father, following the tradition, removed me at the age of one to London. He was in the first war, in the cavalry. After that he wanted to get out of Ireland (I suspect to escape his family, who were Quakers & Plymouth Brethren). He met my enchanting mother in Dublin & carried us off to London where he entered the Civil Service & rose near the top. He was a clever gentle bookish man, a <u>good</u> man. My darling mother who had a wonderful soprano voice, was merry & witty & sweet. I was an only child. <u>What luck</u>. I had this wonderful pair all to myself. I miss them very much.

Enough about me. I don't usually write about myself, but you did ask. John is fine, too much to do (university administration too, now he is a

Prof)—he gave a splendid lecture on Pushkin yesterday (he knows Russian, so do I a bit) and brought tears to eyes.

I love hearing about your children. Write more. You ought to write a novel—perhaps you have? Australia needs you to tell about her. Telling about Australia (by Australians) is really quite different from tales of America by Americans etc. etc. There is an Australian style. (Ah ... Sunny Oz.)

I am writing a novel, also some philosophy (but that's really too difficult).[40] I wonder how you feel about philosophy now? Are you on sabbatical leave from Flinders—or was that, our winter, the summer vac?

I hope you can read this. It is my expensive PEN (a Mont Blanc) which is writing it all. It sends courteous regards to your word processor. I wish you would come over here some time & we could write some songs. Much love, Brian, keep in touch—I

Iris Murdoch to Brian Medlin
[Letter 15]

[Written on Royal Mail Aerogramme]

Brian Medlin
69 Albert Street
5082
Australia
Postmarked ? Jly 1989

New address from July 31 [1989]:
30 Charlbury Road Oxford OX2

Brian, thanks so much for the picture, lovely picture, of the permanent water, and persons there. I'll hope to see your mate—but will be away a good deal on & off in August–September. Anyhow I trust we'll meet. Please note new address above! I wish you were coming too!
    All my best & love

Address till 31st July—
68 Hamilton Road
OXS 7QA

Iris Murdoch to Brian Medlin
[Letter 13]

[Written on Postcard from Bodleian Library, Oxford: *"The creation of the animals of earth and sky*: **from 'The Ashmole Bestiary' made in England, perhaps in the North Midlands, c. 1210. MS Ashmole 1511, fol. 6r (detail)"]**

← "Now let me think, what comes next?"

Dearest Brian, thank you very much for your cheering (and enlivening) reflections! I wish we could meet & have a drink together.

I've been a Dame for a couple of years, it is <u>quite</u> fun. Actually I feel rather like Cinderella, it's all blown over and I've resumed being Miss Murdoch. Au revoir & lots of love

Iris

Letter MDC51

69 Albert Street
Prospect
South Australia 5082
Ph: (08) 269 2483

December 12, 1989

Dear Iris

Thanks for your beaut card and apt comment.

This is to check whether you ever received that mega letter that I'd been promising you for ages. I sent it perhaps two months ago. I'd hate the effort of two years (not solid, of course) to be wasted.

I've just had some terrible news from poor Jack Smart. He was travelling in a car driven by a dear friend whom he'd been visiting in Wells. She was driving. There was an accident in which she was killed. Jack was merely roughed up a bit but, as you'd guess, devastated. Fortunately his wife Elizabeth is with him in England and she is a lovely woman. Jack is a lovely man and a wonderfully mad bastard with it. He'd sent me a copy of his new book and it had arrived just the day before his letter.

I've just spent a week with my son Jake on Retail Island, a place known only to myself. He fishing, I reading. (Amongst other things, Gleik's wonderful book, *Chao*.) When I was Jake's age all you needed to catch good fish in the Murray was a bent pin tied to a skein of hope. He caught three edible fish in days of hard work. I wouldn't be a kid these days. But the Island is a wonderful place still. Many old embattled red-gums. Many birds including white-breasted sea eagles.

I've just brought home *The Book and the Brotherhood* from the Flinders bookroom. Got started on the bus and will push on tonight. My first reaction was an almost entirely subjective one: I am powerfully reminded of those aspects of Oxford that I detested. Balls to Balls! Your sentiments too, it seems. A wonderfully disgusting account of that shindig. I am in just far enough in now to be getting intrigued. And I like the sound of that old bugger Levquist. In a world where most changes are for the worse, real reactionaries can be pretty attractive. How's that for penetrating critical analysis! Don't tell the comrades about the last bit.

Come to Oz and I'll show you Retail Island.
Luv

December 14, 1989: Just finished the novel. Triffic, mate!

Iris Murdoch to Brian Medlin
[Letter 37]

30 Charlbury Rd
Oxford OX2

[no date]

Dearest Brian,
<u>Please forgive</u> my so late reply. I am so glad and moved by your splendid memorial address, the prose and the poems. I put it on a table wondering about my reply (the reply should have come at once), then it was covered up, then we went away for quite a long time in France leaving it behind, then on return I could not find it etc. These were my feeble activities, I had to go away again—etc. Anyway <u>so sorry</u> to have been so speechless. I have read all the pages, your noble speech, and your poems—also Barbara Wall's piece, and To Brian Medlin. I cannot remember John Bray alas. I hope you and Vick are well. I see it is the same address. I love your little mouse. I used to write poetry, but now I can't. Oxford is as ever. John sends best wishes. Do you have another house out in the bush? We have a flat in London. I wish there was also a place in the wilds of Scotland or Wales. How tiny England is, how huge Australia. <u>Much</u> <u>love</u> to you and to Christine,
    Iris.

Iris Murdoch to Brian Medlin
[Letter 18]

[On Christmas 1989 aerogramme]

69 Albert Street,
Prospect

30 Charlbury Rd
Oxford OX2

Brian, much thanks your letter and I'm so glad you enjoyed the novel! I did have a mega communication, partly concerned with the general problems of life, which I much enjoyed reading, imbibing rays from your wonderful antipodean ENERGY. I'm sorry I couldn't come to Retail Island. There are plenty of jolly reactionaries here in Oxford. I wish you'd come on a visit some time.

This to send love and all very best wishes for Christmas and the nineties—Be well
    Yours truly,

Iris Murdoch to Brian Medlin
[Letter 16]

68 Hamilton Rd
Oxford OX2 7QA[i]

Feb 13

Dear Brian

Thank you very much for your thoughts about beating despair; and for your attack on Derrida, whose ideas & rhetoric I <u>detest</u>. The SA Energy forum sounds rather a good spot and the Greenhouse conference a good thing. I wish you'd come to Europe London, Oxford. I hope you sing a lot. Singing seems to have gone out here. Keep in touch. With lots of love,

Iris

---

[i] This letter was apparently written and sent in February 1990. It is addressed to Medlin at Flinders University, and readdressed to 69 Albert St, Prospect. The postmark for redirection is 21 Feb 1990. However, Murdoch had moved to Charlbury Road in July 1989.

Brian Medlin to Iris Murdoch
Letter MDC60

69 Albert Street
Prospect
South Australia 5082
Ph: (08) 269 2483

March 14, 1990

Ms. Iris Murdoch
30 Charlbury Road
Oxford
England, OX2

My dear Iris

I am still powerfully impressed by *The Brothhood and the Book* (*sic*). One thing that is very impressive about the whole corpus of your work is the fertility of theme. The theme of this book is immensely important and it is handled firmly. Firmly, easily, richly. As a theme of course, not as a thesis.

February 16, 1991

That was then and now is now. I wrote a lot of other stuff then which is now out of date. A lot of it was philosophy, but pretty much it was thinking aloud. A small section of it has been worked up into a paper which I've now sent you. The rest is being worked on. It's OK, but it'll keep. I've also sent you a fraction of the work on the fil of language.

I'm finding it very hard to get this language stuff polished up. For one thing Barnett is a very difficult collaborator. One has the same argument and reaches the same agreements and has the same argument over the years ... For another, I keep getting illllll. Too ill even to continue this letter which I'll knock off in a moment. But most of all philosophy is, to use your expression, *too hard for humans.*

Since I wrote all that stuff, Christine and I have had a bugger of a year. We have sat down much and travelled much in the bush. In spite of this, though, it has been a year of intolerable strains—not between us but upon us.

So this is partly to wish you as good a year as we're going to have—at anyrate in 1992.

Add to all this that very soon after the light dawned on us I spent seven days in court suing the State Government Insurance Commission over a motor bike accident in 1983.

February 16, 1991

It wasn't so much the money, as the shearers say, but the bloody insult. I was determined that unless they accepted 100 per cent liability, I'd go for them. The only way I could have avoided that motorist was to have stayed at home in bed—and even then I'd give her an even chance of crashing through the front window. "I'm terribly sorry, Professor," she said as I was lying on the road with my pelvis knocked to bits, "But I do have a PhD in chemistry." And as I was being put into the ambulance, "Please be kind to me. I don't have any insurance." "Then you'd better knock off knocking people off BMWs. They cost." Turned out she didn't have a South Australian license either. "Not at present," she said to the interviewing copper. She visited me a couple of times in hospital to tell me how sorry she was and how bad I was feeling.

My contempt for the medical profession was deepened by the experience of the trial. The Royal Adelaide Hospital had lost all my early X-rays and only after a last-minute blast from one of the surgeons an hour before he was to testify did they manage to find the radiologists' reports. My own orthopod whom I had been seeing privately had also lost X-rays that had been in his possession prior to the accident. He managed to mislay my 1984 X-rays until a week before the trial. At the beginning of 1987, he advised me to retire because of severe and "unremitting pain." At the trial, it turned out that at the same time, he was writing to the vice-Chancellor telling him that I had full movement in the joint with "minor discomfort" at the extremities of movement. Not surprisingly, I had some difficulty which I attributed to the Vice-Chancellor's intransigence.

SGIC managed to unearth a psychiatrist who was able to inform the court that my trouble was liver damage on account of my alcoholism. He was unable to produce any evidence for this claim which conflicted with reports from physicians and endocrinologists and had obviously just thought it up there and then in the box. My barrister was giving him a hard time when suddenly the judge intervened, sent the witness out of the court and, in his absence, told Rob Cameron (in Judgese which I here interpret) to go easy on the poor silly bastard who was obviously the sort of drongo you couldn't take any notice of anyhow.

As their next act in this Greatest Show on Earth, SGIC produced an eminent orthopod, one Mick H[...], a notorious hired gun. Mick took a brief sneering look at a 1984 X-ray, which he hadn't bothered to inspect before. Then to the defending counsel's clear delight, he declared it to be very helpful, showing as it did that I had never had a broken hip in my life. The other X-rays were ambiguous because radiologists don't really know how to take X-rays from the right angle. (He didn't mention the CAT scans and MRI scans.) But this plate was perfectly clear on the matter: the acetabulum was undamaged, the injury had been a minor one not caused but the femur being driven into the pelvis but by a light blow to the pubic region. It had left me with no residual disability. The orthopaedic surgeons who had seemed to detect restrictions in the joint had clearly employed manipulations which are "taught to every student." That I had been treated for many weeks in the Royal Adelaide Hospital for an impacted fracture of the acetabulum merely showed that my condition had been misdiagnosed. That I had recovered in spite of this inappropriate treatment merely showed that the injury had been trivial.

Not surprisingly, the judge was pretty interested in all this.

Next morning it was our turn. After an agonising hour of argument about admissibility, we called evidence from one Tony Pohl of the RAH and University of Adelaide. Tony is a youngish, dapper softly spoken Bokky. An orthopod much honoured and awarded, he had devised the surgical reconstruction of the acetabulum that replaced the conservative treatment that I received. He set a light box up alongside the judge and drew for him thirteen fracture lines through the pelvis, many of them through the acetabulum. Then in confirmation he referred to radiologists' reports (lost till that morning) on the basis of CAT scans, one the day after the accident. Then in further confirmation he put the plate from a recent MRI scan on the box. Then to round it all off, he produced a plastic model of the pelvis with the fracture lines drawn with red plasticene.

All this time talking softly and intensely with small vigorous gestures, thrusting with a softly closed fist, about the "tremendous forces" imparted to the pelvis by the femur. "You can observe the considerable deformation of the pelvis in its healed state. But we must remember that we are seeing the position of the bones after they had rebounded from the soft tissue following the explosion of the pelvis under these tremendous forces. This would account for the considerable bruising to the internal organs, and particularly the bladder, as noted in the CAT scan report of January 1st." And "If we ask how these tremendous forces were transmitted to the pelvis from the femur, the answer must be that they were transmitted through the cartilages of the ball and socket joint. This would have entailed very considerable damage to these cartilages and this damage could not possibly have been perfectly repaired to provide smooth operation. This would certainly have resulted in noticeable loss of function probably accompanied by considerable pain. If we ask further why Mr. H[...] was unable to find his damage revealed by the X-rays he examined, this is because, as Mr. H[...] would be aware, cartilage is translucent to radiation."

Great stuff. Rob Cameron reckoned he'd never had such a morning's fun in court.

Again the judge was rapt. But he also seemed pretty interested in the following defence argument on the matter of liability. It was conceded that I had sustained a severe injury. Even if should be conceded further that I had retired under medical advice as a result of this injury and conceded further that I had been rendered by it unable to do my job ("according to his own high standards"); it still did not follow that it was reasonable of me to have retired for this reason. I was after all a tenured professor. If I had simply done nothing, the University would have been unable to get rid of me—at anyrate only able by a lengthy process which would probably not have been completed till I was due to retire anyhow. Whether the judge was attending to this as a substantial consideration or as a mere moral curio, remains to be seen.

The bugger hasn't delivered yet. (Doubtless, he's rolling in the stuff. I am not, as you'll soon hear.) He's already made it pretty clear that he's likely to find 100 per cent for us on the matter of liability. I'm gloomily hopeful on the matter of damages, in contrast with my solicitor who is engagingly optimistic. (Craig once asked me of a colony of Spinifex Hopping Mice that I was observing while sick, "What are they? Echidnas?" When I told him what they were and that they were rodents he said, "And would they be mammals?" I hope it's because he's been single-minded about the study and practice of law.)

Not surprisingly, after the case was over, I fell sick in a way I'm prone to do these days under prolonged strain and pain. [...]

And oh yes, the bloody war!

Love

Brian Medlin

Iris Murdoch to Brian Medlin
[Letter 38]

30 Charlbury Rd
OX2

[no dateⁱ]

Dearest Brian, so glad to receive your letter—I have been feeling rather overcome by jobs, letters, demands (please give a lecture) etc. You are very welcome. I'm so sorry that you are ill—but you seem to be mastering it. And you & Christine went to the <u>sea</u>. (How near is sea, and what sea?) Also <u>seals</u>.ⁱⁱ I have a little Australian matters (*sic*) in the novel I'm <u>trying</u> to write—and might later ask you about them.

Birds. Here the Magpies persecute the little birds, and the little birds eat the flowers & leaves, the naughty creatures. We have had magnificent flooding of the Thames, and very peculiar weather—<u>brilliant</u> sun, <u>spring flowers</u>, but also raging storms & <u>sudden</u> rain.

Are you writing on the WWI, American Civil War? I am afraid I know very little about it! <u>What</u> are you writing?

Lovely picture of little mouse-like beast.

Much love to Christine, and to you, dearest Brian.

ever

Iris

ⁱ This letter appears to have been written after the change of address in July 1989, and after beginning *The Green Knight*. The notebook for this novel was started on 10 March 1989.

ⁱⁱ Marginal note: "+ sea-eagle."

Iris Murdoch to Brian Medlin
[Letter 32]

30 Charlbury Road
OX2 6UU

Oct 6 [1990?]

Brian, so glad to hear from you with desert picture. (Yes, that's a desert all right.) And you are riding horses (and the pack horses follow, as in "Shift, boys, shift") and flying aeroplanes <u>and</u> doing philosophy. Do send the philosophical thoughts. I am rather short of thoughts at the moment, but if I sit quiet perhaps some will come. Be well. I hope you'll come to England. With love,
   I

Iris Murdoch to Brian Medlin
[Letter 29]

30 Charlbury Road
Oxford OX2 6UU

[no date]

Brian dear, thank you so much for sending me the good stuff (readable copy) about language and Ecology (and a lot of other matters too). I wish we could discuss it all over a few glasses of wine. I am interested in Barnett. (Can't understand it all however.) I cannot get on with Derrida and company. That you are a poet emerges from your writing. (And it is certainly philosophy.) I am struggling with a novel and messing about with some lectures I gave long ago. Write me a letter.

What are you thinking about politics? What did you think about the Gulf War? What a century. Just when we thought everything was turning out so well in Eastern Europe we have Iraq etc. I hope you are writing poetry and singing as well as doing philosophy. I haven't been anywhere in particular. Perhaps you will visit England (Europe anyway.) Thanks for keeping in touch. Be well.

With much spring time love & best wishes

Iris

Brian Medlin to Iris Murdoch
Letter MDC71

69 Albert Street
Prospect, 5082
Phone: (08) 269 2493

April 8, 1991

My dear Iris,

Saw you on the telly yesterday. The rotten ABC showed it before the advertised time so I missed about fifteen minutes of it. But wonderful all the same.

Christine said, "How could anybody not love her!." Iris, you were beautiful! And so sensible and straightforward. To see again the happy countenance of that lovely man John.

Byass's[i] (*sic*) remark about being afraid of you. She may well be a pretty sensible woman and is certainly a pretty good novelist—though, I assert, not in the same street as our Iris. But that surely is a bit daft. I've met few people so perceptive. That doesn't have to make you intimidating. Nor does it. (Am I a poor subject?) I think your friend may have a bad conscience tucked away somewhere.

No. I haven't written any poetry for many years. One of the last good poems I wrote, in 1971, is the following:

A LOVE POEM
dedicated to my comrades throughout the world

When I was young I used to make
Intricate verses and would take
Pains to get the music just
Exactly so. Putting my trust
In God knows what, I thought the sense
Would somehow shape itself. Immense
Voices bellowed in the night
From hill to heart. Yet by daylight
Not even I could read the page

---

[i] Presumably A.S. Byatt.

Purporting to record their sage
And profitable revelations.
Now, many years and many passions
Later, I have come to know
It pays to let the music go
And unambitiously to break
Your small heart for the mere truth's sake.
And that is why I cannot tell—
Out of this enduring hell
You and I inhabit—the plain
Unvarnished truth about our pain.
I cannot tell the world the world
's history, for I have held,
For half my life, hard to the faith
That a clear mind can do something with
Any known phenomenon,
And everything that can be done
Will be done, if only we're able
To render the world intelligible.
In this faith I have written well
And for it lost the clumsy skill
Of setting down upon a page
Those inarticulate cries of rage.

That poem might indicate what some of my dissatisfactions were. But it wasn't just that the passion was missing, so was the mere truth. Let me use you to try to bring to consciousness what I found wrong with my work. Let me give you an example from the collection I sent you once.

Now I hear nothing from you, day
Follows night, night day, no word.
I work at my work and draw my pay
For proving the sublime absurd.

For less they poisoned Socrates.
Now it's a humdrum good profession.
Day and night I watch my trees
Grow tall and unpick his confusion.

The world has altered, I know more
Than Socrates who only knew
That he knew nothing. But, what for?
I know nothing now of you.

Day and night the argument

Elaborates and every move
Is hard. But something that I meant
Was simple once, worth talking of.

To that I shall return and all
Digression will be relevant.
What's left undone, we can't recall.
Tomorrow is our element.

I walk my garden, think my thoughts,
Essaying rationality.
I think of you more than I ought.
The winds have spoiled another tree.

Paradoxes I can solve,
And I know why the sky is blue,
And I know how the heavens revolve.
But I know nothing now of you.

I know the structure of your flesh,
Whence you come and where you go,
The meaning of your blood and breath,
But I know only what is true.

Now Socrates is dead and gone
The work is done by little men.
Today, tomorrow, we live on.
Tomorrow we shall meet again.

A pretty bad poem, though with a competence lacking in most poems published in Australia. The competence contributes to its tawdriness. It's about profound matters, but isn't itself profound. It's profoundly superficial, failing to express the passion and to speak truth. I was unable to speak plainly, passionately, accurately, convincingly through aphorism and symbol as I think I can when I speak discursively. Then aphorism and symbol fall into place within a natural rhetoric, they illuminating rather than obscuring. (Compare the utterly reactionary Yeats who, for all his crankiness, is profound and compelling. And, mostly correct, what's more.) I don't want to write as half a man and even less as no man at all. Yet when I write poetry, it's not just that the philosopher is imprisoned. The philosopher kills the poet trying to escape and, since philosopher is the poet, they die together. Writing discursively, however, the two are one and work as one. (A friend, himself a poet, said recently, "These papers of late years are your best poems.")

I may write poetry in the future. I have things I'd like to write. But not rubbish, not even polished rubbish. If I do write poetry again it'll be because I've changed in ways that I would like to bring about, but which you can't produce by will power.

(As for philosophy, I don't give two hoots about being "important." I seem to be entirely without ambition in a way that often exasperates my friends and surely pisses off university authorities. But I'm determined to be as good as I can. Some of even the great philosophers wrote too much and published too much of it. Kant, e.g., did more harm than good. And when it comes to us mediocre academics—the little men—the demand that we should keep pace with the scientists has led to grotesque results. Mediocre scientists can grind out useful work by mere intelligent application. There is a scientific method. There is and can be no **philosophic** method. (Only methods.)

By contrast with their tinniness, the objectionable ideological content of the poems isn't a problem. I was appalled years back to find out just how vilely sexist they are. That in itself would have caused me to suppress them; yet in spite of the opinion of many feminists I regard this as an fairly corrigible defect. Deeper than my aversion to coloured cricket gear, yes, but still not down to the cellular level with the other problems.

(I've suppressed those poems as well as I can. There are copies in some of the libraries around Australia. I've managed to restrict access to all those I know about.)

I'm working on the same themes as the poem at the moment. The result will be a lecture given next August—in the Distinguished Scholars Lecture Series at Flinders to celebrate the Silver Jubilee of that ancient university! So the poem isn't all lies. To that I have returned and **one** digression (constituted by the poem itself) is relevant. I'll send you a copy of the lecture when it is sendable. You may be interested to compare it with the poem. (Or not.)

I think I'm clearer now about these matters than I've ever been before. Perhaps you're not, but thanks mate.

How interested are you in cricket?

Bill Ponsford died yesterday. He was still playing when I came to be conscious of cricket. His last tour of England was in 1934, the one where he topped the Australian averages and put on that stupendous fourth wicket partnership with Bradman.

I have a friend, a lawyer now retired, now getting on a bit too, one John Davies. Davies used to open the bowling for Adelaide. His first ball for South Australia bowled Bill Ponsford. He went blind soon afterwards. (These days, he'd have become an umpire.) While he was fatally ill a group of his friends, including Bray, called on him in hospital. He was too sick for visitors, but the doctor reckoned what the heck. "Anything you'd like before you kick off Davies?" "Well, I could go a Cooper's Ale." So they brought in a cargo and everyone got rotten. Davies made an immediate and complete recovery—except for his sight. And he has never forgotten that lesson.

I just thought you'd like to know that.

Singing: I still like to sing. But I don't sing in pubs any more. Christine and I used to call into bush pubs and play music when we travelled on the bikes. Not now since my bad smash in 1983. A lot of things have had to give way to coping with pain and keeping in practice is one of them. Don't play at all and don't sing well. And when I'm sick, as I have been for the last few months, I can't sing in tune. But I still try when I'm well.

I seem to be recovering. Into my seventh straight day of not feeling desperately ill. Still desperately tired and that isn't yet improving, but not ill. The change occurred clockably. I had to give a paper long ago arranged. I was driven by Christine, being too ill to travel by bus or drive myself. Walked into the restaurant where I was meeting the committee— late, too ill to eat dinner. Sat down ill and started talking. Within sixty seconds I noticed that I was behaving animatedly. I concluded that I must be feeling better and, what do you know, I was. And have been ever since. Romped through the paper and the discussion, though dog-tired. Since then hardly a romp, but nonetheless a great improvement on ill down to the least significant molecule. Some precious bodily fluid was suddenly turned back on again—doubtless by the collapse of the eastern regimes.

[…]

Iris Murdoch to Brian Medlin
[Letter 7]

30 Charlbury Road
OX 2 6UU

[no date]

Brian, dear mate, thank you for splendidly long letter. I am glad to know
that Christine is better after that strange interlude. How odd the mind is.
One is lucky if one does not have to think about it. It's so good that she is
with you again. I recall your telling me about your accident (and that awful
casual female) but I had not realised how serious it was. I'm so sorry.
Your account of the trial was amusing, though I can imagine how much it
was not an amusing matter. I hope there is better news on that front—
about your claim and of course about your progress in getting better. I
hope Bruno is putting himself together.

Jake seems to be entirely good news.

I'm afraid I can't place "too hard for [deletion] humans." It might be in
<u>Message to the Planet</u>, though I can't find where.[41] It's a great task
anyway. <u>You</u> must carry on. I have tried to do some lately but stopped. My
novel, now resumed, has been at a standstill. I have a <u>very</u> <u>nice</u> minor
character who is Australian. I have quite a lot of vocabulary, but might do
with more.[42] What are Australian terms for "bastard" (as well as
"bastard")? Also any terminology about "a really good guy." Any
oddments welcome.

What is an "orthopod" by the way? It can't (from the context) mean
right-footed. (Well, it may be sarcastic.) Certainly not the same as a
drongo.

I love your long reel of a letter coming off your word processor (sorry
about the burglary, but glad you got that machine back). I stay with pen
and ink—but fear that ink will soon be obsolete. The word "knib" (*sic*) is
already archaic—young people in shops have never heard it.

Brian, I do hope you are getting better—do so. Wish you were here!
With much love as always

Iris

Brian Medlin to Iris Murdoch
[Letter MDC71 continued]

April 19, 1991

Your lovely letter today. I shan't make a practice of crowding your doubtless busy life with correspondence, but I'll send this off reasonably soon because of the TV show. As Christine said when heard about your remark on my account of the trial, "The way to write an entertaining letter is to have plenty of grief." We once got a humdinger from Roy Edgley. Ever since, when there's something from Roy, she says, "I hope things have been going badly with them."

No news of the claim yet. I wonder whether I told you **all** about the egregious Doctor W[…] K[…]. Asked by the police whether she held a current South Australian driver's licence, she replied, "Not actually at the moment." ("Have you written that essay?" "Not as such.") She used to visit me in hospital till I told her to hop it. She'd sit by the bed and stare at the steel traction pin screwed into my shin. "It must be terrible!" I asked her why, once she had turned across my path, she then braked in front of me. If she'd gone right on I'd have got around behind her. She was concerned that I'd hit the car at the back axle and she'd braked so that I'd hit the back door instead. Which indeed I did.

The Royal Adelaide hospital was amazing. I woke in a trauma ward full of bikies got up to look like wind-jammers and Dutch mills. We swapped lies about what we rode and about the idiocy and depravity of motorists. There was a little bloke in the bed alongside me silent through all. Finally, the big bloke with the tats says "What do you ride mate?" "Oh I don't ride a motor cycle. Far too dangerous." "Then what the fuck y' doonere then?" "Oh, I jumped off the roof of my house." And nobody said a word.

One of the coppers at the accident asked me if there was anyone I'd like notified. A modern cop—"Your wife or the person you live with perhaps." I asked him to contact Christine. Also to be sure to make it clear that I was alright. "We've had lots of experience with this sort of thing, Brian. You can be sure it'll be done properly." The phone. "Miss Vick?" "Yes." "It's the Adelaide police here Miss Vick. I have to advise that Miss Christine Vick was involved in a motor-cycle accident at 9.30 this evening and is now in the Royal Adelaide Hospital." "I don't think that can be right. I haven't been out tonight." "Well that's what it says here, Miss

Vick!" "But my bike's still in the shed. I can't have been in an accident."
"All I know is that's what it says here." Spike Milligan wrote the world.

Maybe Bruno is improving, though it'll be a long haul […] I suggested
that he and I should spend some time together in the bush just trying to
enjoy ourselves and one another. A little to my surprise, he jumped at it
and suggested, too, our old camp at the Coorong. That may mean
something. We have a lot of history together in that place. […]

Christine is well and truly back. It now seems inconceivable that she
should have a repeat. Subjectively, that is: it would have been
inconceivable before, had one conceived of it. We can now bear to be
apart for half a day or more—just. She's a bit nervous about going back
into that country without me. In fact she's just passed up an opportunity to
go classifying plants for a fortnight or so in the Coongie area. That would
have been in a couple of days' time and she doesn't feel ready. But she is
off on Monday for a coupla days with her daughter Alice. So how about
that! She'll go up, probably to Lake Blanche and probably in October. By
then I should be well enough to tag along with the computer—and even if
not, she should be confident enough to go it alone. She's off on Monday
for a coupla days with her daughter Alice.[i]

Iris, I cannot tell you what a beaut (and beautiful) woman Christine
is—how conscientious and loving and wise and considerate to all and how
tough-minded with it. Nor how full of joy I am to have her here and
making this place as much hers as mine. I was struck by your reply when
asked why you had married John. "Love," you said—I believe somewhat
surprised. "I thought, 'Why not be happy? Why not?'" Why not indeed!

Yes, too hard for humans. Yes, a great truth. (I can't find it in **Message
to the Planet**. It's earlier, in an unlikely place.) Three kinds of hard, aren't
there? All hopelessly muddled up together and often impossible to sort out
for one's own case. You can sometimes do it moderately well for others—
when you seem to know where they've gone wrong. There are the absolute
limits of the human mind—and of course one reaches one's own absolute
limits long before them. There are the historical limits—imposed by the
state of learning at the time. Then there are the other historical limits, the
ideological ones—imposed by ... what? Class struggle? Well, yes, but
what else?

When you encounter pervasive error, like what can fairly be called the
bourgeois view of human nature, it's no good just refuting the offending
thesis. That simply makes people hate you, as someone says somewhere to
Socrates. You have to show what's wrong with the argument. And it's no

---

[i] This sentence is repeated in the original file.

good just doing that either. It doesn't destroy the power of the error. Look how often scepticism keeps on cropping up amongst people who know what's wrong with it, how often you get unnecessary reductionist attempts to escape from it. Ryle. Kant (not mainly reductionist though). "The panic flight from scepticism," as Charlie Martin calls it. Somehow, one has to grub out the ideological roots, the structuring of experience that keeps on nourishing the error. No news. John Wisdom was saying something pretty much like this (was it so long ago?) though his conception of the roots would have been very different from mine.

But there's an odd thing about philosophy. It **is** hard. It can **seem** hard: sometimes you stand at the very edge of reality looking down into a swirling conceptual chaos. But often when you get something right, just as often when others get something wrong, it can seem ridiculously easy. The points that are so hard to see are sometimes so simple that we tend to look straight past them. And when you do see them it's as though you must have known them all your life. What's all the fuss been about?

... and mysteries
Are like the sun, dazzling yet plain to all eyes.[43]

Another odd thing, and it's what makes philosophy especially difficult—how is it that we can't easily say just *how* bloody hard it is?—**"difficult"** for Chrissake!—another thing is that truth and falsehood are intertwined and interwoven so intimately that they seem identical. Donne was right that they be near twins and that Truth the little elder is. But, more than that, they be Siamese twins. What do we make of Sufi mysticism, for example? Of Junayd's endeavour to recognise God as He was prior to Creation? (Cf. Goethe on Creation and action/contemplation.) Of the consequences of that attempt—that God becomes the sole agent, the one who alone can rightly say "I." Put that alongside Descartes, who seemed to be the **only** one entitled to say it. They're both dead wrong, but how right they can both look standing incompatibly side by side. And Hume for whom **no one** was entitled to say it? I could make some sense of all that for you, but it would take longer than this is going to be. This isn't yet philosophy, it's **doing** philosophy—what has to go on before all the lucid formulations have any point.

(The complaint in that poem: "But I know only what is true." It comes out smart-arsed, alas.)

I too like pen and ink. But I broke my thumb in 1981. Did myself a good turn in the event. Word processors are miraculous. Christine remarked on your comments that you seem not to like a change of thrush. Don't let Clovis hear.

And your nib problem reminds me of a charming affectionate poem,
To Bonnie Elspeth that begins:

> I canna thole those fleechin' folk
> Wha ca' a lassie "Goddess"
> When a' their meanin' is tae poke
> Their neb inside her bodice.

I've forgotten the author, I've lost the book it's in and hence the poem
that's in it. I can remember other lines, but not the whole. It finishes:

> Syne fainness follows flesh an' bluid
> By Nature's dear designin'
> Let's mak the inclination guid
> By hazard o' combinin'.

Do you know this bonzer little poem? Does John? Please. There's more.
The first stanza concludes, to the rhymes of "muse" and "wreaths o
myrtle," with "Parnassus" in there somewhere:

> Aye, but the mount they hae in view's
> Her ain beneath a kirtle.

The second stanza I hae in fu':

> Wi' sic, an they be gi'en their boon
> The compliments they've paid ye
> Are dangit aff-hand like auld shoon
> An' barefit gaes the lady.
> Sic phrasin' flatteries I abhor
> An leave tae ither gentry:
> I'd rather be tongue-tied afore,
> An', after, complimentary.

The poet is not paralysed by the passion for consistency: a third stanza
declares that her **beauty** would **E'en juvenate Auld Clooty**.

What do I think about politics these days and the Gulf War? Briefly.
First, What a Century! as you say. The liberation of Eastern Europe was
necessary. But to what have they been liberated? All that blood, all that
oppression and nothing achieved except capitalism. The liberal rejoicing
seems to me to be both heartless and simple-minded. Heartless because it
takes in its stride the horrors of capitalism. Simple-minded because it
brushes aside the obvious fact that the classless society is the only rational

long-range political objective. Class society is at best a fools' paradise. Socialism was destructive enough for god's sake. Capitalism will **certainly** destroy the world and we now know that we don't know what to do about it.

This has been mentioned in some of the papers I've sent you. More about it in my Flinders Jubilee lecture later in the year.

The Gulf War was fought against a power that had been largely created by the West and before it became obvious that it was necessary—even allowing that war is still an option. I believe that Bush had domestic reasons for wanting an early war. He was very clever at taking the UN with him. (Australia and Britain don't count of course. *Of course* they went along.) Bush and the US military were also very good at controlling all sections of the media. The fact is that the war, for all the vaunted humane concern, was fought with the brutality we have come to expect from the US. For all the skiting about smart bombs, the great bulk of air-borne ordinance was dumb. The "collateral damage" was systematic and part of a deliberate tactic of dismantling Iraqi society. Then, having got into the war, we stopped too soon. I'm not suggesting that the coalition should necessarily have continued attacking Iraq. But the United Nations could have continued the state of war, could have resisted a formal cease-fire until all sorts of conditions had been accepted by Iraq. I mean mainly conditions upon the regime's treatment of its own citizens. Once US objectives had been achieved, that was it. I welcome the very recent intervention in Northern Iraq, but the East and South will be lucky to get either protection or relief. It seems to me, too, that a country with the interventionist history of the US could without qualms have imposed some useful conditions upon the Kuwaiti Emir as a price for restoration.

That of course wasn't what the War was about. Otherwise why US the support for Indonesia, the butcher of East Timor? Do you know that Australia has recently signed an agreement with Indonesia to collaborate in the exploitation of off-shore East Timorese oil? Why the not-all-that covert US and Australian support for the Khmer Rouge? That's a real "Why," not rhetorical. I don't understand that one.

I believe Bush to be less vile than Saddam Hussein—certainly but marginally. They are both canting pious hypocrites. For what it's worth, Saddam, "The Modern Saladin," has a militarist religion to give him some consistency. (Did you know that Saladin was a *Kurd*, by the way? And that Saladin didn't leave enough to pay for his own funeral? Bet your boots here again time will prove that Saddam fails to resemble him.) Bush, the oil man and CIA director, recalls to my mind the advice of the old actor to the young actor, "Son, once you learn to fake sincerity, you can fake anything."

The Australian language thing is hard for two reasons. For one, there is no Australian language any more, though G. Wilkes would prove me wrong.[44] We're thoroughly Americanised. My kids talk of "dudes" and use the American vowel to do so. Make sure that when you character sings, she does so with an American accent.

For another thing Australianness resides, not just in vocabulary, but in the phrasing. Not just in set phrases like "flat out like a lizard drinking," but in the **style** of phrasing. (This isn't necessarily distinguishable from some kinds of American speech.) "Wet as baby-shit" might be said of a person. Adelaide water might be described as hard enough to cut glass with. I have been told about the first by an American and about the second by an English couple that they are "very Australian." You are free to use them if they are useful. I suggest that you absorb the Barry Mackenzie comics, which are brilliant from that point of view. Then make up your own phrases. You'll doubtless need to tone them down and redirect them to suit the nature and preoccupations of your character. If you like, you can try them out on me (or someone else) to see how they ring.

I don't think there's anything **peculiarly** Australian about such phrases. That only appears when they are pronounced. And it's not just in the pronunciation either, but rhythm and intonation. Unfortunately you have only a one-dimensional script to work with.

Words for "bastard." My friend Charles Jury, dead alas since 1958, once compressed Christian theology into this limerick. You shouldn't go through life without knowing it.

There was a young man from Cape Cod
Who didn't believe in a God.
His name was Ken Tucker,
The bleeder, the fucker,
The bugger, the bastard the sod.[45]

Those epithets are still current amongst the articulate. "Cunt," I fear, is still about the strongest term of abuse amongst those who use it (Not I!) "Absolute bastard" has the advantage of explicitly rejecting moral relativism. "Bugger of a bloke" would seem to most people fairly strong condemnation. "Fair bastard," "fair cow," "rotten cow" of persons and situations and things, still linger. You still hear "dingo!" for coward or cheat amongst those innocent of natural history. "Numbat" can serve for drongo. Oh and "nong." As can "Wombat." Oh, and "Nong"[i]. I don't know whether "fuck-wit" is used overseas, ("off-shore" as we have to say these days) but I'm sure it originated here. Indeed, I think I know the man who invented it ("Great little fuck-wits") in Canberra in 1966. Plenty of scope for it there. You still hear "Cunning as a shithouse rat." "No-hoper" and "ratbag" get plenty of air still, but don't mean just "bastard" either. "Shit" is fairly common amongst us. "Prick" is acceptable amongst ideologically sound, but not lady-like, females. "Prick-face" is used, especially in the vocative, to register disapproval, not necessarily of the addressee's appearance. It is sometimes a term of endearment. "Dick-head" is used,—more for dick-headedness than mere bastardry and never or rarely as a term of endearment. The odious Paul Keating has popularised "scumbag"—the nearest thing to a scalpel in his analytic tool-kit. I suspect it's a recent import.

As for "a really good guy," the national experience is so poor in examples that we haven't developed any language to accommodate them. "Alright" said in the right way is about as good as you can get. "She's alright" or "You'll do"—but pretty nonchalantly. "Extra grouse" (meaning excellent) is an expression I'd use myself, but it's now a bit old-fashioned. "Corker," meaning the same, is even more old-fashioned, but again I'd use it. One might say just "Corker bloke" as the whole sentence. Or "Extra grouse" on its own in response to an enquiry. "Humdinger" is still heard, not always favourably applied though. "Good bloke" is still the main stand-by. Depending on intonation it can mean anything from "not quite an utter and absolute bastard" to "a superlatively virtuous and charming gentleman." "Bonzer"'s another term of approbation. "Bonzer bloke" is high praise indeed. Suggests good nature and charm rather than strict virtue. "Really nice (good) fella" still has a place and is probably as high praise as you could get. The pronunciation is important, if it is to mean what it says, even in a mouth that would otherwise say "fellow." You might say to or of some one that their blood's worth bottling.

A term of approbation always used ironically is "the sun shines out of his arse" (or "arsehole") (or "navel" for the more realistically inclined). "He thinks the sun shines out of his (own) arse(h)ole" or "She thought that the sun shone out of his navel, but it was only a monocle."

An interesting expression is "good man." I first noticed it consciously when I was nineteen and working horses and cattle in the Northern Territory, where it could be life or death to know whether a bloke was good at his stuff. Virtue was irrelevant and always improbable. "Good

---

[i] This sentence is repeated in the original file.

man" was a common expression amongst stockmen. Even without context being spoken in, it always meant "Good at the stuff." When I came back to Adelaide, I noticed that my father used "good man," in talking about the First War, to mean a reliable soldier. Being a Metho, he was conscious of virtue and its importance in life. But I never heard him use this expression to mean "a virtuous man." He was a man of great and varied manual skills and he often used it to describe a competent tradesman.

General terms of approbation. "Corker" is a good one but, as I said, not much heard in these evil times. (Christine says that one of the things she first found attractive about me was that I spoke the same language as her father. Actually Murray and I went to the same school, God help us.) "Beaut" is still a commonly used adjective. "You beaut!," "You little beaut!," "You little beauty!" are still acceptable exclamations. "Beauty!," though is used mainly by car salesmen and real estate agents. "Bloody beauty!," however, would pass unnoticed anywhere except in church—and even then it would probably have to be a funeral service. Another general term of approbation is "bobby-dazzler." An exclamation of delight is "Whackothediddlo!" It's used by Guineau in **Come in Spinner.** Other exclamations—"Starve the lizards!," "Stone the (flamin') crows," "Buggeration!" "(Well) fuck (bugger, stuff) me (dead, sideways, but never with 'stuff')," "Fuck me up a gum tree!."

For "everything's fine" or "ready to go": "She's apples," "She's Jake," "She's the berries."

For indifference: "Hooley-dooley," "Six of one and half a dozen of the other" (of course), "Bob's your uncle," the last also for "She's Jake" etc.. For passionate indifference, all three strung together.

For "Don't come the raw prawn": "Don't come the raw prawn," or "We had one of them at home but the wheels fell off."

As for terms of general disapprobation, disgust, disapproval, for some reason that escapes me we seem to be light on. "Shit!" isn't very inspiring, whether as exclamation, form of address, or description and doesn't add much local colour. "Yuk!" which appeared in the mid-sixties is surely North American.

"Mate" persists, both vocatively and descriptively, in spite of unremembering hearts and heads. My acquaintance, male and female deal in it. My children call me "mate"—except, I think, Margie. Christine and I use it towards one another as a matter of course.

Greetings.—"G'day!," of course. But often enough, "What do you know," to which the reciprocating courtesy is "Fuck all!" "Not much" will do. Just. At Flinders a few years back. Brian Matthews to Joost Daalder, "G'day, Joost. What do you know?" "Well, first ..." "No, you don't get it.

It's a kind of greeting like 'How do you do'." "But how could there be a reply to such a question." "Easy. What you say is fuck all." "Surely you are pulling my arms." "No. Dinkum." Enter Syd Harrex. "Look, I'll show you. G'day, Syd. What do you know?" "Ar, fuck all!" Joost was wiped out.[46]

(Compare the experience of an English-born mate of mine, an Iris Murdoch fan. First game of district cricket here, he was bowled neck and crop. "Well bowled!" "Fuck off!")

Dunno how restricted these expressions are to Australia. Not really the point, though.

But in any case, the language can't really be captured through its vocabulary. Inventiveness and style thereof is all. For example, I once heard an attractive young woman described approvingly as our bucket of cowshit. The point was that she drew off the flies in country pubs so that the rest of the party could get on with serious drinking. A friend, proposing to testify for me last year, promised not to be a loose cannon on my deck. I won Christine's heart with the claim to have frightened twelve colours of shit out of (whoever).

A lot depends on your character. Whether she's witty or demonstrative or broad-mouthed, tight-lipped or what. To some extent also on her social background. And on her age. If she's twenty and talks like me it'll be something like describing the kangaroos in the main street of Adelaide.

Oh and try browsing in Wilkes' dictionaries if you haven't done so. There's a new one, I believe. If I had one here, I'd look through it myself.

It may be worth-while bearing in mind that there is a certain kind of Australian who eschews Australianisms. Not colloquialisms, but Australianisms. I'm sure, though, that your friend, being very nice, would not be one of those.

You've made me feel like the centipede who was asked how she walked.

"Orthopod" means orthopaedic surgeon. They don't like it too much. And it does indeed mean right-footed.

April 22, 1991

Still recovering slowly. Perhaps I can forget Ben Jonson till next time:

> But what we're born for we must bear;
> Our frail condition it is such,
> That what to all may happen here,
> If 't chance to me, I must not grutch.

Else I my state should much mistake,
To harbour a divided thought
From all my kind: that for my sake,
There should a miracle be wrought.[47]

Dear Iris, again it was lovely ("bottler"!) to see you and hear you. (Forget "bottler." You never hear it from the young.) I am keeping at least one bottle of D'Arenberg 1982 Burgundy for when you come to Australia.[48] It should be good for a few years yet, but don't push your luck. D'Arenberg doesn't make a wine like it any more—big as a house and knee-deep in velvet. They've gone over to the modern light style— girl's wine, as we would have said in those lovely old days before the women's movement.

Much love, dear friend

Brian Medlin to Iris Murdoch
Letter MDC80

69 Albert Street
Prospect
South Australia
5082
Ph (08) 269 2483

Iris Murdoch
30 Charlbury Road
Oxford, OX2 6UV

June 3, 1991

Dear Iris,
    Now that you're interested in cricket:
    (That reminds me of a story, by the way. I'll tell it when I'm through with cricket.)
    Did you ever see Ponsford play? I must have, but I would have been very young and all my memories from before I was, say, seven are very properly dominated by Bradman. I still have visual images of Larwood bowling and of Jardine on the field and of batsmen (not Bradman) getting hit. (Fingleton seemed to think that it was somehow wicked of Bradman not to get hit.) But that's about it.
    Certainly I can remember the Ponsford legend from very early on— and especially the stories of the famous Leeds innings. By one account, there was a bunch at Woop-Woop following that test on the radio. At stumps on the first day Bradman had scored 309 not out and Ponsford however many. "Jeeze," says one station hand. "What'd the bastards do in daylight!" Ponsford is still the only player with two scores of over 400 in first-class cricket. His average for 29 tests is a mere 48.22. For 43 Shield[49] games he averaged a more respectable 84.57. So that must have been a reasonable ball of Davies'. McGilvray says that his footwork was the best he's ever seen and Ian Johnson rates him as one of the three greatest Australian batsmen, Trumper and, of course, Bradman being the others.
    (What a pity by the way that you missed Trumper's 300 not out at Brighton in 1899. Trumper nearly missed that tour as a matter of fact. Joe Darling and another of the three selectors were against him, because he

was doing nowt in Shield games. Then at the last moment, he knocked up a score against South Australia and Darling recognised him at once for a great batsman. So Trumper was dragged into the squad two days before the ship sailed. Did you know that he took 20—or was it more?—wickets for just over 20 each on that tour? Joe Darling wouldn't bowl Trumper because of his health, but said that if he'd been fit, he would also have been a great fast bowler. And did you know that Trumper once batted for five weeks straight in lunch-hour cricket at school.)

But Ponsford ... He was notoriously hard to shift, yet, unlike Boycott, say, he used to keep things going while he was there. (Did you know that it took Boycott 9 years to hit his first four against Australia? And that then it was a 5 which included 4 overthrows?) Grimmett used to reckon Ponsford was even harder to shift than Bradman: Bradman, he said, always gave you a chance because of his daring.

I suppose you won't have heard of David Hookes' testimonial match that was played here at the Adelaide oval on Sunday April 7th? There's good reason to believe that Hookesy is a bugger of a bloke, but then so was Frege and he was pretty good at his job too.[50] Hookes has been arguably the most talented Australian batsman since Greg Chappel retired. Nobody could say that he has been as good a batsman as Border, but he has a hell of a lot more talent. He's been given opportunities in tests and in a sense has wasted them; but that he never established himself as a test batsman speaks to the folly of Australian selection policy during the critical years from the late seventies into the second half of the eighties. In the years since then we persisted with Steve Waugh, for example, for season after season when he was hardly earning his keep. No doubt this was wise, but meanwhile Mark Waugh, a much better player, was left to mature in shield cricket for about three years. (Mark has much better footwork than Steve, plays more correctly, yet just as aggressively. He is an equally brilliant field and a phenomenally successful bowler—especially in the one-day game.) Anyhow, Hookes. ...

Hookes is now the top run-getter for South Australia—with 9909 (average 48.10, 28 centuries) in 126 matches. In his opening season 66-67, he scored five centuries in six digs. In 1976-77, when Victoria had set South Australia an impossible target, he promoted himself to open and scored a century off 43 balls to win the match.

His benefit match was between the Australian Centenary Test side and a Rest of the World eleven. Players included Pollock, Barry Richards, Garner, the Crowes, Lillee, Rodney Marsh, Doug Walters and of course Hookes. And, bugger me, I wasn't well enough to go. From a financial point of view it was a fizzle—$19398 grossed from 4788 spectators.

Hookes will see very little of that. The attendance was a disgrace. But for various reasons not surprising. The one-day game, Readers Digest cricket, is killing serious cricket in this country. What's more, now that cricket has been integrated into the capitalist system, it's being promoted as a blood sport. Very few people are going to turn out to a match where the quicks are too old to kill anyone.

And then too there was the Crows match. South Australia has this year fielded a new Australian Rules team, The Adelaide crows. This isn't a naturally evolved team, but a designer club to participate in the Australian Football League. The AFL is the Victorian Football league slightly expanded. The VFL, being wealthier than other leagues has been able to buy up players and in this way has been able to usurp the national competition. Now the bastards have started to compete with cricket. On the day of the Hookes' testimonial game, the Crows were playing their third game in the AFL and this was telecast live.

But the match was a humdinger. Hookes himself made 104 and Doug Walters 50. (You would never have seen Walters really going.) Terry Jenner (remember Jenner?) got 5 wickets for 104 of 14 overs for The World. (Jenner recently did a stretch for embezzlement, having become a compulsive gambler, and this hopefully will do something to rehabilitate him.) Martin Crowe put on 83 in 39 minutes and Pollock 61 in an hour. And Lillee (another bugger of a bloke) took 4 for 56 off 13 overs. Joel Garner hit a six off the last ball of the day to tie the scores at 293. Who that could have been there would have been elsewhere?

Talking cricket, the West Indians are a bunch of bloody cheats. Their behaviour makes even the Australians look innocent.

And now the story which you thought I'd forgotten. The same Iris Murdoch fan, that got bowled neck and crop in his first match here lives at Semaphore—so called because there used to be a semaphore station there for the ships entering and leaving Port Adelaide. There's a fairly large community of blacks at Semaphore. Indeed the strip of lawn just outside the local police station is a favourite drinking spot and a few years back had the highest murder-rate per square yard of any patch of turf in Australia. But Henry, for that was his name, as you novelists say ... Henry was (and is) a smoker and boozer and generally a reckless liver—even for a professional actor. (In Australia, he's quite famous, not by name, but as a monkey.) To illustrate—but this isn't the story—he once bought an exercise bike. Seeing it, I told him he was a fuckwit, why didn't he get something he could ride around The Semi. "Ar no," says Henry, "This way you can watch the telly and have your ash-tray and whisky alongside while you exercise." On the occasion in question, Henry must have been putting in a long spell, for he ran out of fags. So he hoped into his clapped out old Holden, as I'm sure it was then, and drove a couple of blocks down to the deli. He double-parked outside, leaving the keys in the lock and the motor running. He came out to find a black bloke, as total stranger, just about to drive off. Henry, who is a strong bastard, grabbed him by the collar. "That's my fucking car, mate!" "Sorry mate. I didn't know it was yours." Henry dragged him out and started to get in himself. "Now that I don't have a car, could you give us a lift to The Port?" Henry did.

Henry is one of my literary executors, but I reckon I'll outlive him, sick as I am.

July 2, 1991
Big mistake appointing Salter as a literary executor. Means he's got to outlive me. And that's got to mean an early death.

Iris Murdoch to Brian Medlin
[Letter 28]

30 Charlbury Road
OX2 6UU

May 28 [1991][i]

My dear creature, thank you so much for your wonderful letter, so beautifully printed and looking like a magazine. So much in it. Excuse rambling replies. I am very interested in cricket, or rather I just love cricket. I don't go to see much of it. I spent 10 years (summers) of my life playing it, at prep school and boarding school and was in the first eleven. A noble game, so good to look at and to hear. And so (or was) gentlemanly.

I am glad to hear you are recovering and I hope that has <u>gone ahead</u> and that your claim has been justly dealt with at last. Let me have news. And how altogether good about Christine—a very good egg—I am glad to hear about her too.[ii]

I hope Bruno is better and that it was all OK at the old camp at Coorong.

And may philosophy and poetry (Plato said there was an old feud between them) co-exist peacefully & creatively. I like your poems. And <u>thanks</u> for the terminology, and I like the thing about Ken Tucker (somehow that cheers one up.)

I am touched that you assume that my character (who wanted the terminology) was a "she." (And the centipede is "she" too.) In fact he's a rough man who keeps a pub. I hope he can be suitably eloquent.

The enclosed shows the state of philosophy here. It was sent me by a Swedish child psychiatrist friend. The word written in (*sic*) "Aspberger" refers to a psychologist of that name who discovered a syndrome (hence Aspbergers Syndrome) which my friend thinks Witt[n] had.[51] He certainly

---

[i] Apparently written before the immediately preceding letter from Medlin was received.
[ii] Note written sideways in left margin: "Yes, I know Saladin was a Kurd. Very significant (in some way). Can't trace the Scottish poem. Wish you, and Christine, were here."

had <u>some</u> of the symptoms, anti-social, very touchy etc. but then that covers a lot of people—and Witt^n was perfectly sane, only capable of being rather nasty. (Perhaps just not suffering fools—only for him most people were fools.) I wonder if you feel, or still feel, deeply or at all interested in Witt^n? I drift away but tend to come back—not that it matters I'm not really a philosopher anyway. (The idea of "reading him as poetry" would annoy him very much.) I <u>do</u> like your poems, I have been rereading them—they are real poetry. It is very difficult to write that. Why not write more. I wish I could.

I do hope you are really put together & all right. I picture that hospital ward with the bikies. Polx:[i] I think there is real liberation in East Europe, basically being able to say what you like at last. (Tho' in Romania at least the old gang seems still in power, after their palace revolution.) Sorry not an eloquent letter. I am feeling rotten—flat out like a lizard. It's a lovely spring here, North Oxford (that must seem far away) full of flowers (& marvellous trees with flowers on) the sky remains <u>low</u>, not like the great Australian high sky.[ii]

---

[i] i.e. politics.
[ii] Letter finishes here at the end of page 2. Possibly the marginal note on page 1 is the conclusion.

Brian Medlin to Iris Murdoch
[Letter MDC81]

July 2, 1991

Dear Iris

Thanks for your lovely letter of May 28. I won't reply to anything in it except to say that you are not flat out like a lizard. You are flat out like a lizard *drinking*.

I have a favour to ask and that is why I am sending this inchoate bunch of stuff. My health is quite bad and getting worse. I've moved back into investigative mode. And at last I've found a physician who isn't a pompous opinionated prick and doesn't tell you such things as that your trouble is that you can't stand the thought of your body aging. David Bowman is one for thorough enquiry and untrammelled truth.

There are a number of options, most of them pretty nasty. The most likely, to my mind, is very nasty indeed. I won't know for sure about that for another fortnight. But in the meantime, I'd be stupid to act on any other assumption—if it turns out positive then I don't have any time to waste *now*. I've got to start ordering my priorities and get going on the twenty years work I have outstanding. I've been tending to put things off until I began to feel better, but now it seems that may never happen.

Recently, before all this came to a head, I found myself planning a book as the result of some casual conversations I'd been having with a mad bastard called Henry, a very good mate of mine. I now think that this book would be a nice thing, amongst others, to get finished—if I have the time. But I don't want to waste time working on something just because I'm infatuated with it.

Do you think that you could glance through the plan and the accompanying letter to Henry and let me know what you think. Is it likely to make a nice book? Don't worry if you can't follow it all—as you won't be able to. Don't worry either about getting it right. You'll know that nobody can be sure of that.[52]

I'm sorry, I suppose, to put this on you, but you're not alone. I'm trying it out on two other people whose opinion I value. As a matter of fact I don't regard very many people as qualified to pronounce on this matter.

By the way, I'm rediscovering Thomas Hardy to be a very unmoving poet.

And by the way too—as a reward for your trouble, which I hope you'll minimise. Do you know about the Queen Mother's inspection of the Chelsea Pensioners. There they were in wavering, breeze-blown line, she passing down it. She stopped in front of the most ancient of them all, a mere skeltonised leaf of a man.

And how are you today, my good man?
Ar, not too good today, Mum.
I'm sorry to hear that. What seems to be the trouble?
Well, Mum, do you remember the Crimean War?
Well, no. Not really.
Do you know that stuff they used to put in the water to stop us chasing after women?
No, I can't say that I do.
Well, you know ... I think it's beginning to work.

I think I could use that somewhere.
Love

Letter MDC90

69 Albert Street
Prospect
South Australia
5082
Ph (08) 269 2483

July 14, 1991

Dear Iris

Given the contents of my last letter, I should write this one pretty soon. I had some more neurological tests. The results were bad enough, but given what had been expected quite good. I have a demyelinasing peripheral neuropathy. There! That's certainly better than ontological relativism! If one knows what myelin is the expression is self-explanatory I think. The condition is likely to be progressive and degenerative, but it's one hell of a lot better than motor neuron disease, which is what I was thought to have. In any case, I now realise that I've had the condition for some eight or ten years (on at least three occasions in the past it should have been picked up) so it seems to be progressing fairly slowly.

The underlying cause of the loss of myelin has yet to be discovered. It may be curable or it may not. If it is then there may be some regeneration of myelin. The underlying cause may also be what is making me so ill or it may not. What is making me ill is still up for grabs and finding it is getting more and more unlikely. My physician likes the idea of cancer but nobody can find one and I am now convinced that there are too many things against it. Certainly, I haven't had a cancer (still unfindable and remitting without therapy) since 1982.

The physician also expects the attacks to get more frequent and more severe—though how they can be much more severe puzzles me. Even if the cause can't be nailed, it may be possible to control the illness with steroids. So you may expect me to turn black and set a new 100 metre world record for fairly soon. This is fairly important: even though I recover fairly well, get very fit again and recover muscle mass, I'm never quite as good as I was before the illness.

I seem now to be pulling out of this attack, the last month of which was very bad. Within two weeks of the worst of it I was loading a trailer with mallee roots. I'm still very weak and tired and on past experience likely to be convalescent for two or three months. But the delight of being able to work up a sweat, and generally doing physical things that I had thought I might never do again is intense.

This has so far been a very interesting experience. My first thought on hearing that I probably had motor neuron disease was to take up physics. But then I learnt that you only live with it for as long as Stephen Hawking if you get it as young as he did. My first act was to ring up Henry Salter[53]—whose corrigible errors on mortality have been very useful to me—and pull rank on him. I found the prospect of dying of motor neuron disease very unpleasant, but once I had decided that if it came to that I wouldn't go the whole course, I found that I had no detectable fear of death whatsoever. At the same time, every minute became precious and both Christine and I found that we were really enjoying life—in spite of the disappointments that cropped up by the minute.

This feeling of the preciousness of everything is unlikely to leave me, I think. I'm also powerfully motivated to work. To have left one's life work till one is dying, as I seemed to have done, was (is?) bloody irritating. There won't be another minute wasted if I live to be a hundred.

Christine has been bloody marvellous through all this. Now that the pressure's off a bit, she's tended to flop a bit. That's fine by me. Just to be able to do the dishes, cook the tea is marvellous.

One deprivation: I had to tell Bray that he would be better to find someone else as a literary executor. That is a real loss to me and, it seemed to him also. I really will be pissed off, if I survive him in good health by some forty years.

I'm sorry to have bothered you with my last letter and shall be especially sorry to have done so if I outlive God, but it wasn't done lightly. For that matter, I still have to think rigorously about priorities.[i]

Do you know about the bloke who went to the doctor? I'm going to use him in the mortality book.

> Well, sir, I've got some good news and some bad news. Which do you want first? PATIENT: Give us the bad news. DOCTOR: You've only got a week to live. PATIENT: Jeeze! What could be good after that! DOCTOR: Did you notice that receptionist on your way in? PATIENT: Well, yes. DOCTOR: Did you see how beautiful she is? PATIENT: Yes, but ... DOCTOR: Did you notice just how extraordinarily beautiful she is?

---

[i] The preceding 2 paragraphs were repeated in the original file. The repeated section has been deleted.

PATIENT: Yes, yes, yes, but what's this got to do with good news?
DOCTOR: I'm screwing her.
Be, like the doctor, of good cheer.

Love, mate,

Bugger. I have received today notice of a review of the Discipline of Philosophy at Flinders and an invitation to contribute a submission. I'm not sure how big a job I should make it. It seems to me proper that even though I'm not yet dead, I ought to lie down. One thing, I will need though is some independent comments on my research (and other writings) over the years—particularly since I have rather cussedly set my face at premature publication. Do you think that you could provide a short document, saying first of all who you are, what your acquaintance with me has been. What work you have seen, and what your assessment is of this work.

To remind you: Since I've been at Flinders, I've sent you some poems, some stories, some articles and other documents as follows (I think)

Unpublished:

Rationality and Communism(??)
Notes for two seminar papers on the Philosophy of Language
Notes for a book (now to be called) Mortality and the Meaning of Life

Now published:

Nuclear Disarmament and the Defence of Australia (???)
Rationality and Ratiocination (?)
Objective Despair
Objectivity and Ideology in the Physical and Social Sciences
Ideology for Extinction
Ecological Crisis and Social Order[54]

I'll also send you with this a print-out of a Public lecture I'm giving in a week or so at Flinders. I shall, if this is ever published, give a correct interpretation of "too hard for humans." Strapped for space in this version.

Human Nature and the Prospects for Human Survival

It will give you some idea of why I don't want assessments from merely professional philosophers.
Your statement should go to

Ms. Tessa Hodson
Secretary to the Review of Philosophy
The Secretariat, Academic Services Division
The Flinders University of South Australia
GPO Box 2100
Adelaide 5001
Australia.

It should arrive by September 11.

I'm sorry to do this to you. There's a bit more involved than my own self-esteem though. I shan't keep it up forever. Don't spend a lot of time on it. A page or so.

Again, love.

But no. Do you know of the expression "crook and" (pronounced *crooken*) used as an intensive? "crook and rotten (on him)" would mean "very angry (with him)." "crook and rotten (with the booze/piss/turps)" would mean either "extremely inebriated" or "suffering severely from the after-effects of strong drink." "crook and decent"—"very good." This expression goes over very readily into ironical usage: So "crook and likely" would almost certainly mean "highly improbable." Also with additional intensives as in "crook and bloody/fuckin' ..."

LOVE, MY FRIEND

Iris Murdoch to Brian Medlin
[Letter 30]

30 Charlbury Road
OX2 6UU

Aug 15

Dearest Brian, dear Mate, I am so sorry I did not write sooner, in answer to your earlier letter. I was away a great deal of July, and bothered by other on-the-doorstep and less important obligations! I am very sorry. I enjoy your letters and reading them is a treat, and I put them in a special place. I am also now very grieved to hear of your serious ailments which you treat with your usual brave and characteristic wit. (I note it should be "flat as a lizard <u>drinking</u>" but I have forgotten which it actually means—is it good or bad? Also: I know "crook" as in "the plonk's crook"—has "crooken / crook and" superseded "crook" or do they both coexist? Of course I understand that "crooken" is an ambiguous intensive—as in "bloody good" and "bloody bad" etc.) Sorry about this interlude.

I very much hope that the doctors are sorting out this myelin problem: I hope you are not in pain. At any rate you have got over the weakness and tiredness—and you have Christine. And you are working. I am sending /posting/ with this letter, a letter to Ms Tessa Hodson, saying I think your sort of philosophical thinking is what we need in this time when philosophy is menaced in so many ways—being fragmented into philosophy, sociology, psychology etc., or simply treated as otiose (closure of philosophical departments etc.). I also mentioned in the letter your possible book, and I hope that's OK too.

I'm sorry to hear you are unmoved by T. Hardy, poet.[i] I hope you are writing poems. (Well, I know you are, you have sent me some recent ones, and I expect more.) I am sorry too that I have never heard of Ponsford. At this very moment our cricketers are playing the West Indies at the Oval. It is a noble game—it has a mystical magic absent from tennis and <u>a fortiori</u> football. (Football has become so rough and commercial and boorish and generally crook and awful.)

---

[i] Note in margin here: "I like him a lot."

As I write I am staying with friends down by the <u>sea</u> and getting some longed-for swimming. I forget if you are a swimming addict—your seas are warmer and the waves are higher. (Of course you also have sharks.)

Please write to me again soon—I'm so sorry about delay—I so very much hope you are steadily better. All very best wishes and much lots of love from your old mate

I.

Brian Medlin to Iris Murdoch
[Letter MDC000]

August 24, 1991

Oh my dear Iris, what are we going to do with you!!!!!!!!!!!!!!!!!
    Not, repeat NOT flat as a lizard, but

FLAT OUT LIKE A LIZARD DRINKING

The words are fixed and fossilised into an imperishable beauty destined to remain in midst of other woe than ours and no more to be tampered with by pommy novelists than are the legs of Phar Lap to be redesigned by a merry-go-round proprietor.

Talking of Phar Lap, how could anybody not have heard of Bill Ponsford! You'll tell me next you haven't heard of Spofforth or Victor Trumper. Hazlitt says somewhere in his Table Talk that he has no desire to have been alive in the last century or during the reign of Queen Anne. That would seem reasonable to me. But that was before 1991 and before Trumper had been dead for 76 years and before his 1902 tour. (Do you know the prayer of the young Neville Cardus before the fourth test at Old Trafford? "Please God, let Victor Trumper score a century out of a total of 137 all out.") I also wish that I had been standing alongside Bradman to watch Stan McCabe make that 232 at Trent Bridge in 1938—instead of sitting in the front desk under the eye of that bullying drongo Parnell. (Not the one who loved his country and loved a lass. This Parnell was perhaps a proud man, but surely not a lovely one.) It seems to me that if I can wish myself to have been (or to be) in another place, I can regret not having been at another time. Now fear, that's another matter. As I remember, Hazlitt doesn't distinguish what I can't rationally fear from what I can't rationally wish and doesn't distinguish either from what I don't in fact wish.

I suppose that most of us would prefer not to be flat out in this manner, but it's not necessarily bad. We've all known people who are never really happy unless they're flat out like a lizard drinking. Yes, No I mean, "crooken" hasn't replaced "crook" and couldn't. And one could certainly say "crook and crook," though I've never heard it.

Thank you for writing to the committee. It's a routine enquiry of the kind held periodically and certainly whenever a professor leaves. There are some good people on the committee—especially Graham Nerlich—but a couple I'm not so happy about. [...] Given the harshness of the times and the amount of trouble that the philosophers at Flinders have caused the authorities, both civil and academic, it's fairly important to get this one right. I feel limited as to what I can properly do. Though not dead, I feel I ought to lie down a bit.

And don't worry about not having answered earlier. I didn't worry. And I'm glad you enjoy the letters.

The address I sent you was delivered on August 15th. I was very ill that night and my throat was partially paralysed from the neuropathy. (I now understand, by the way, why I have been progressively losing my ability to sing over the past ten years. And to play the flute and piccolo.) But it was a splendid night. The speakers in the series so far have been people like ex-vice-Chancellors and ex-deputy-vice-Chancellors. For the most part grey, boring power-brokers who from the cradle have never had an idea that might have cut across their career. They have been pulling in audiences of thirty or so composed of people like themselves. My audience amounted to more than all theirs put together. (Childish to enjoy that, but why not for those of us anxious to enter the Kingdom of Heaven?) The lecture produced such a burst of applause as has not been heard in the Matthew Flinders Theatre since the production of Brecht's Galileo and The Mother in the Moratorium days. (Childish again, but you little beauty.) There were drinks in the foyer afterwards and the atmosphere was superb. One nice thing was that a lot of one's old mates had shown from the anti-war days, people who had largely dispersed into despondency since then.

The events in Moscow have been inspiring. A pity of course that there is nowhere to go but back to capitalism. But that is certainly to be preferred to that bunch of vice-Chancellors who tried to take over. (How quaint it is to see the public media describing social fascists as right-wingers. They've got to get it right occasionally, just by accident.) I don't like Yeltsin. He is going to prove bad news within three years and has certainly behaved since the collapse of the coup with a total lack of magnanimity. But there's no doubt the smarmy bastard has guts. More important, the Russian people are indestructible. And what a joy to see Father Felix's statue come down.[55]

As you might gather, we haven't got very far at finding out what's behind the loss of myelin and it doesn't seem to be improving. My physician now thinks that I am also guilty of chronic fatigue syndrome. But I've had a few little trips to the mallee lately, the last of them last week-end.

[…]

But I'm working. Not as much as I'd like, but I'm pleased with what results I produce. And Christine is very excited about all her projects. They are limited these days by her need to look after me a bit, but she's getting a lot done nevertheless. A main project is the establishment of indigenous plants—trees shrubs and grasses—on our block. This means the identification and collection of plants and (mainly) seeds from remnant areas nearby. The remnants are left mainly in areas that have been thoroughly neglected. Corners of cemeteries, industrial sites, railway lines. As civilisation spreads out come the mowers and sprays. In come the exotic weeds—cultivated and uncultivated. All this has meant largely remaking the beautiful garden I wrote to you about some time ago. Apart from its productive side, it was planted with natives. But in a continent this size, for any given place most natives are exotics. Further, the favoured natives tend to be few in number, so that the planting of natives is itself a way of eliminating species. There's been some heart-break involved, and plenty of compromise, but project is an important piece of conservation and the result will be worth it. The result will be worth it aesthetically.

The visits to the mallee have come about partly because Christine is involved in a survey of the mallee fowl population in a conservation park in the Murray Mallee. Do you know about that wonderful bird, the mallee fowl? If not tell me and I'll tell you all about it.

Dear Iris, thanks for your lovely letter. Good to think of you swimming. I used to be an adventurous swimmer till I got into my forties. I used to like swimming on my own or with just one other companion in wild surf and rips. I always used to believe that if you just kept your head and never struggled against the sea, nothing could happen to you. I gave it up when I got kids. Just swimming I find boring and the water is never warm enough for my skeleton these days. And just between us I've always hated the idea of sharks. You can tell yourself about the probabilities till your blue with cold, it doesn't help.

Just over a year ago, we landed on the beach at Wentworth on the Gulf of Carpentaria. We camped there in the sheoaks overnight. We knew that there were crocs there, of course, and that you didn't go into the water. In fact it wasn't all that clever to camp near it. The water looked so innocent it was hard to take seriously, what one knew very well, that there could be any danger in it. Then when we took off in the morning and flew low over the shallows, we saw what we'd been camped by. The whole sea was a thick soup. The kind that eats you. Crocodile mainly but turtle too with just a pinch of dolphin. We were very glad that we hadn't brought life jackets.

August 26, 1991

Bruno has been keeping in touch. […] He says he'll come to lunch sometime soon. Perhaps yet another good thing.

[…]

Jake has fallen on hard times. […] He came to lunch yesterday and I must say I admired him. He is certainly free of what I call the Ken Sievers heresy, namely that being depressed is an excuse for not being cheerful. He's decided to give up study […]. He has a lot of ability that gets frustrated in a class-room.

This seems to be a very domestic letter. […]

Iris Murdoch to Brian Medlin
[Letter 22]

30 Charlbury Rd
Oxford OX2 6UU

[no date]

Brian dear, many thanks, and about the now clarified lizard. (At least, I'm still not /quite/ sure what it means.) I can't do Spofforth or Trumper—But the name of Don Bradman is eternal, a great link between our two great cricketing countries.[i]

I'm very glad to hear of your August 15th triumph—huge audience, cries of joy. Most uplifting—one does need it sometimes. I like to hear of Christine's indigenous plants project.[ii] I think of your country as mainly <u>untouched wildness</u>—alas not the case here.[iii] Well, there are great unspoilt places—but motorways increase, and "housing developments." One actually, I note, <u>remarks</u> <u>upon</u> places which have been left alone.[iv]

Swimming cold here but no sharks.

I am sorry to hear about Bruno.[v] I hope he is still organised and in touch. Hope Jake better too.

I can't picture Prospect (nice name)—is it town or country? I hope you are writing poems & singing.

Much love,

I

What about plans for desalinating the sea and flooding the bush? What birds do you have in your garden?

---

[i] Marginal note here: "And what is a mallee? Just a wild place or a special kind of wild place? Tell me about the mallee fowl."

[ii] Marginal note here: "Crocodile soup."

[iii] Marginal note here: "especially in Wales and North."

[iv] Marginal note here: "Still the Cotswolds aren't bad, 20 minutes drive from here."

[v] Marginal note here: "At least it's better news. I needn't be sorry."

Brian Medlin to Iris Murdoch
Letter MDC020

September 19, 1991

Iris Dear

The lizard: It means that you are extremely busy. Even to the point of being frazzled.

Australia as untouched wilderness. A myth that is contributing to the continuing destruction.

As for *untouched*. In two hundred years, we have devastated this continent. The full extent of the damage isn't always obvious to the untutored eye. For example, in the Strzelecki Desert, you might well think that the country looks well. What in fact you are seeing is Dillon Bush, a plant that takes over because it is inedible. Everything else gets cleaned up by the rabbits. (They are back in force again and have recommenced on the destruction of the remaining inland vegetation.) There are plenty of obvious signs. As you fly over even very remote areas, you are hardly ever out of sight of vehicle tracks. And wherever you fly there are geological survey lines running straight from horizon to horizon. At least two-thirds of our arable-pastoral lands are now considered to be seriously degraded. The cane-toad is rapidly moving south into New South Wales and West into Arnhem Land. Last year the blacks on Bentick Island in the Gulf of Carpentaria told us that it had arrived there. After the rabbit, the cane toad is the most destructive animal to have been introduced by us. (I'll tell you the saga of the cane toad and its properties, if you don't know.)

As for *wilderness*. Where we used to cross the cattle over The Ord River on the Wyndham Stockroute, there are now *No Camping* signs. Huge areas of South Australia—millions of hectares are about to be closed to camping—to preserve them as wilderness. The point is that they are no longer wilderness and can no longer take the abuse dealt out to them by your urban Aussie-tough four-wheel drivers. Infuriating for me. I've been throwing my swag down wherever I chose since I was twelve years old.

The crocodiles: Twenty years ago the Australian salt-water croc was almost shot out. They have been protected since and have bred up again. (There is also a pretty harmless, though not inoffensive fresh water croc.) The salt-water croc will be quite happy to eat you in fresh water. It is mainly an estuary animal, but can travel long distances overland. You're not really safe till you're up over a scarp.

But yes, all the same, it is different from England. My friend Douglas Muecke has an Hungarian friend who loves Australia because, as he says, he can get out into the bush where he can get to feel "a little bit completely lost."

Iris, no, I'm no longer singing. The neuropathy partly paralyses my throat and seems to be speeding up alarmingly. Unless we can find out what causes it, I'll be quite happy to be still talking in five years time. And at the present rate of progress, my voice could fold up much more quickly than that. The prospect of sitting around listening to some of the bullshit that comes my way without being able to speak appals me even more than the prospect of losing the use of my legs. I'm just coming down off a course of steroids which we hoped would check the neuropathy, but in fact it still seems to be progressing at a fair clip. I still have a couple of strings to my bow yet and shall draw it again this coming Tuesday.

Iris, I'm going to send you a tape of my lecture. The technician was a bit of a dunce, I'm afraid and the chairman ... well, the less said. But having heard and seen you on telly recently, and bearing in mind that my voice is going quite fast, I'd quite like you to hear it some time when you have leisure. I was desperately ill that night and it shows in question time, but it was still great fun.

You'll notice that I refer copiously to Iris Murdoch—and even more so in the monograph that is coming out of the lecture. I have got so much from your novels, especially in recent years, that they have become, like Yeats' close companions, a portion of my life and mind, as it were. I am deeply your debtor, mate. I love you lots, Iris.

Life with us is good. Hard, but good. I don't know how it should be possible to find so much happiness in such an unbelievably foul world, but we manage.

I am at present working on a paper called *The Critique of Reason, Pure and Practical*. It has to be delivered at a conference on October 3. I think it'll be a good paper in time, but whether by then I don't know. The trouble is that I have a ration of six thousand words to write a fair sized book in.

Oh and thank you for writing to Flinders.

Where does Sir Thomas Browne say, "And so when God forsakes us, Satan also leaves us." It should be in the *Religio*, but I can't find it. I suppose worse things can happen than having to read Sir Thomas Browne through.[56] I did it once in 1948 camped on the Finke River and that was pretty nice. Does John know?

I would send you stars if I could. Instead, I'll send you overleaf a map of what they look like overhead right here, right now.

Good luck.

But no, I'm not finished, am I? The square cursor in the centre of the map is pretty much Adelaide. To the North you will see the moon in Capricorn and just to the South-west of the moon, the planet Saturn. (West is to the right on a star-chart—as you probably know.) South-west of Saturn, in Sagittarius, is the planet Uranus. At a magnitude of about 5.7, Uranus is hardly visible to the unaided eye—and certainly not with so much moon about. On a reasonable clear, darkish night, you can see it with a small pair of binoculars. The object marked with a cross just to the SW of Uranus is the globular cluster M22 in Sagittarius. This is allegedly a view of 180°, but we need a wider angle to see everything that's visible even from my backyard. Lets try 210°. Yes that's about right.

Prospect is one of the first districts of Adelaide, just to the North of the city proper. It was the first farming area. There are still some of the original almond trees, one in our backyard. The Northern suburbs have become notorious for breakins and general hoonishness. Annie and I moved here in 1976. About 18 months after we separated I moved into this place (that was in January, 1981.) Prospect is not country. It is suburbia.

Been reading with some sadness of the antics of the young in Oxford, etc. Bloody goons. But I dunno what you can expect. One of the many legacies of Maggie.

My house is about 120 years old, a small cottage of the kind the English call detached. It is pretty full at present. Rebecca, Christine's nineteen year old daughter, has come to live with us. She had moved in with her boyfriend […], stupid bugger. So now she's with us and I get a double ration of cuddles and hugs. Suits me fine.

Birds in our garden. I'll send you a print-out of some very unconscientiously kept notes. The common names may not always mean much. Ask if you want to know what, for example a willy wagtail is.

(Note in handwriting: I did a print out and it was so awful I shan't send it. Christine is going to put the material into a data-base and I'll send it then. But I will send you my little submission for the Review of Philosophy. It's been an interesting time and I hope it reads interestingly.)

Mallee. 1. A kind of Eucalypt.

Characteristically eucalypts are fire-adapted. An important trick is the epicormal bud that stays dormant under the bark. These are stimulated when the tree is defoliated. After bushfires you will see the new growth sprouting like candle flame all along the main trunk and lower branches. The mallees take this adaptation one step further. They grow their trunk underground, thus reducing again the chances of the destruction of the epicormal buds. The mallee "root," a very gnarled, dense object, and a famous fuel, is really this ligno-tuber, the underground trunk. This adaptation produces the mallee habit: branches arise straight from the ground. The basic mallee shape is a fairly regular vase with between three to a dozen straightish branches radiating out from the base and rising to a set of leaf-bearing twigs that form a regular sparse canopy. This shape also serves to direct moisture to the base of the tree. In a good mallee scrub, the canopies will pretty much touch one another. Most mallees grow to about fifteen feet high. They are tough, casual, hardy, but elegant, graceful, pretty.

The mallee, after fire shoots up, at first bushily out of the ground. Usually the old branches will still be radiating out bare from the new foliage.

(You may remember that in 1988, I wrote to you about camping in Billiatt after fire. We were going to do a monthly survey of regeneration, but too much else has happened—including my non-happening health. But we were back a few weeks ago. This is pretty dry country the mallees are none of them three feet high yet.)

The basic shape and size vary with conditions and also from species to species. The curly mallee, *E. gillii*, that grows in the Northern Flinders bends under its own weight as it grows, forming bizarre shapes. I planted one maybe eight years ago and it still hasn't managed to stand up tho four feet tall. Instead it's snaking off across the yard. The red mallee, *E. socialis*, which grew in this area and which Christine has now planted here, is a very substantial and very irregular tree, rough-barked and warmly red. Not a tree of The Mallee in sense 2 or 3. A wise, generous tree. Though it branches low from the ground, you wouldn't at first take it to be a mallee.

Mallee: 2. A kind of community.

Mallee is sclerophyll woodland, light but not usually open. It is good stuff to get a lot completely lost in. It will contain only about a dozen or two dozen plant species, few grasses amongst them. Mostly, plants other than mallee will be small to medium-sized shrubs with hard water-conserving foliage. The ground will mostly be bare between them. For the most part walking through even the densest mallee is easy enough, though riding a horse among trees of that shape is hazardous.—

The daddy of all the stockmen as
ever come musterin' here
Killed in the flamin' mallee
Yardin' a scrub bred steer.[57]

Extensive mallee scrub has a quality all its own. Not threatening, not hostile, not friendly, not even indifferent, but manifesting the utter a-theism of the universe. There is no room in the mallee for pathetic fallacy. The mallee is beautiful, harsh and pretty both. Starlight through the mallee! It is the right medium through which to view the eternal silence of those infinite spaces that so terrified Pascal. (Without his expectations, the godlessness of the world isn't terrifying. Similarly, it is the expectation of life that makes death fearful.)

Mallee: 3. A district.

These communities once stretched in a huge unbroken belt from eastern Victoria and New South Wales (but inland on the Great Dividing Range) well into South Australia. Most of it all has now gone, cleared for farming. Low rainfall farming on light not too fertile soils. For many miles, the mallee survives only along verges. But there are a few patches left where you can get to feel what it must have been like when there were hundreds of unbroken miles of it.

Mallee fowl or *lowan (Leipa ocellata).* A most interesting bird of the family Megapodiidae (Galliformes). The other Megapodes are the scrub fowl and the brush turkeys. The "turkeys" are also found in Australia. All three are mound-building birds, hence the big feet. The mallee fowl has somehow got itself stranded with this practice in dry conditions, so its life is very laborious.

The mallee fowl is the size of a very big chook, light brown-grey. It can fly pretty well, but is basically a ground bird.

The mound is an incubating device, built maintained and serviced by the male. The mound can be 4-5 metres across and a metre or more above the ground. In the centre is an egg chamber, dug to perhaps a half metre below ground level. This is filled in with vegetation much of it seeming very unpromising—containing quite thick sticks and twigs. This is also spread out over the top of the chamber. Once the vegetation gets wet, it is covered with earth. The male maintains the temperature of the chamber somewhere in the low thirties and always within a three degree range. This requires constant work, raking out sand to heat up in the sun or cool off in the shade. He constantly monitors the temperature with a thermometer in his beak. Only when he is satisfied that all is well, does he allow the female in to lay. He must excavate the chamber for her to do so and then cover it in again. During the season, she will lay 30-40 eggs. The chicks, when they hatch, have to fight their way up through about a metre of material to the surface. Once there, they tumble down the side of the mound and scurry off into the scrub. From the moment of hatching they are self-supporting, receiving no parental care whatsoever. They can fly within a couple of days of hatching.

The species is big trouble. They are vulnerable to feral cats and foxes which infest this country. In addition, the remaining mallee communities are seriously degraded so that chicks released into the wild find it hard to make a living. The area where Christine has been working is one of the few places where they seem to be well established. And to maintain that requires a continuous poisoning of cats and foxes.

I haven't read all this through. (Christine did in the end.) But to make up for this neglect, you'll find overleaf a plot of your stars as they will be in a week's time. If they don't match up, then it's not my computer but the heavens that have gone wrong. Not for the first time either.

Love, my dear friend

Brian Medlin to Iris Murdoch
[Letter MDC040][i]

It was recently remarked to me, in regard to the underground trunks of mallee and the underground nests of mallee fowl, "You'll be coming up next with underground flowers, I shouldn't wonder." Well and why not.

Here is something that might interest you concerning the plants of the heathlands of south western Western Australia. This is an area of meagre soils that alternates between waterlogged conditions and extreme dryness. The quotations are from John Vandenbeld, *The Nature of Australia*, Collins Australia & Australian Broadcasting Corporation, Sydney. If ever you get a chance to watch the television series, *The Nature of Australia*, don't miss it.

Selective pressures came from the frequent climatic swings of the past two million years, from wet and warm to cold and dry and back again. They had their greatest impact—and produced the greatest number of species—in the transition zone between the wetter southwestern corner and the arid region.

The result is one of the most diverse floral communities in the world, with 3600 species identified so far (of which 2450 occur nowhere else) and many more to be described. There is greater variety here than in the rainforest: in fact, in many places the heath resembles a miniature forest, with many plants dwarfed forms of their rainforest progenitors (pp. 152-3).

Cutting back on nectar production—or cutting it out altogether—is one way of conserving resources. Another is to seek supplements elsewhere and several plants have turned to trapping insects, not for pollination, but for food. It is not restricted to heath lands: sundews which catch flies in their sticky tentacles, grow in many areas of nutritionally poor soil in Australia, but the heath has produced a remarkable example of evolutionary convergence in the Albany pitcher plant.

It is not even remotely related to the large group of insectivorous pitcher plants found in other parts of the world, but is a member of a family of Australian plants that elsewhere grow in conventional forms. Yet in the isolation of the heath, selective pressures generated by a particular nutrient deficiency have produced a plant with almost identical features to those of the pitcher group: a leaf shaped like a jug, filled with a sweet-

---

[i] This is in a separate file but has no salutation or date.

smelling digestive liquid that entices ant and other insects into a fatal plunge.

Eating insects is among the more visibly dramatic of the many ways heath plants make more effective use of available nutrients. The processes are usually underground, out of sight. There, plants have set up chemical associations through their root systems; with fungi to provide phosphorus, and with bacteria to produce nitrogen. One plant has taken this to the extreme. The underground orchid (_Rhizanthella gardeneri_) lives an entirely subterranean existence: a fungus supplies the carbohydrate that the rest of the plant world derives from sunlight. The orchid blooms underground, too; its flowers grow upward to just below the surface, where they are pollinated by a tiny insect that reaches them through cracks in the soil (pp. 156-7).

Why not come to Australia? If you went to Coober Pedy, you could live in an underground house.

There is at least one other underground orchid, Chryptanthemis slateri, but I don't know anything about it.

The standard pitcher plants are of the family Sarraceniaceae with two genera _Sarracenia_ and _Darlingtonia_ in North America and of the family Nepenthaceae with the one genus _Nepenthes_. Species of this last genus extend from South East Asia into Queensland to about 17+ degrees South. The Queensland species is _N. mirabilis_, so variable that is has received at least ten different species names.

All these plants, as Vandenbeld makes clear, are completely unrelated to the Western Australian pitcher plant _Cephalotus follicularis_, the sole species of the family Cephalotaceae. For all the resultant similarities, the mode of development of the pitcher is quite different. The foliage of _follicularis_ is of two kinds, with normal leaves between autumn and spring, these withering and being replaced by the pitchers which mature in summer.

I think that it is highly probable that the olive has epicormal buds. Certainly it is highly resistant to fire—at least as effectively so as any eucalypt. I wouldn't mind betting that it has an underground trunk too. Whatever the reason, it can't be killed merely by chopping it down and will survive many years of regular mowing and grazing to ground level. Frequently, you will see, on mowed ground, a couple of tiny olive shoots. On trying to pull them up you'll find that they are spouting from a deep stock thicker than your wrist. I have no doubt that for these adaptations we are indebted to the Spartans and their behaviour in Attica. The eucalypt and other native trees don't manage nearly so well in such circumstances. A result is that the olive is a rapidly invasive weed forming thickets in the remnant bush of the Adelaide foothills, on disused—and even used pasture—and along the few remaining stretches of wildish creek of the suburban plains. I don't see the olive as a symbol of peace, but as an agent of degradation. The same goes for the turtle dove. Extirpate the bastards root and branch with grunting bulldozer. Visit upon them clouds of toxic spray. Trap them with nets and massy jaws. Dash their little ones against the stones. Bestrew their path with poisoned wheat.

You may like to read something I have recently written to Jack Smart.[58]

Thanks Jack for your nice paper. Beautifully written as usual—lucid and simple. There are some points, though.

1. I think that I agree with Broad.[59] I think that it is highly probable that there are phenomena that we will never fully understand. I think it is pretty likely too that there are phenomena of which we cannot even become aware. My reasons for this—knock down or not are given in the last paper I sent you—the one on reasoning. I don't think that there are phenomena of which we are aware and of which orthodox science can tell us nothing. In fact I think that this is contradictory. I haven't seen the Schilpp volume on Broad[60] so I don't know exactly what he meant.

2. Maybe you can eliminate anthropocentric perspectives from metaphysics, but I bet you can't from epistemology. That you can't—if you can't—from epistemology, is no reason at all to believe that you can't from metaphysics. All too often, I think, people oppose ontology with epistemology. Dogmatic and gnomic, I know. But life is short.

3. Geach's position, if I have understood, it is surely pathetic.[61] (I think, by the way that it is like Geach's nerve to have a robust faith in human reason. People like Geach reduce me to despair about human reason. Suppose that the future is to be explicated in terms of tendencies. Well, it seems to me that, if the universe isn't simply going to run away from itself, then for every tendency there will be a countervailing tendency. Perhaps that's not so, but no matter ... Because, for plenty of tendencies there are countervailing tendencies. Take the last eucalypt that Christine has planted in the back-yard. There is a present tendency, which will almost certainly be thwarted for it to live for the next five hundred years. But there is also a present tendency, which again will almost certainly be thwarted for it to be killed off before the end of summer. Doesn't this give us two incompatible futures? We get a unique future, which is the same for all times prior to us, if we assume determinism and constitute the future out of the sum total of all (the relevant?) tendencies.

But then this future can't be changed. Geach may well not mind multiple present futures. To the extent that the futures simply are tendencies, then they can be opposing as are tendencies without being incompatible. (Beliefs provide another case.) But then that seems to me to be positivism. And if it's not positivism and the future (state of affairs?) is somehow distinct from its corresponding tendency, then that future is indefinite—not just epistemologically, which is no problem, but ontologically, which is. This is all compressed and I haven't really thought the expansion out explicitly, but I bet it's there for the unpacking.

4. In what sense could there be a knock-down argument in philosophy? Anthropological? Well, if all arguments were knock-down, then I doubt that we'd need argument at all. To the extent that argument is needed, there is disagreement. I suspect that [it is] _no_ surprise [to] us that no argument is absolutely knock down. Certainly the argumentation which establishes the theory of evolution by means of natural selection isn't. And, it is my belief, that many people (including many professional biologists) who take themselves to be knocked down by the theory don't really know what the argumentation is. It shouldn't therefore surprise us that some kinds of disagreement are much less readily resolvable than others and that some are particularly obdurate. Being unsurprised doesn't however constitute the knowledge of what characterises the most obdurate kinds of disagreement nor the knowledge of why these kinds are obdurate.

5. I think we may mean different things by philosophy. You say, of the conception of metaphysics as not wholly an intellectual pursuit but as something that informs our whole lives, "Quite why this should be demanded of philosophers is unclear to me." And I say "Because otherwise they would not _be_ philosophers." In one sense of the word philosophy is the determination to avoid what I call in the Flinders lecture "a purchased and partial objectivity, a servile scientism." You talk of it as though it's a trade like industrial chemistry, or at anyrate as though it can be defined by its intellectual content. Which it can't. Now if philosophy were merely a profession, like medicine, then there would be no obvious reason why the disagreements amongst us should be at once so vexed and at the same time, as Hume observed, so calmly canvassed. The latter fact needs explanation along with the first.

But suppose there were a species of people, like yourself, just suppose it, who hated illusion and scorned to be self-deceived, and who were determined, to the full extent of their ability to live without either. This would entail, I think, a determination to live the good as opposed to the prosperous life. Would we not expect to find such people characteristically, systematically exercised by those very questions where illusion and self-deception are most common, where the dangers of these misfortunes are greatest. (And would this not be the hardest intellectual life of all. I am not at all intimidated by the superior cleverness of successful scientists. Quite frankly, I think that you and I can run rings around self-indulgent, soft-minded creatures like Paul Davies.[62]) And would we not find such people, with the best will, in the world differing radically amongst themselves. And would we not expect to find that, for all their differences, and for all their passion and their sinful pride of intellect—would we not expect also a proper humility and a common respect?

And of course there are such people, you among them. Let's call them philosophers. Or what have you—Jack, say.[63]

But the situation is more complex than that. For we would also expect to find, masquerading as philosophers, people who cherished illusion and self-deception. And such people would naturally busy themselves with the same problems as the philosophers. For it is just the illusions associated with those problems that are most precious. Such people ape intellectual honesty.

And we would also expect to find others who fear and hate the whole philosophical enterprise. Some of these, fascists, will try crudely to stamp it out. But others, in these times mainly Frenchmen and North Americans but increasingly Australian, will try to corrupt it from within.

In the light of these last too considerations we may expect to find that "philosophical" disagreement sometimes gets heated as well as passionate.

The philosophical enterprise, disturbing and disruptive as it may be, is in the long run socially useful. In fact, I think we have brought ourselves to a pass where it is socially necessary. Even fairly philistine minds can be dimly aware of this. Hence pursuit of the enterprise is institutionalised—we have philosophy departments. Hence we have people posing as philosophers who are mere careerists. The bloody universities and the bloody journals are aswarm with them. I'm convinced that this institutionalising of philosophy is more good than bad: I'd resist attempts to abolish philosophy departments. But nonetheless, it *is* bad.

I'm still being too simple. For being human, none of us is simple. It depends on how the philosopher, charlatan, anti-philosopher, careerist are mixed in us whether we be philosopher, charlatan, anti-philosopher, or careerist.

Iris Murdoch and John Bayley at Cedar Lodge, Steeple Aston. *Iris Murdoch Collections at Kingston University Archives* (we have been unable to trace the copyright owners of this photograph and we would appreciate any information that would enable us to do so)

Brian Medlin in the arms of the South Australian Police, 1970s. *Medlin Collection, Flinders University Library*

Iris Murdoch in London 1988. *Miriam Berkley*

Iris Murdoch and John Bayley in London 1988. *Miriam Berkley*

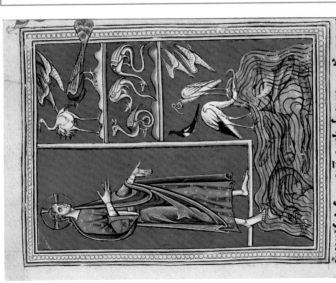

← "Now let me think, what comes next?"

Dearest Brian, thank you very much for your cheerin (and interesting) postcard. I will be relieved to see me drunk together.

Iris has a Dome to come to [rescue], it is quite fun. Much ? I feel better like Candlelight. I ?? all to learn very... Miss you very much darling remember... lots of love Iris

Facsimile: Card from Iris Murdoch to Brian Medlin [Letter 13, 1989]. *Medlin Collection, Flinders University Library*

30 Charlsbury Rd
Oxford OX2 6UU

Brian dear, many thanks, and about the now clarified lizard. (At least, I'm still not quite sure what it means.) I can't do Snuffboxe or Thorpe — But the name of Don Bradman is eternal, a great link between our two great cricketing countries.

I'm very glad to hear of your August 15ᵗʰ triumph — huge audience, cries of joy. most uplifting — one does need it sometimes. I like to hear of Clathue's indigenous plants project. I know of your county as recently untouched wilderness — alas not the case here. Well, there are great unspoilt places — but motorways increase, and 'horrid developments'. One achieves, I note, reverence upon places which have been left alone.
Swimming cold here but no sharks.
I am sorry to hear about Bruno. I hope we a shy organized and in touch.
Hope Jake better too.

And what is a mallee? Just a wild place or a special kind of wild place? Tell me about the mallee fowl.

Crocodile soup

especially in Wales and North. Still the Cotswolds aren't bad, 20 minutes drive from here.

at least it's better news. I needn't be sorry.

Book launch at Flinders University, 1992. L to R: Brian Medlin, Sue Hosking, Brian Matthews, Syd Harrex, Katy Hasenohr. *Flinders University.*

Brian Medlin with Syd Harrex, Flinders University, 1992. *Flinders University.*

Christine Vick in the Wirra in her Prospect garden, 1993. *Prospect Heritage Collection, City of Prospect, South Australia.*

Brian Medlin with 'Truth' statuette given to him in 1970 by a supporter, 1993. *Prospect Heritage Collection, City of Prospect, South Australia.*

The house in Hamilton Road, North Oxford, where Iris
Murdoch and John Bayley lived from 1986 to 1989. Photo
taken in 2010. *G. Dooley.*

Iris Murdoch and John Bayley in Japan in 1995. *Professor Muroya.*

Brian Medlin picnicking on McKenzie Creek, Victoria: a self-portrait taken with his new digital camera. *Estate Brian Medlin.*

Brian Medlin just before his death in 2004. *John Schumann.*

Iris Murdoch to Brian Medlin
[Letter 25]

30 Charlbury Rd.
OX2

[no date]

Brian dear, thanks so much for letter, and your bold submission to the Committee. You <u>write</u> so well. I hope they noticed that among other things. I think it's fine, its form & tone just right. I much look forward to reading <u>Morality & the Meaning of Life.</u> You're <u>serious</u>. How much Marxism is still with you I wonder. And you are a real <u>teacher</u>. There's a lot I don't understand (well, things are being mentioned not, since the Committee knows about, explained.) (Eg re Barnett & Lewis.) Your classes much have been fun too. Wish you were here for talk about <u>art</u>. (I suspect we might disagree about art—tho' maybe not. I expect I am by your standards <u>bourgeois</u>.)

Thanks for your letter, as I said above, with information about cane toads and crocodiles, I like that. By the way I hope the <u>Crit of Pure & Practical Reason</u> went across well. You are certainly well into the centre of the problems of life. I can't find the Thomas Browne quote (at the moment anyway). How does religion stand with you—were you <u>brought up</u> as an Anglican, Evangelical, atheist?

Thanks for Mallee news, and also "stonkered." (I'll pass stonkered on to the chap in my novel—I sorry now he's not a main character.) Thank you for the <u>stars</u>, by the way. I haven't been able to check since think rain clouds have occluded them for some time. I recall some Aussie, perhaps you, saying that clouds in England were all <u>too low</u>, whereas in Australia they were in the right place, very high up. Still that wouldn't affect the stars. Though I imagine your skies are usually clearer than ours. Starlight through the mallee—yes. And what interesting habits your creatures (eg Mallee fowl) have.[i] From where you are Europe must look small. (It can kick up a lot of trouble however.) I hope you are writing lots of poems. It seems not long ago that you were at New College, and that you read out a

---

[i] Marginal note here: "And the Mallee's habits are bizarre—so clever about avoiding fire."

love poem sequence at the Mermaid Theatre. (Alas I wasn't there.) I am trying to write a little philosophy and am as usual pushing along a novel. Good that you are pleased with Christine. I hope your submission was received with warm appreciation. And I do hope you are feeling <u>better</u> and getting <u>well</u>. Be it so.[i] The gods be with you. (There must be a lot around down there. There's been a splendid Abo exhibition in London. Perhaps they should be called "spirits.")

    Much love, my dear, ever

    I

---

[i] Marginal note here: "Let me know."

Iris Murdoch to Brian Medlin
[Letter 23]

30 Charlbury Rd
OX 2

PS Brian dear, thanks very much for <u>Pure and Practical Reason</u>, you have certainly given the rational and the irrational a very thorough going over, with refs to Braithwaite, Nietzsche Keats and Ryle! I like a lot and will read again. Reason as making the best of things and sorting out inconsistent desires. Hume too of course. Bless him.[i]

What is a "what have you"?
I hope you enjoyed giving them that talk.
With all best wishes & love
ever I

---

[i] Marginal note here: "<u>And</u> Blake, and …"

Brian Medlin to Iris Murdoch
Letter MDC030

69 Albert Street
Prospect
South Australia
5082
Ph: (08) 269 2483

November 11, 1991

My dear Iris
   You'll find enclosed an anthology that is pretty self-explanatory. I hope you enjoy it. It does Syd great credit, I think, being largely a product of his work as founder and director over the years of the Centre.[64]
   You'll also find the tape of my Silver Jubilee lecture. [...] I was desperately ill at the time and my throat was partially paralysed. By question time I could hardly talk and hardly stand. But it was an exciting night all the same.
   Some remarks about your last two notes.

   1. "Morality and the Meaning of Life," while indeed a pertinent title, should be "Mortality and the Meaning of Life," which is the revised title of the proposed book "Philosophy and Mortality," the plan of which I sent you some time back.
   2. Was the exhibition you saw "Dreamings"? If so, it was indeed splendid. It was put together by a bloke called Sutton of the South Australian Art Gallery.[65]
   3. Religion? Complicated. A convinced atheist and materialist. Determinedly hostile to religion, but not implacably so. I believe that the religions are partly rooted in something very important. Were it not so they could hardly be such effective instruments of control and such breeding grounds for irrationality and bigotry. I have a special aversion to Christianity and Islam, (though also a special emotional connection with the former). To start with, they are both utterly silly. To finish with, they are appallingly evil. More later, perhaps. You? I suspect that you are a bit soft on religion.
   4. I wouldn't be surprised if I were to find your views on art "Bourgeois." Some of the best views abroad are. And what Marxism can

be made to tell us about art, in so far as it is correct, is at least woefully incomplete.

5. The Braithwaite quoted in the Reason paper, by the way, is another Braithwaite, a contemporary and a journalist.[66] He was writing about the Gulf War.

6. A what have you is like a what's'a name except that what is unknown or in doubt is not so much the correct description of the thing as its nature. Another difference is that the former expression is standardly used as a noun, in spite of being a noun clause. A far as I know, mine is the first use of "What have you" as a noun. Which is probably what caused you difficulty.

More to the point.

Christine and I went up to the Mallee again this week-end. We took a friend, Maureen, as a birthday present. Maureen is a Derbyshire lass who once worked for the miners' union—whatever it's called. She's now a woman in her late forties. She was a Politics and Art student of mine about ten years back, which is how I got to know her. She is now the principal of the school for adolescent boys and girls under penal detention. So you can imagine that she lives a hard life. On the one hand she has to battle the retributive bureaucrats. On the other hand she has to endure frequent disappointment from the kids themselves. All this in the knowledge that our society lacks both the competence and the will to change the circumstances that produce those kids.

Anyway ...

Maureen was bloody lucky, for we saw a mallee-fowl. Something impelled me on this occasion to walk straight past its nest instead of stopping to examine it. About two hundred metres further on, there was a grunt off in the scrub and there fifty metres away at most was this beautiful bird.

It moved off quietly after the manner of mallee-fowl. But then, before long, it began to feed. First of all from the ground and then from a 1.5 metre-high shrub. Not from that height, of course, though it was sporting a surprisingly long neck. This was an education to me as I had always imagined these birds as feeding off the ground. I had often wondered what they found to support them.

We all had the glasses on this bird for some minutes and for Christine and myself it was certainly our best sighting—for Maureen her only one. It (he? she?) was beautifully marked above in a rich, subdued way. The underparts were superb, a plain sumptuous buff-beige, slightly puffed but not frivolously so. There was a dark marking running down the neck and breast, somewhat too striking on such a subtle bird. The eye was large and dark. The legs and feet were massive. The whole animal blended into its surroundings. After a few minutes, it took itself off more or less absent-mindedly.

The shrub it was feeding off turned out to be a pale turpentine, *Beyeria leschenaultii*. The fruits are small capsules about as round as your (my) little fingernail. They have a tough skin, rather than flesh, which encloses seeds that are as hard as bullets. That bird must have one helluva gizzard.

A couple of interesting facts that I didn't mention last time. Each individual egg takes seven weeks to hatch. And the male works at the nest for a total of nine months in the year.

This part of the scrub where we saw the bird is rather prettier than where we camp. It is on a bit of a ridge which grows spinifex. Spinifex is a tough prickly grass that is nonetheless very delicate and pretty in appearance. It softens the whole appearance of a landscape. It is inedible when mature, but the new shoots make good green pick, so it is often burnt off for feed in pastoral areas. The blacks, too, used to burn it to bring game to the new growth and in the areas still (or again) under their control, they do still (or again).

But the whole understory there is richer and prettier than where we camp. I don't know why that should be since this part of the scrub too has been harvested. I suspect that it is because the soil here is sandier and so less compressible.

Near our camp the soil has been quite badly compressed by heavy machinery. There are tread tracks everywhere. I imagine that the trees were knocked down by bulldozers. Many of them were uprooted and the larger tubers are still lying about. Most of the trees have regenerated. It is now quite a respectable scrub again, perhaps forty years old. There are few ancient trees though and those that were left standing were mostly spared because they were too beat up by the centuries to yield much fuel. And, as I say, the understory there is pretty poor. There are a couple of kinds of salt-bush scattered sparsely about, but that's pretty well it.

The other area supports a wealth, by our standards in arid Oz, of flowering plants.

And even that area isn't a patch on Billiatt, which is the prettiest mallee I have ever seen. But, alas, we have only ever found one mallee-fowl's nest in Billiatt and that has been disused since 1981. (In that year Christine, making a motor-bike trip into New South Wales, found a dead bird killed by the road about one kilometre away from this nest. That was almost certainly one of the last birds in the Billiatt scrub.)

There is a long disused nest very near to our camp and it was nearly Maureen's undoing. My fault because I usually give newchums a five-minute lesson in not taking risks as soon as we arrive in such a place. You'll remember that I told you that mallee is good stuff for getting lost in? Well Maureen did just that. She went off to look at the nest I'd told her about. It was just on the other side of the (vehicle) track and only forty metres from the camp. She walked past it and on into the scrub. At some point she saw a couple of mallee ring-necks (parrots) and followed them to get a closer look. After they'd flown off, she realised that she didn't know where she'd come since she first saw them, which direction was which and where the camp was. A case straight out of the text books. After about half an hour I realised that she'd been gone a longish time, but thought that she'd probably taken a stroll along the track—she being a bit of a walker in town. The track was too marked by all our foot prints to be much use to me and the ground around the old nest was too compressed to leave tracks that I could make out. I coo-eed off in the direction she'd taken with no response. At this time she was probably of in another direction altogether, having crossed back over the vehicle track without noticing it. We decided to have our breakfast and then, after she'd been gone an hour to begin taking the matter seriously. We weren't especially concerned since the scrub is of finite size and there are a number of tracks in it. But it was beginning to be a warmish day and Maureen had certainly needed water early in the walk the day before. Exactly on the hour we heard a faint call. So we sounded the horn. A bit later, a bit stronger. And so on until Maureen emerged from the scrub to the North having previously gone off to the South.

There was once a time when we could have got high-up about Pommie new chums, but now that we're a multi-cultural society even our English brothers and sisters have to be endured with forbearance.

I realise that this is a rather boring story. A tragedy would have been more exciting, but this was after all our dear friend Maureen.

Our guests seem to be lucky. Perhaps a couple of months back, I took my friend Peter Hicks to the same place. He was going through a bad patch at the time and the idea was to help him over it by bringing him back to the real world. Peter too saw a mallee fowl. Got quite a good look at it. I was very ill at the time so he saw it on his own. No need to instruct Peter in the elements of not getting lost, as he's spent a lot of time in the Mallee. Amongst other things, some years back he was writer in residence in the Tatiara. The Tatiara is a South Australian district on the Victorian border. It is famed in song.

From Billabone, Murray and Lodden
To the far Tatiara and back
The mountains and plains are well-trodden
By the men on the wallaby track.

Refr: With a raggedy old swag on me shoulder
And a billy quart pot in me hand
I tell you we'll astonish the new chums
For to see how we travel the land.[67]

Peter too was a student of mine, one of the original intake in 1967. He is
the author of the poem for me in the anthology I am sending you, a poem
of which I am very proud, written as it is by someone for whom I have so
much respect.

Peter was (one of) the author(s) of one of the most elegant pieces of
political theatre I have ever encountered. At the height of the Vietnam War
he and others announced that they proposed, on the following Friday, to
napalm a dog on the plaza at Flinders. The purpose was to demonstrate the
horror of this particular weapon. For days thereafter, the university
switchboard was jammed by humane protest. The registrar proclaimed that
it would be a breach of university discipline to light a fire on the plaza.
The day after Peter's announcement, the morning paper carried a photo of
him fondling the dog, Plato by name, and a statement to the effect that
Plato belonged to a friend who didn't mind him being publicly burnt.
Came the day and every sensationalist journo in South Australia turned up
at Flinders. No principals, however. It took a long time for the point to
sink in, but in the end I think most people got it. Peter Karmel who was at
that time vice-Chancellor told me that soon after the event, he was having
dinner with Jim Cornell, Professor of French at the University of Adelaide.
Peter remarked that he thought that the youngsters had made their point, to
which Jim replied, "Nonsense! You forget that we are not at war with the
dogs." And presumably, if we had been, it would have been bad form to
prefer a grown dog for immolation over bitches and puppies.

And why don't I tell you about the Brisbane brush turkey?

Well, first the two other megapods, as I've partly said already, are the
orange footed scrub fowl, or jungle fowl, Megapodius reinwardt, which is
confined to the narrow Northern coastal regions and the brush turkey,
Alectura latharmi, ranging through the tropical and temperate forests from
Cape York Peninsula to south of Sydney. You will understand that the
latter bird is no more a turkey than is the flying fox a fox. (Do you know
of the theory by the way, which I find very plausible, that Flying foxes are
primates?)

I was actually in jungle fowl country just in July of last year. How can that be? I that in heill wes and gladnes, can hardly now believe that I was ever in that condition, in that place, and just so short a time past. Howbeit ...

And second, when I went to live in Brisbane, in 1964 I think, I built a house on a scrub block on the outskirts of Brisbane. (More of that wonderful house perhaps another time.) The area had been cleared of its understory about five or ten years earlier by developers whom god rot. But it had grown back vigorously. The tall timber, stringybark, ironbark and spotted gum had been left. The blocks were of 2 1/2 acres each. There were originally only 3 of us in the whole area, all living there because of the dense scrub. As it happened we were all academics.

But very soon the aspiring young business people moved in. They knocked down every blessed living thing less than 30 metres tall and set about pommifying the joint. Lawns, rose gardens, white-painted iron garden furniture.

An immediate effect was to bury in wild-life those of us who'd kept our scrub. Quail and bandicoots especially. But also red-back spiders which made their way inside. (And there's an interesting story to be told about the recent hybridisation of red-backs in the Brisbane area, too. But again, another time.) Since the red-back is highly venomous and since it is a lurky little bastard and since we all had kids of an age to poke their fingers into every possible spider-refuge, this was a worrying time. But the quail and the bandicoot were a delight. Not that they could last, we knew. There were too any of them for the space available. But then the accursed dogs and cats, also of the aspiring business caste, discovered them and cleaned them all out in a fortnight.

That was bad enough, but one family of the three originals defected to the enemy and cleared their block too. This was a bitter defeat and especially so as they were my direct neighbours. It happened like this. They were English. One day he came to me and said that they were thinking of clearing their block. "Why would you do a thing like that?" It turned out that they had seen a snake near the house and were frightened that the children might get bitten. "Have you ever met anybody that had been bitten by a snake?" I am sure to this day that there was no trace in my voice or expression of that well-merited scorn of the sturdy Australian for the effete and timid Englishman.

Well bugger me dead, if within a week he doesn't come to me with accusatory air and complaining tone. "Nicholas was bitten by a snake today." "That's interesting, what kind?" Well, it was interesting and I did want to know. But he didn't speak to me for weeks after that. He did, however, clear his block. And put in a bloody swimming pool.

I bet the damn kid had been meddling with the snake. And the reason why is that the only snake in the area likely to attack unprovoked is the Taipan. If a four year old kid gets bitten by a Taipan, then he's very sick indeed and lucky to survive. So it wasn't one of those. (If you can call it luck growing up amid cast iron furniture in a de-snaked suburb.)

Well, I was back in Brisbane in 1985 and 6. I think. I know the first date is right because that's when I got skittled off my bike at Wanaaring by a feral pig. Anyhow ... I went up to have a look at the old house. Apart from my fury at finding that the present owners had built a bloody stupid boxy room onto my beautiful blank front wall, I was delighted. As you doubtless know, Brisbane though not tropical, is pretty hot and fairly wet and things grow there at a fair clip. The householders of the area were now young middle-aged, past their physical best. They were now all junior execs., exploited for all the multinationals could wring out of them, and busy as buggery. Their properties had, for the most part got completely away from them. The bush had returned. It was coming up through the swimming pools and there were 10 metre eucalypts on the tennis courts. And marvellous to see and relate, there perched in the scrub and peering in at the windows of my former house with clumsy tail and implausible red head was that wonderfully ugly old brush turkey. And others clinging incompetently to the branches through the scrub all about.

And talking of developers and such people, as we nearly were a while back, I was once talking to one. This too was in Brisbane. I mentioned a particular area to him. Acre upon acre of superb secondary scrub was being shaved to the bedrock by bulldozers. The scrub was just being pushed into huge piles and burnt. I said it was a tragedy. He agreed with me, as for a moment I thought. "You should have seen it twenty years ago, Brian. It was all pineapple farms. Beautiful land! Not a tree on it."

Dean Jones has just made a quick 218 against South Australia. His two previous innings for the season so far have yielded 243 and 144. This is the best start to the season for a long while and perhaps the best since 1927-28. Then Bill Ponsford kicked off with 133, 437 and 202. His first five innings notched up 1146 runs. I was born in 1927. Bugger it. A few years earlier and I could have seen all that.

To add to our woes here in South Australia, the Vatican seems to be on the verge of canonising Mother Mary NACELLE—of whom no doubt you have never heard. I have nothing against Mother Mary who seems to have been a good sort—far too good for the company of dreadful types like Augustine—and who certainly stood for no nonsense from archbishops.

She even managed to get herself ex-communicated for a while. And I don't much object to the concept of canonisation, silly though it be. I do object to the routine subservience of my compatriots. The gush over a saint of our very own. Not as bad as the annual crawl that we get every October-November over the international celebrities here for the Grand Prix. (Washed out again this year. Another triumph for the argument from design.) And what I object to most is that the canonisation will ruin another nice Australian town—Penola where she first flashed her black, shiny heels. Penola is a small place in South Australia's South East. It is on the road to Casterton, so I have had some interest in it over the years. The area was originally entirely pastoral, but now Penola sits on the edge of the Coonawarra district where the sheep have given way to vineyards and some of our best wines are made. So far Penola has managed to survive a moderate tourism with credit. The main result has been to generate a couple of very nice quite unpretentious restaurants. Now, however, it is anticipated that the place will be buried in tourists. I don't suppose that too many of them will be Japanese, but I am sure that the event will serve to intensify my anti-Americanism, which is a sort of bonus.[68]

November 23, 1991
Australia is becoming a very interesting country. At present there is a bloom of toxic blue-green algae in the Darling and Barwon. (Eighteen months ago, the Barwon was in flood. We were ringing our friends at Tilpa on the Darling about floods. They had then been three years in drought—still are—and were watching the river go past hoping it would break out. Heigh ho!)

There have been minor, but ominous blooms in recent years. But these have been in places like Lake Alexandrina, from which (roughly speaking) the Murray flows into the sea. This time the bloom is in North Western New South Wales. At present it stretches for 1000 kilometres and is advancing at the rate of 40 kilometres a day. Consequently it threatens the greater part of the Murray-Darling system. There is a severe drought in the whole of Western New South Wales at present. This is a normal state of affairs, a fact which hasn't so far penetrated the consciousness of this nation of slow learners. The river is very low at present and is about the only source of water along most of its length. The algae feeds on phosphates which are generously provided by cockies in the form of super-phosphate. The toxicity cannot be reduced by boiling and even if it could it would be impossible to provide every sheep with its own little quart-pot.

This is only the beginning of summer. Short of a miracle, the algae will eventually reach the lakes at Menindee. These hold more water than Sydney Harbour. So there is some chance that the infection will be absorbed. There is also a chance that it will take over the lakes, in which case the main water supply for the city of Broken Hill will be poisoned. Bourke and Wilcannia will have lost their supply before then. If it gets into South Australia, then it will affect our supplies too for our water too. That includes Adelaide which depends heavily on the Murray. Fortunately, local reservoirs are pretty full at present. But there are large areas of the State that depend almost entirely on the Murray. Maybe this time, maybe next time. Unless we stop using phosphates, which will enormously reduce productivity, we can expect to get caught by a toxic river system on top of a three-year drought in South Australia. We are setting ourselves up for the greatest emergency in the nation's history—including the war against Japan. (Which I wish we'd won by the way.)

Watch this space!

[…]

One thing that might save S.A.—In the drought of the early 80s—an extension of the drought of the early 60s, in turn an extension of...—the Darling flowed backwards from its confluence with the Murray. You could tell because the beer-bottles went the wrong way.

Also, a nice story about the Paroo flowing the wrong way. But, alas, another time.

November 24, 1991

I've just rung a mate of mine who has a station near Tilpa—I might once have written you from Terrible Tiny Tilpa. The river at his frontage is only 3 feet wide and six inches deep. And putrid. This is a stream that has taken paddle steamers up to Bourke. There is plenty of water held upstream in Queensland dams. The Queensland authorities won't release water to flush the river. They maintain that it has all been sold for irrigation. The river is no lower now than it would have been before it was managed. The water stored upstream would all have been in the sea by now. As a a matter (*sic*) when Sturt hit the Darling in February 1929,[69] (*sic*) it was so salt that he thought that he must be near to his inland sea. Nonetheless, I think it could be fairly claimed that the Queenslanders regularly let the river run lower than it should. And certainly that is a main cause of the present problem which amounts now to a national emergency. Colin has been out shooting sheep today. His wife has had to go back to teaching in Broken Hill, some hundreds of miles away. (Lucky to get the job actually.) There is a big meeting in Bourke tonight. He reckons that if that doesn't produce results, they might have to graduate to shooting bureaucrats.

Iris Murdoch to Brian Medlin
[Letter 26]

30 Charlbury Rd
OX2

[no date]

Brian dear, just to say I will certainly look out for Margie, she sounds splendid, I hope her search will be OK. Perhaps she cd telephone me after she arrives, then we cd meet in Oxford or London. I hope that you are well and getting better. There has been a splendid Abo exhibition in London. How those chaps can paint! Lots and lots of love

I

Iris Murdoch to Brian Medlin
[Letter 24]

30 Charlbury Rd
OX2

[no date]

Dearest Brian, thank you very much for the Super Flinders Anthology, and especially for your fine POEM therein.[i] A comrade thanks you. Since writing last I have met lovely Margie, so very nice, so clever, so beautiful. After much difficulty, going up down various stairs and into the jewellery department, I found her in her lair in Theatre Design, and we went out and drank coffee. She is so absolutely <u>there</u>. I hope she will find work for her talents quickly here. Yes, I'm soft on religion, though not on God. (He is the great barrier to true religion.) I think Buddhism is best. I have some Buddhist friends. (Of course Buddhism comes in all kinds, from Zen to walking on the water.) I think it would be terrible to lose Christianity, I mean the mystical Christ kind. No god. (No heaven, no survival etc.)

(Ken Tucker would agree.)

I'm glad you saw the mallee-fowl,[ii] he sounds good. (Maureen too.) We only see town birds now. (Though in very cold weather lately we saw a plover (lapwing) in the grounds of Lady Margaret Hall.) The river Cherwell is frozen.

So you think my views on art are "bourgeois." I wonder what you mean by that? Here we are <u>menaced</u> by deconstruction, minimalism, anti-art art (real hatred of art). Huge sums of money are paid for pictures which consist of (they have to be <u>very</u> <u>big</u>) canvases consisting of a few random lines of paint. At the Tate Gallery (which houses such pictures, taking up yards of wall space, while the French Impressionists are in the cellar) contestants for the Turner Prize exhibited a bath, partly concrete, a piece of faintly chipped stone, a sort of sofa, etc. In a way, these things may be said to be already old hat, lagging after genuine (Pop art) artists—not that I care for most of them, but they are artists (I mean Lichtenberg[70] etc.). But

---

[i] Marginal note here: "And Peter H's poem for you. Sorry about the English girl p. 93. + pommification"

[ii] Marginal note here: "megapod, good name."

what comes next—what is after Post-Modernism? This afflicts literature too. But perhaps you have not had this affliction. I mean Derrida and his followers. <u>He</u> is very clever, learned, interesting, but a false prophet and a pseudo-metaphysician. His followers are crude and often <u>very aggressive.</u> This then gets mixed up with the women's movement, which it damages. (The full-blooded post-modernists <u>condemn</u> as "bourgeois" Dickens, Tolstoy, Jane Austen etc. etc.)

I think what you have & are thinking of is a much more liberal open-minded & <u>in a way</u> traditional kind of free literature. Not hating the real /truth-telling/ art of the past. Good art tells truth. I like the Tatiara song.[i] I connect you with songs. People don't <u>sing</u> much in Oxford now. Except for the Warden of New College who is a talented pianist, and sings a lot of Cole Porter etc. if encouraged—and even if not.

I am trying to write a bit of philosophy and also as usual a novel. I hope you are feeling better. Write soon. You are my Australia. Give my love to Christine. Much love to you, friend in a hundred guises, splendid magician.

Iris

---

[i] Marginal note here: "+ your pal Peter."

Brian Medlin to Iris Murdoch
Letter MDC050

February 5, 1992

Dear Iris

No so much a letter as a set of curses—not loud perhaps but bloody deep.

First on the heads of that damned Phil review committee to whom we are going to take the long handle at the March Council meeting. I'm sorry now that I wasted your time, as I shall say in my response. I have already had—after loud complaint—a partial apology from my mate Nerlich who should have known better. Little better could have been expected from Pettit and Taylor, who were amongst the targets of my remarks about the pressure to publish. Part of the fault lies with the department. Their submission was pathetic. I hope the result enlivens them to do a proper job.

Bruno […] is fascinated with crime, fascinated with the idea of heroin and convinced he can try it once and give it away. […]

You will have seen the political news from Oz and that we have recently exchanged a rogue for a knave.[71]

I have many other things to complain about, including the bloody weather.

But thank God for Christine the Beautiful.

And I did have a nice couple of days with my son Barney. He caught the bus from Melbourne to Casterton and joined me in my camp on Meath. It's one of the Hawkes' paddocks. Ivy H. is Irish. Beautiful paddock with a lovely billabong off the Glenelg River. (Bloody Australian names! Bloody "Glenelg"!) Barney had come as well to talk to Bob about parrots and keeping them. That went well. We also visited three women called The Girls who have a property, Falconstoop, downstream from Tolka—the H.'s place. They have just started keeping alpacas. Astonishingly beautiful animals. Astonishingly expensive. I had come down—and the rest of our household had scattered—to give Bruno a week alone in the house at his own request so that he could demonstrate his responsibility. Jeeze! It was something of a last desperate throw as far as I was concerned. […]

Down with bourgeois philosophers and all their works!

Love

Iris Murdoch to Brian Medlin
[Letter 27]

30 Charlbury Road
OX2

Brian dear, I am so very sorry to hear about Bruno. What very sad business—when you had tried so hard. I hope it may be that somewhere someone will—but that begins to sound like a film. I am so sorry. But thank God for Christine—and for Barney and his parrots. Have you ever had a parrot? (And could you tell me what an alpaca is—I feel I sort of know, but couldn't pass an exam on it.)

I don't think you should curse all bourgeois philosophers. I even think that bourgeois, as a term of abuse, is beginning to belong to the past—or rather it is so <u>used</u> like an old penny. Curse all structuralist, deconstructionist, post-modernist pseudo-philosophers by all means. I wonder whether Derrida has taken root in Oz? I hope all will be well at the Phil Review Committee. I have run out of large sheets of writing paper— it's even difficult to get really <u>good</u> writing paper now. Perhaps everything is being faxed—also I fear there may soon be no more <u>ink</u>. Write to me again soon. I hope you are recovering from the Bruno episode. Be well, reflect, see birds, animals—with love

I

Iris Murdoch to Brian Medlin
[Letter 42]

April 29 [1992]

Brian dear, much thanks your letter 8.iv about your mate. I have indeed heard of him. But he hasn't got in touch so I suppose he decided to hasten on. Our telephone is ex-directory I shd say, see it above.[i] I'm sorry not to see him. And Margie must I think have left too.[ii] I hope I shall receive your letter, which you speak of in your letter. I have had a sort of pneumonia-bronchitis bout which made me feel very exhausted. I still suffer from a tendency to want to lie down flat (like those lizards).

I do hope you are feeling better and are enjoying some (not too much) bush. I look forward to seeing your lovely word-processed news—your type is much nicer than the local type here. I do hope you are well, that you are both well—I wish you too would come across world. Also I would like to hear you sing.

Much love

I

---

[i] Phone number removed for privacy reasons.
[ii] Marginal note here: "She said she was leaving in March, I think."

Brian Medlin to Iris Murdoch
Letter MDC060

69 Albert Street
Prospect
South Australia
5082
Ph: (08) 269 2483

February 28, 1992

Iris Murdoch
30 Charlbury Road
Oxford OX2
England

Dearest Iris

May 4, 1992
I'm sticking in here a brief reply to your latest of 29 April. Iris dear, I'm sorry that you have been crook. I hope you are much better now. Margie, is still in England, though I haven't been able to contact her myself for a couple of months. She keeps on moving to different answering machines.

My law suit drags on. I don't know whether I told you, but the judge found in our favour as far as liability was concerned, and awarded damages for pain and loss of capacity. He awarded nothing, however, for financial loss. We are appealing. Whether I ever get to England depends on how that goes. I would love to see you again, mate. But take warning. The neuropathy has left me unable to sing in tune—or to play the flute either.

Be well, love.

Back to Feb 28
Many thanks for your lovely letter in reply to my whinging one.

The news about Bruno is just a little better than it might have been. […]

I really have two letters of yours to answer, I think.

Yes isn't Margie nice. And clever. And beautiful. And *there*. I spoke to her by phone the other day […]

[…] [W]e have at last got judgement in my case before the Supreme Court. Fourteen months! […] my lawyers have more or less persuaded me to appeal. [...] They, no more than myself, cannot understand how a bloke can be advised by his specialist to retire and yet be found not to have suffered economic damage. His judgement is somewhat obscure—I'd give it a C- as a Philosophy One Lecture—but as far as I can tell, he bought the defence line that, as a tenured professor, I could have kept my job and done absolutely nothing. (Tell John!) I don't really want the fuss, but there's four and a half years of a professorial salary involved. What's more, the bastard has got my wild up. […] If we appeal and win then it'll be possible to come to England for a bit—which it certainly isn't now. In that case, I could prove to you that I can no longer sing in tune.

Being soft on religion, but not on God (God, Ugh!), you may be interested in the little thing on the nature of philosophy that I'm sending. I'll print this out on the back of it.

I wasn't the first to say that your views on art are bourgeois. You said I'd probably find them bourgeois and, being an accommodating chap, I merely agreed. You wonder what *I* mean by that. I wonder what you mean by that. I've now got a little appendix about the word "bourgeois" attached to my monograph on human nature—which should be out soonish. Anyway, one could have worse views than bourgeois views—that poets "feign," for example. So I won't go into that anymore now. Briefly, without reason here, I agree that the word bourgeois isn't much use as a mere term of abuse. And my curses upon bourgeois philosophers were doubtless frivolous—what provoked them, I wonder? I've just looked up the file and found it was that bloody Committee of Review. So down with bourgeois philosophers again. Those bastards anyhow. I'll throw your way the memorandum, I wrote on The Report. Have you got a copy—you should have. A bloody disgraceful document. My colleagues, who can be bloody wet, dealt so inadequately with the working party that followed up the report, that I felt compelled to burst into song myself—so here goes. You should like the banyan tree at anyrate.—Actually, I'm now sending a separate copy with this. Also a little foreword that you might find fun. It has some bearing on the stuff about religion. I think we probably share a lot of ground there.

The trouble with all this is that if it is convincing—to whom?—then The Committee—are a bunch of drongoes. And that discredits the one substantial recommendation they make that is of any use to the philosophers—the one concerning the centre for applied philosophy. The rest are mostly out of date.

My friend Graham Nerlich will probably be a bit upset. But then he should have known better. And bugger it! I'm upset.

Yes, *of course*, we are plagued by post-modernists. Why do you think that I routinely abuse Derrida? And what else would Dickens etc., be except "bourgeois"? (At anyrate, in some sense.) I don't think that it's hard to show that the kind of relativism that characterises the postmodernists and the de-constructionists is itself objectively as bourgeois as buggery and much more perniciously so than, say, Dickens and Jane Austen. The worst that the great bourgeois novelists can be accused of is "critical realism." But the modern relativisms—in addition to the pretentiousness of their presentation—lead straight to a paralysing nihilism.

I'll send you with this a copy of a poem by Douglas Muecke about deconstructionism. You may remember that I suggested that Douglas visit you when he was in Oxford, but it didn't come off. He's a lovely man Douglas. And it's a nice poem. His son Stephen says it's reactionary. I don't believe that "reactionary" is always a useful term of abuse, any more than is "bourgeois." Against some things, surely, it is good to be reactionary. It is to some extent my conservatism that makes me politically radical.

So the Warden of New College plays and sings Cole Porter! Thank God I left Oxford. I'm reactionary about Cole Porter.

Yes I have had a parrot. Well not quite a parrot—a cockatoo. A wonderful galah. Do you remember that flock of galahs when we went to Henscke's winery at Kyneton? I had this bird for about three years when I was in primary school and it used to ride everywhere on my shoulder. It had a clipped wing when I got it, but I let it grow out. If it flew away, I reckoned, then it wanted to. It did fly all around the place, but it always came home. It had our cocker spaniel bitch bluffed and our white cat. The cat in her turn had every dog in the neighbourhood bluffed, except our Peg, but Cocky very quickly sorted her out. He/she had a big cage that she used to fly into at night. It was as big as a small room. She used to hang upside down and start screeching to be let out at dawn. We soon got to leave the door open. He was a bit destructive on fruit—tending to strip the buds as they appeared. So she wasn't too popular with the neighbours. But such a wonderful bird. Such a good mate. I don't think he knew that he was a cocky. She was really a human being. I don't know his history, but I'm sure she'd been hand reared. (The Hawkes have a red-rump parrot, a lutino actually, one Jeffrey, who also is a person. They put him out into the aviaries to breed, but he insisted on coming back into the house to live as a man should.) Cocky got sick in the end and my Dad killed him. Nobody ever thought of vets in those days.

My mate Henry Salter tells a story about me. According to Henry, I was in a pub, plastered, and talking about Cocky. Rodney Allen[72] said, "He must have been a lovely cocky. Did he outlive you?" "No," says I in tears. Two things about that. One: if ever I was drunk in the company of Henry Salter, then he was long unconscious. Two: Henry once told me a story that I'd told him about something that had happened to me on the Wickham River, in the Northern Territory in 1949. In Henry's version, it had happened to him at Paringa, on the Murray, a couple of years back. Henry is one of my literary executors, but I suppose he won't ever read this, worse luck.

An alpaca is a lamoid camel. **Lama pacos** of the family **Camelidae** and the order **Artiodactyla**. Peruvian mainly. About three feet high at the shoulder. Long vertical neck. A quizzical, surprised look, rather than the haughtiness of the camel or lama, very expressive eyes with a direct gaze. I'm sure that they were much studied by Dr. Seuss. They have recently been introduced for their wool into Australia. The wool is very fine and very strong. They are soft-footed, so it's hoped they won't knock the place about as much as sheep. At present they cost many thousands of dollars per beast. So there you go. Plenty more to know if you have to do a stiff exam, but that'll probably keep you happy.

The girls got into alpacas and out of ostriches. They had a complicated bit of luck with their ostriches and cleaned up a small fortune. Bob Hawkes was thinking of getting rid of all his cattle and getting thirty alpacas. He could then have run them in a small enclosure and let the rest of his property revert to bush. He found that by selling his whole herd, he could afford <u>three</u> alpacas.

Christine has just been to Melbourne to visit a dear friend of ours, Leigh. Leigh is having some strife, so Christine took her to Casterton to visit Falconstoop and Tolka. Leigh is originally from the United States and, though as lovely as anyone can be, a bit of a towney. And there she was belting around the paddocks on the back of a truck, bottle feeding a young kangaroo, patting alpacas, and Nubian goats, marvelling as a magpie chased a dog and stole its bone. Not all simultaneously, you'll understand. Leigh has a smile that runs three times round her head. I can imagine her with a joey in her lap. Barney fed it too when he and I were at Falconstoop.

Jake and I had a couple of days at Deep Creek while Christine was away. Deep Creek is the name of a smallish national park, containing

Deep Creek, very near to Cape Jervis on the Fleurieu Peninsula. It looks across Backstairs Passage (Flinders' name[73]) to Kangaroo Island. There's a fair bit of remnant vegetation, interspersed with the farmland as well as some organised regeneration. The country is pretty steep, though not rugged. I fear my days of serious walking may well be over. This is the first tough country I've tried since I fell sick in December, 1990. I've really worked hard on my legs since I began feeling a bit better last year, but didn't think I was making much headway against the neuropathy. This trip confirmed that. In the end, Jake finished the walk down into Deep Creek Cove on his own. If I'd gone down, I could have got back up, I'm sure, but only at a very high cost. As it was, I could hardly walk for many days. My hip was on fire as it always is in steep country. I'm used to that, but my bloody quads and calf muscles simply won't function. Disappointing, but not a great surprise. And it was beautiful watching Jake go down into the Cove. The face was not quite vertical, not quite a climb, but steep enough for a fatal fall. He bounded down it upright and confident. That tall beautiful young body. I was close to tears watching him. All is not lost. There is still plenty I can do in the bush. I can service a walk for Christine and Jake, for example. Putting them down in one place and picking them up in another, doing day walks myself, perhaps going in to meet them, or philosophising on the computer.

May 5, 1992

Hey, wanna hear more about me legs? I went down to Deep Creek again with Christine, this time taking a stick. Found I could power myself up precipices with it. Went off again to the Lower Flinders[74] this time on my own and with a back pack—easier grades though. Carried a lot of water so it was hard, hard, hard. But the stick has certainly given me a few more years bushwalking. And I'm beginning to think that with hard work, I'm gaining on the neuropathy. Didn't have to use the stick at all in the easier stages—which were still hard enough to have defeated the kind of mates Jake thrives on (see below).

The obnoxious Mr. Keating has at last got something right. He didn't actually kiss The Queen's bum when she was here. (A first for an Australian Prime Minister. Your rugged Ocker individualist can be a crawling creature.) And, horror of horrors, his missus didn't curtsey to H.M.. And then young Paul sounded off about Britain's (Churchill's attitude to Australia) during World War Two. And about Britain abandoning her old trading relations with Australia to join the common market. The point to be made is that we are an Asian country. The political advantage to be gained is that of representing the opposition parties as still in the grip of a servile Menzies-ism. As for Keatings' republicanism—apart from being a republican myself anyway—his point that in the 1960s Britain declared Australia to be a foreign country is well taken. He hasn't yet gone on to say that, in consequence, The Queen is a foreign monarch.

Now don't get me wrong. Some of my best friends are Brits. But some Brits are not my best friends—amongst them Harold Macmillan and Betty Windsor. Though Philip is—or used to be—a mate of Bob Hawkes, mateship isn't all that transitive. Another who is not one of my best friends is—god his name has suddenly gone—he used to be the New College chaplain in the sixties—Gary whatsisname—and I wonder of which ric he is now bishop. I remember talking to him at lunch one day. I had just got a letter from my dad who had been sounding off because Australians were now going to need visas to enter Britain and were not going to able to hang around indefinitely. The Old Man had fought on the Western Front during World War Two. (Did I ever tell you that at the end of the war he'd been selected from the A.I.F. buglers to sound the Last Post and reveille at a memorial service in Salisbury cathedral?) "We were welcome enough in 1916." Bennett, that was his name, asked, "And what happened in 1916?" Having been reminded, he said, "Oh, I don't think that sort of thing counts for very much." "You're bloody right, mate."

We're good learners, though, in Oz. We're dishing it out to the East Timorese with both hands. We recognised the Indonesian annexation almost immediately, we train the Indonesian military, give them military aid. We have a treaty with Indonesia to exploit oil in the Timor Gap. Gareth Evans (our foreign minister, if you don't know) had the crosses removed that the East Timorese in Canberra had planted outside the Indonesian Embassy after the Dili massacre. Etc., etc..

May 5, 1992
Iris dear,

I'm gunna continue this because a) I won't be at Flinders for a day or so and they can pay the postage; b) I have a nice (or nasty) story worth telling b) I have some ready-made cricket anecdotes. I'm taking them straight from letters to Graham Nerlich. The first lot aren't so much anecdotes but a slab of philosophical argument, but they embody some anecdotes. The second is an anecdote told to drive home a point. The third is a set of anecdotes written to sweeten a rather bitter letter. This latter was written in reply to a rather hurt but insubstantial note from Graham about my memo on the Review of Philosophy. Graham was a member of the Review Committee and in my view got himself hijacked by the reactionaries. But enough of that.

March 7, 1992.[75]

Well, we've survived Michaelangelo's birthday!

What happens to courage, to courageous persistence? In the face of the knowledge that nobody ever does fail, that all I have to do is plod on, courage becomes irrational, because fear becomes irrational. And since irrationality is ruled out of the case, all virtues and skills are degraded to mere doggedness.

But worse than that cricket becomes a bore and for that I can't forgive you. All batsmen become Don Bradman and all bowlers Bill O'Reilly. That sounds exciting, but not so. Yesterday Frank Devine in the *Australian* remarked that over the past fifteen years Botham had made the marvellous commonplace. That is a figure, of course. An oxymoron, in fact. Botham's performances still are marvellous, because they are not inevitable even for him and are outstanding in the context of international cricket. There was a marvellous England-Australia test in Adelaide over Christmas 1958. It followed the Gabba test of early December which Jack Pollard describes as one of the dreariest ever played. In Adelaide Ian Meckiff and Neil Harvey demolished the Poms who held the Ashes. Pollard says, "The glorious uncertainty of cricket was intact." It's in the last volume of his big history of Australian Cricket. (As I remember "Meckiff" doesn't appear in the index. Another falling-short.)

But *your* batsmen become run-making, your bowlers wicket-taking automata. Every batsman scores six off every ball and never gets out. This means that keeper and fielders become pointless. Every bowler takes one for none off every ball—preferably, and so certainly, by demolishing the wicket. This too means that other fieldsmen are unnecessary. For the batting side the innings lasts indefinitely, they score at the rate of thirty-six a six-ball over and need a team of just two. They can, of course, declare at any time after the first ball of the innings, since they are going to bowl the other side out for a total of nought within just ten balls. For the fielding side the innings lasts just ten balls before the opposition is all out for nought and they need a team of just two bowlers. In fact, given the guaranteed shortness of every innings, the economical thing to do would be to introduce the ten-ball over and dispense with the second bowler. So cricket becomes pretty boring. It also becomes impossible.

Meckiff probably wasn't a chucker by the way, though Colin Egar no-balled him out of the game. Lindsay Kline may well have been a chucker and Charlie Griffith certainly was. But Meckiff had a frozen bend in his left arm and a double-jointed shoulder. This is not just anecdotal. There are uncertainties about what people are going to do or have done—Historical problems. There are also uncertainties about the *application* of standards. In Meckiff's case, this was a matter of whether what he did actually breach a standard not itself in doubt. So, given the standard, this is still an historical problem: how did Meckiff actually move his arm, and in particular did he straighten it as he brought it over to deliver the ball? The answer seems to be *No*. He *couldn't* straighten his arm. But, while still considering problems of application, there can also be uncertainties about the standards themselves. These in turn can be of two kinds.

First simple doubt or ignorance concerning what the standards actually are. A nice illustration is the recent run-out of Jones in the Caribbean where nobody on the field seemed to know the relevant rule and certainly the umpires didn't. (That before we even consider the standards of sportsmanship as they apply to this case.) Second, though, the standard itself may well be unclear. In a world which relentlessly confronts us with novelty any finite set of standards is going to require continuous revision and interpretation. It can be easy enough to settle what the laws and playing conditions of cricket *are* at some given time. What they *ought* to be is a different kettle of fish. This too is complicated. There is at present great difficulty finding fair playing conditions for rain-affected one-day matches. What would constitute fairness isn't the problem: how to achieve it is. But there can also be questions as to what constitutes fairness in certain cases, questions which bring to the fore fundamental differences in outlook. Regardless of the rules, was it sporting of Carl Hooper to have "run out" Jones in those circumstances? Should more able people be paid more than less able people? What do you think of the GST proposal? How do you spend your salary? And such questions certainly are involved in our daily life at all levels.

Given these facts it is inconceivable to the realistic imagination that we should ever live in absolute harmony and agreement. And I don't mean logically impossible.

It is for such reasons as those canvassed a couple of paragraphs back, that heaven as described by Julian Barnes in *The History of the World in 10½ Chapters* contains a lot of illusion. Committed as I am to the ideal of objectivity, I want no part of it. In fact, everyone in Barnes' heaven eventually, after some centuries, opts to die permanently. There is another option available: they could become the sort of people who don't mind the illusion and don't get bored. But nobody chooses this option, as I remember. For that amounts to becoming *somebody else.*

On this interpretation of your position, it really does look like a logical impossibility. I'm not claiming that, though. What I am claiming is that you owe us, not just an abstract remark about what can be envisaged, but a concrete description of a mode of life. This mode of life will have to embody and exemplify your claim. The description will have to be free of inconsistency—as my description of the New Cricket is not. And it will have to be a description of a kind of life that is recognisably human. And that I'm sure it won't be.

George Couvalis[76] is of the opinion that there won't be cricket in heaven. For me a heaven without cricket would be hell and more so for Jack Smart. But the point isn't really one about competitive sports. You can't do philosophy in heaven. You can't *do* philosophy.

> ... On a huge hill,
> Cragged, and steep, Truth stands, and he that will
> Reach her, about must and about must go ;
> And what the hills suddennes resists, winne so.[77]

How can I do that, **win** her, knowing that nobody ever fails in their assault on the hill? Nobody ever falls off a real hill so that mountaineering requires no courage, only doggedness. It would be irrational to ascribe courage to somebody where it would be irrational to fear, for in this world nobody ever is irrational. Nobody ever falls off John Donne's hill either, so that philosophy becomes a mere mechanical plodding with success assured. And if I can't do philosophy in heaven, *I* can't go there. *The person I am* can't go there. If I can't do philosophy badly, then I can't do it all. That goes for you too, young Graham. I'm not being modest here or, alas, even offensive! To do philosophy *is* to do it badly. That's part of doing it well. Philosophy *is* the unfinishable business of the intellect, what we generate as fast as we do it, what we leave unfinished by completing it. (Or so my Foreword maintains.) Neither of us can go to heaven, then. Only some lobotomised automata of similar appearance. The air there is too rare, too unpolluted for human lungs.

You may object to the heaven bit, but I have used only those conditions postulated by yourself.

The second is neater:

March 10, 1992

Dear Graham

At the risk of driving you crazy here is another cricket anecdote. It illustrates very nicely how standards rise with performance, but it's worth hearing for its own sake.

In the Sheffield Shield match between Victoria and New South Wales at Melbourne 22-27 December 1928, Victoria made 376 in their first innings. New South Wales were 9 for 113, 263 behind, when Hooker the number 10, joined his captain, Alan Kippax, late on the Monday arvo. They proceeded to put on 307. This is still the world record for the tenth wicket. Hooker made 62, his highest first-class score. Finally, at midday on the Wednesday, with Kippax on 260 and the NSW total at 420, Hooker attempted his first aggressive shot off a'Beckett. He put up a catch to Ryder which was gratefully accepted. As they walked off, all Kippax said to Hooker was, "I was counting on you to make a hundred."

Cheers

The third:

Then (I must add) there was the famous prayer of the small boy—Neville Cardus, no less. It was the first day of the Old Trafford Test in 1902 and

Cardus' first time at a Test match. As Trumper and Duff walked to the wicket, he prayed through the palings, "Please, God, let Victor Trumper score a century for Australia against England—out of a total of 137 all out." Half his prayer was answered. Trumper scored a century before lunch—the first in a Test—but Australia made 299. By the end of the day, England were 5/70. In the end, Australia pulled off a spectacular victory by three runs, bowling out the Poms for 120 in the fourth dig. Trumper's batting put an early end to the Test career of Fred Tate, father of Maurice. Tate was hammered in the first innings, but came back to take 2/7 in the third when the Australians collapsed for 86. However, he did drop Joe Darling, Stephen's great grandfather. In tears, he said, "I've got a little lad at home who'll make up for that!" All this, and more in Ashley Mallett's beaut book on Trumper.[78]

Next this here story. Coupla Sundays back Christine and I visited Ferguson Park. Ferguson Park is a very important precious and fragile conservation park—though it's only the size of a small farm. It contains one of the two remaining stands of remnant bush in the whole of Metropolitan Adelaide. It is of course much corrupted by exotics, both Australian and European. But over recent years The Friends of Ferguson Park have laboured greatly to restore it to something like its original condition. When we arrived, we noticed a woman—prosperous middle-class looking—one of Earth's owners—collecting sticks for the boot of her Mitsubishi. Being a determined dobber in such matters, I immediately took her rego number. Then I spoke to her in my politest tones—which are really quite acceptable as I hope you will remember, "Excuse me. Do you know that you shouldn't be removing wood from the park?" She turned to me a large and florid face. "No I don't know that. And what harm does it do!" (I think "!" rather than "?") Christine began to explain what harm it did, starting with the fact that it *was* a conservation park and just starting to move onto the micro-organisms when the woman shouted her down, "You're interfering bastards!" I: "Well, if that's your attitude, I'll have to report the matter to the Council."

Then off we went to have lunch. Very pleasant it was too. We sat at the very beautiful stump of a huge old olive that our friend Waldo Bushman had helped remove ten years earlier. (I'm not kidding, his name *is* "Waldo Bushman." He's Ukrainian, of course.) Happy couples, jolly families, beaming loners all greeted us in passing. It was very like *not* being in England.

Exactly one hour after our encounter with the woman, we were about to leave and I was standing about twenty yards inside the park fence with Christine about twenty or thirty yards to the North of me. A small gentleman approached the fence. I noticed him particularly because he seemed very intense. Prosperous middle class again. Certainly not a horny-handed child of toil like you and me, Iris. He glared across at me. "Did you abuse a woman down the road just now!" ("!" again.) "I didn't abuse anyone." He got through the fence and came at me almost running and reviling me as he came. I was sure that he was going to attack me. I was standing relaxed with a day-bag slung over one shoulder and stayed that way throughout what followed. For one thing I was sure that I had enough judo left in me to make a mess of him. For another, I noticed that he was wearing soft shoes that would be no match for my walking boots when it came to interviewing his feet. And for a third was certain that if I made any sort of move, he certainly would take a swing at me. By the time he got to within two or three paces of me, it was clear that he was going to limit himself to bluster. By this time it must have been pretty obvious that I was looming over him.

Still he was a cocky young bantam, I'll give him that. Young—forty. His face and voice were distorted with fury. He came right up to me, thrust his face within six inches of mine. Meanwhile he was pouring out, almost incoherently such poeticisms as "You fucking slug. You cunt. Fucking arsehole. You fucking small-minded cunt. It's fucking small-minded slags like you that... What about the real problems of the fucking world! What about er Libya. You real fucking slag ..." And so on with his gob in mine for thirty or forty-five seconds. Me trying to show a polite interest.

Then he turned and walked away. As he did so, I said, very politely, "How do you do." He wheeled around and for an instant I thought he was going to charge me. But he checked himself. And said, "No!" Half choked. At the same time he gave me the fingers, but he was so incoherent that even the gesture was half-choked. "No," he said. "I wouldn't fuck you." Or—he was very agitated it could have been "No I wouldn't. Fuck you!" I called out to Christine while he was leaving, "Hey Christine, did you hear that?" "What I could make out"—something like that. "The bastard's mad!" I was rather hoping to get a charge out of him by this time, but no such luck. The Moratorium taught me physical restraint and discipline, and I sometimes regret it. Certainly I would have loved this joker to have taken a swing at me.

In face I wonder how he has survived to this advanced age. If he'd have tried it on with Jake, for instance, he'd have probably got himself pulverised. Jake has the makings of a martial arts champion, but he's only a beginner and I doubt that he yet has the discipline to handle something like that.

But in spite of this minor disappointment, it made our day. It was like walking straight into a Monty Python film—actually being in it. It had its darker side of course—such a person is capable of being the camp guard—but what doesn't. We kept on wondering all day where we could go next to get abused. In the end, we thought we'd have to fall back on one another.[79]

Jake. We went to Jake's Yellow Belt exam in Tae Kwan Doe. Iris, he was beautiful. Actually, I think Christine's forms are neater and more precise. She has the containedness and footwork of an old table-tennis champion. But Jake was bloody good all the same. Terrifyingly powerful. And wonderful to see him concentrating three hundred percent. At the end of the exam, Chris, the master, set Jake and his mate Garth free-sparring—something unheard of with white belts. Garth is another large lump of a lad, heavier set than Jake but at 6' 2" about three inches shorter. They were stunning, for novices both obvious naturals. They lacked accuracy, of course, and occasionally landed some sickening blows when they were not supposed to be making contact. Jake was amazingly light on his feet and elegant. At the end of the bout Chris stood them up and said that they both had exceptional ability and application, especially Jake and that if they continued to apply themselves, they could expect extraordinary promotions at future exams. I was pretty proud of the lad of course. But more than anything, delighted for him. He hasn't had too many wins in life and a fair bit of bad luck. He did very well in his mechanics exam, for example, but couldn't get an apprenticeship because he was a year too old and he'd have had to get an adult wage for the second year. He's been out of work now since the flood and it's marvellous to see him making something of it rather than going under. (When Barney was out of work for two years in the last recession, he turned himself into a fine percussionist.)

Another nice thing was that Annie, his Mum, was there. Annie's feminism has often seemed to me to be unthinkingly anti-macho. But she has certainly encouraged Jake in his training and she was obviously very impressed.

His mates were out in force too. There were Jake and Garth on the floor alert and athletic. And there in the corner was this absolute shower of beer bellied uncouth yobboes. Apart from being strikingly ungilded, they powerfully recalled the famous lines of the famous Banjo.

> There were some gilded youths that sat along the barber's wall
> Their eyes were dull, their heads were flat, they had no brains at all.

Enough skiting about me kids. But with Bruno about, you've got to enjoy the ones you can.

May 5, 1992

Leaves me room to celebrate a lovely outcome of the Ferguson Park incident. We've met a corker young woman, a ranger of the Lofty area called Gill Peacey. She called to take statements and thoroughly enjoyed the story. Also the fact that our front verandah was piled high with firewood—obviously not bought commercially. Most of it grown in our own back yard. She's lean, boyish, rangey, with close-cropped dark hair, dark intelligent eyes (her head not flat!) unmade-up, unpretty, handsome, firm-voiced, straight-forward—laughs from the diaphragm, meets your eye. An all-round no bull-shit girl. She said that it's possible to expiate such offences with an on the spot fine, but "I reckon I'll just prosecute straight off. The only way to teach buggers like that." While she was there each of us knew that the other would reckon she was a ripper. Soon as she left, each of us burst out, "What a beaut young woman."

Iris Murdoch to Brian Medlin
[Letter 1]

30 Charlbury Rd
OX2

[no date]

My dear, thanks [for] your welcome letter and your spirited memorandum and splendid foreword.[i] I like your: "philosophy is about the texture of human life. Philosophy is about getting life right and making life right." Russell is good too, though I don't*[ii] care for him at all points. (What you quote is fine.) I agree with you that there is no God, but I do believe in religion, that is some kind of Buddhism or Christian Buddhism. (No "gods" or "elsewhere" etc but some kind of everyday—mysticism à la Eckhart.) I forget if I told you—I am trying to put together my old dusty Gifford lectures into some sort of book. I love your fighting stuff. I think philosophy should be rescued from the present analytical stuff and also from Derrida and company. I hope D. is not <u>rampant</u> in Australia.

I've talked to Margie on telephone. She seems to be enjoying London. I'm glad Bruno news is better. I hadn't made out (picked up from Margie conversation) that he was so young.[iii] I hope he is getting all ways better. I'm also very glad and hopeful about, judging from your reckoning, your lawsuit and its prospect of bringing you to England! (I mean—I see it's still in the balance. But you are so obviously in the right. However etc.) You would disapprove of our government of course, and our weather, which I'm sure you remember.

I recall being sorry too when Britain decided to leave its commonwealth trading partners and join the common market. Sometimes things seems unavoidable, "the will of history." (My old college Somerville, last but one Oxford College being women only, has just been forced or "forced" by some probably economic circumstances to <u>admit men</u>. The Junior Common Room, from the undergraduates, voted 200 or so against 10 NOT to have males. I'm entirely with them. I wouldn't have

---

[i] Marginal note here: "+ J. Donne."
[ii] Marginal note here: "in general*."
[iii] Marginal note here: "How old is Jake?"

liked them around. There are plenty of the creatures outside in Oxford and easily found.) I think poor Britain is being forced in a "federal" Europe run by France Germany and governed from Brussels.

I liked hearing about your galah—I remember seeing them—and all your animal talk. You down there are so much closer to nature than us up here. Your nature is more powerful, dangerous too of course. By the way, do you have gingkos in Oz? Perhaps they've always been there. (You are Asians, as you say.) Also (for the Australian, small part, in my novel, I think I told you) could you provide me with various words for "girls"? The Ferguson Park episode is very Aussie. You are a tough lot, but good ending. Give my love to Christine. Be well. Much love ever I

Brian Medlin to Iris Murdoch
Letter MDC070

September 9, 1992

Dear Iris,

Lovely to talk to you on Saturday. So long ago?

Thank you for agreeing to do the book. I'm honoured actually. I think I have some idea of how you cherish your time and I'd been prepared to be knocked back. Brian Matthews is making the arrangements now and I should hear something within a day or so.

I expect it to come off, though there may be some impediment. [...][i]

Before this morning, I could have said that I hadn't heard from Bruno for two months [...] He did ring this morning with a [...] question. [...]

Christine continues to improve, though for a couple of weeks it was awful. There is much to be said though for my looking after her for a change. [Her] [...] doctor [...] failed to give Christine the right advice. Christine treated the matter as trivial [...] and bloody nearly died in consequence. Jack Cade was right about the lawyers. How he came to omit the medicos defeats me.

You said on the phone that you were trying to picture the scene. Little house, single-fronted, broken down, conscientiously unrenovated. Large kitchen the width of the house: gas stove, wood stove. We grow our own wood and—with a bit of help from Casterton are getting near to being self-supporting. Back-yard a dramatic contrast between vegie plot and indigenous (as opposed to merely native bush). Two very beautiful two thousand-gallon tanks just installed to add to the out-back effect. Another eight hundred gallons storage in modular tanks between shed and fence. Lovely old galvanised iron fences mellowing into the bush, the Western one blown over in last month's winds and needing repair (next week-end?). The front of the house buried in citrus trees and native, as opposed to strictly indigenous vegetation. But you can see it all for yourself when you visit.

Our old faithful tank at the back-door began to collapse at the beginning of winter. So we went the ecologically sound wholish-hog and

---

[i] Passage deleted here as it contains potentially offensive comments about an individual.

put in a lot of storage. Also the financially sound hog, given the escalating cupidity of the Engineering and Water Service. You have probably not heard that because of financial mismanagement in the context of economic rationalism, the State Bank of South Australia has gone through the hoop to the tune of some billions of dollars. As a result of this alone, the state debt for every man woman and child in South Australia amounts to over A$5000. On top of the Government has been glitz (*sic*) its way along the years by financing, not merely capital but the daily running of the State by borrowing. As a result 62 cents of every dollar in tax goes into interest payments alone. Add to this the Federal picture, which is kept obscure— there hasn't yet been a scandal big enough to provoke a Royal Commission into Federal finances—one can only hope that John Dawkins as Treasurer will add this to his other notable achievements—and, if you can remember where this sentence started, the picture is bloody scary. But water is beginning to cost more than whisky in this state. I don't mind that much, actually, since enormous quantities of it run down storm-drains every year and the sooner we start harvesting water locally the better. As it turns out, the hog we went wasn't whole enough. I should have sat down with a calculator beforehand. We've had a bit more rain than usual since the beginning of August and have now almost filled our storage. We should have made the backyard tank twice as big, i.e. 4000g.

I'm sending you a package with this. If you ever get round to playing the tape, I hope you savour the presence on it of John Skinner, as David Askew asks lovers of the paradox to do. Skinner is the grey power who makes the grey speech. As Dean of research, he was a main target of the memo I distributed on The Review of Philosophy. And right rotten he was about it too. After gnawing the carpet at the Board meeting that received the document, he wrote me an unctuously courteous letter thanking me for my interest and saying that the Board had regarded my memorandum as a submission to the Review, which of course was no longer in existence. Subsequently at lunch I congratulated him on a piece of bureaucratic legerdemain the equal of any thing I had seen at Flinders. I told him that I couldn't emulate his courtesy, but I that I could improve on both his grammar and his logic. I told him the story of Neville Cardus, a small boy at his first test match at Old Trafford in 1902. As Victor Trumper and Troop walked to the wicket on the first day, Cardus, his face pressed between the pickets prayed, "Please God let Victor Trumper score a century for Australia against England today out of a total of 137 all out." The Almighty was half obliging. Trumper went on to make the first 100 before lunch ever in a test match. I told John Skinner that, by the logic of the Board, that story could be of no conceivable interest to anyone, since occurring as it does in Ashley Mallett's biography of Trumper, it is addressed to a dead man. It took him a little time to catch on, though I thought he was quite quick for a medical man. Then he began to talk of Cardus as a music critic.

Aboriginal art. We have a friend, one Waldo Bushman, born in the Ukrainian (*sic*), for long ashamed of his racist heritage, now reclaiming what he can endure of it. Waldo is probably the greatest expert of the plants and animals of the Adelaide plains and hills since we wiped out the blacks. Waldo is the "inventor" of the concept of the Wirra, the re-established indigenous bushland. Christine, having read his book rang him up a few years back. And excellent move. Waldo does a lot of work with blacks, particularly in the Flinders Ranges and has got to be half Abo in the head. They exchange a lot of knowledge (and ignorance too I bet) across the cultures. Well we had a little gathering over Sunday lunch a while back attended by Waldo and like-minded people. Carol, an ex-Englishwoman, an out-of-work architect, put up a board exhibit of photos of the vegetation of Folland Park. Folland Park is about five miles from here and is one of the two largest remnants of near-indigenous scrub in the metropolitan area. I recited two ballads which I here resent to you.

JONES'S SELECTION

You hear a lot of new-chum talk
Of goin' on the land,
And raisin' record crops of wheat
On rocks and flamin' sand.

I 'ates exaggerated skite,
But if yer likes I can
Authenticate a case in which
The land went on the man.

Bill Jones 'e 'ad a mountain block
Up Kosiusko (sic) way;
He farmed it pretty nigh to death,
The neighbours used to say.

He scarified the surface with
His double-furrow ploughs,
An' ate its blinded heart right out
With sheep an' milkin' cows.

He filled its blamed intestines up
With agricultural pipes,
An' lime, and superphosphates, fit
To give the land the gripes.

Until at last the tortured soil,
Worn out with Jones's thrift,
Decided as the time was come
To up and make a shift.

One day the mountain shook itself,
An' give a sort o' groan,
The neighbours was a lot more scared
Than they was game to own.

Their jaws was dropped upon their chests,
Their eyes was opened wide,
They saw the whole of Jones's farm
Upend itself and slide.

It slithered down the mountain spur,
Majestic-like and slow,
An' landed in the river-bed,
A thousand feet below.

Bill Jones was on the lower slopes
Of 'is long-sufferin' farm,
A-testin' some new-fangled plough
Which acted like a charm.

He'd just been screwin' up a nut
When somethin' seemed to crack,
An' fifty acres, more or less,
Come down on Jones's back.

'Twas sudden-like, a shake, a crack,
A slitherin slide, an Bill
Was buried fifty feet below
The soil he used to till.

One moment Bill was standin up
A-ownin all that land,
The next 'es in eternity -
A spanner in 'is 'and!

They never dug up no remains
Or scraps of William Jones—
The superphosphates ate the lot,
Hide, buttons, boots, and bones.

For this here land wot Jones abused
And harassed in the past
'Ad turned and wiped 'im out, an' things
Got evened up at last.

From this untimely end o' Bill
It would perhaps appear
That goin' free-selectin' ain't
All skittles, no, nor beer.

So all you cocky city coves,
Wot's savin' up your screws
To get upon the land, look out
The land don't get on yous.

(Gibson, G. H. ("Ironbark"), 1955, 279-281.)

FIVE MILES FROM GUNDAGAI

I'm used to punchin' bullock teams
Across the hills and plains,
I've teamed outback for forty years
In blazin' droughts and rains.
I've lived a heap of trouble down
Without a word o' lie,
But I can't forget what happened to me
Five miles from Gundagai.

'Twas getting' dark, the team got bogged,
The axle snapped in two.
I'd lost me matches and me pipe,
Lord what was I to do?
The rain come down, 'twas bitter cold,
And hungry too was I.
And the dog he shat in the tucker box,
Five miles from Gundagai.

Some blokes I know have lotsa luck,
Whatever way they fall.
But there was I, Lord love-a-duck,
No flamin' luck at all.

I couldn't make a pot a tea
Or get me trousers dry,
And the dog, he shat in the tucker box,
Five miles from Gundagai.

I can forgive the blasted team,
I can forgive the rain,
I can forgive the dark and cold,
And go through it again.
I can forgive me rotten luck,
But hang me till I die,
I can't forgive that bloody dog,
Five miles from Gundagai.

Well, all that now is past and gone,
I sold the team for meat,
And where I got the bullocks bogged
Is now an asphalt street.
The dog? He musta took a bait,
I reckoned that he'd died,
So I buried him in the tucker box,
Five miles from Gundagai.

Yeah, all that now is past and gone,
And things are lookin' sweet,
For now I drive a big Mack truck,
In fact I own a fleet.
I churn out lots of diesel fumes,
Turn peoples' faces sour,
And drive through bloody Gundagai
At ninety miles an hour!

(Traditional Ballad, but the last two stanzas added by the Bushwackers about ten years ago.)

Really you should hear me do these ballads. I can't sing much anymore, but I can still do that sort of thing.

But more really, you should have heard Waldo. He produced a beautiful dot painting of the Ruby Salt-bush Dreaming and then told the dreaming. Not authentic of course. The local Kaurna people are near as dammit to extinct (and were reckoned extinct within about thirty years of the foundation of South Australia). Their dreamings have certainly been lost.[80] And anyhow, they never did dot paintings—a western Desert form. (But for that matter the Western Desert paintings were originally done on the sand and danced on!) Authenticity has its place alright, but only where it belongs. And yes those abo painters are great artists.

And great blokes too! Many stories, but one in particular. I saw a film recently recording the visit of a group of women from the Western Desert to that great cosmopolitan centre of the arts New York. The plane circled Manhattan before landing. They were impressed, but not particularly favourably. Without it being said, I suppose that large-scale white-fella construction means to them utter destruction. What did strike them was the poverty of New Yorkers, and particularly the begging. Through flash-backs to their own settlement showing them sitting in the dust, as they always do, amongst naked kids and lean dogs and a minimum of everything except litter, they kept saying, "Here people so poor they gotta beg for tucker. Back home we got everything what we want." They want very little. That they've got that is the result of the painting.

But just in passing, they have no more idea of living sustainably than we do. They go through cars, for example, like some people go through fags.

Margie rang from the States recently. She should be back in England now working with her computer. She says that it has become her god and that she worships it.

Bronchitis? Better, I hope.

Keep well, my dear old mate

Much love

Iris Murdoch to Brian Medlin
[Letter 2]

30 Charlbury Rd
OX 2

Brian dear,

Sorry for hasty previous letter. I am glad Christine is better. And I hope you are steadily better too. I am very sorry about Bruno. One must hope for some sudden ray of light.

Thank you for the ballads! I like these offerings very much. I often think about the Man from Snowy River and Shift, Boys, Shift![81] You chaps are unique.

I am still rather run over by interviews and discussions[i]—one should say <u>no</u> to all these things, but often there is some particular reason why one can't! (Old school pal etc.) I hope to have more reflection before long.

I have an Aussie (minor) character in a novel I'm writing, hence the question about the police! (As in British "Fuzz" etc.)

I'll write again—much love to you.

I

---

[i] Inserted above line here "re philosophy book."

Iris Murdoch to Brian Medlin
[Letter 41]

30 Charlbury Rd
OX2

[No date]

Dearest Brian,

Your super <u>Human Nature Human Survival</u> book has arrived just as I am leaving for some sojourn in the wild west of England. I will take it along with me. It looks like <u>what the age requires</u>. It is a kind of poetry too. I hope lots and lots of people are reading it. May you carry on with glowing life purpose and meaning, we can do with that.

Aborigine (*sic*) art is becoming popular over here, several large shows have been put on. It is wonderfully beautiful. Brian dear, be well. Thank you for your message! With much love from your mate, ever

I

Iris Murdoch to Brian Medlin
[Letter 6]

30 Charlbury Rd:
OX 2

Oct 11

Dearest Brian

Just to report work in progress. I have been away, and rather overwhelmed with instant (*sic*) tasks. I am reading H. <u>Nature H Survival</u> with greatest interest & pleasure. I hope I can write a suitable and worthy piece. Perhaps not <u>very</u> long—I shall have to see. It's such wonderful stuff and difficult. Let me know if there's a deadline. Thank you so much for asking me.

If you receive a longish Book with a pretty cover from me don't feel you have to read it—it is (being based on lectures) all bits & pieces, there are some jokes, some lit. criticism etc.[82] I wish you were here. I love the argument & the sound of your voice, which I hope is heard all over Australia.

Will communicate again before long. Much love, Dear creature, and to Chris

I

Brian Medlin to Iris Murdoch
Letter MDC080

69 Albert Street
Prospect
South Australia
5082
Ph: (08) 269 2483

Dearest Iris

Lovely talking to you again mate.

Business before pleasure though. As I had more than half expected Barry Oakley of *The Australian turned* down the proposal that you should review *Human Nature Human Survival*. I had a number of reasons for expecting this. He and I have crossed swords in the past. He is a Murdoch (Rupert, not Iris!) lackey. The book is anti-capitalist and actually mentions Australia's favourite export unfavourably, though not by name. You may be interested in our correspondence this time round. Looking over it I seem myself to have been infected with Oakley's feline insincerity.

(In passing, there is a review by Jack Smart soon to appear in the Adelaide (and Sydney) Review. It's quite "favourable," but a bloody mess. It's hard to sort out what he's saying from what I've said. Alas! And, alas, he makes the same silly point as Oakley about capitalism, though not with Oakley's condescension.)

No matter, we always had *The Age* as a second string. Not quite so useful from a "business" point of view. *The Age* is a much better paper, though, and I'm happier about that. Melbourne-based but it is semi-national. When we finally managed to contact her, Louise Carbines agreed, just on Matthews' recommendation, to the take it on without seeing the book.

She wanted your phone number, but I didn't think you'd be crazy about my handing out your phone number to journalists. And anyhow, it was an excuse to ring you myself. I am, however sending her your address with this mailing.

I have written saying that you won't be able to start working on the review until mid-November, though you have been reading the book. She would prefer you to fax it to her—as would I. The fax number of *The Age* is

670 7514

The fax number of the paper's library whose line is likely to be less congested is

670 1059

You would also need the Australian prefix. I mentioned your Luddism to Louise. The address of *The Age* is

25 Spenser Street, Melbourne, 2000.

That would take a week longer. I'm sure that there is a fax machine in St. Anne's College and perhaps even somebody who can use it. Be that as it may, anything headed *Attention Louise Carbine* will find her by one of those three ways.

Iris you thank me for asking you. Thank you in turn for taking it on. I hope that the extent of my admiration for you shows at times. I very much look forward to hearing what you disagree with. I was a bit discouraged to hear that you were finding it difficult—it was supposed to be easy. Ah well.

I'm being interviewed by the South Australian ABC on the day Jack Smart's review appears. And probably also by National ABC after your review appears. Julia Lester, who will be doing the interview here, suggested that the National people would probably want to talk to you too. I told her that you almost certainly would think that you had better things to do. I even quoted you before you'd said it yesterday: "People keep on asking you to do things." I hope I was right to discourage her.

As I said, your beautiful big book arrived a few days ago and I have been dipping into with pleasure. So far I think I disagree with what you say in "Wittgenstein and the Inner Life," but I'll have to make sure that I've understood you aright (so there!) before I launch into a complaint.

Your book now has a third competitor—besides Bullock on Hitler and Stalin,[83] Desmond and Moore on Darwin.[84] Today I picked up for thirty bucks the complete stories of Steele Rudd. Do you know Steele Rudd? If you don't I promise I'll record some for you. You'll see why the competition is pretty stiff.[85]

Talking about *So there*, do you know the story of Tennyson and Jowett? It's in Harold Nicholson's book,[86] I think, so you must know it. But just in case.—Tennyson showed Jowett a sonnet (or whatever). "I don't think much of that Tennyson." Well if it comes to that, Master, the sherry you gave us at luncheon was filthy.

Don't read the long paper on Love Mortality and the Meaning of Life that I sent you. By the time it's fit to be read it will be much shorter.

[…]

Christine has been very ill indeed. I was able to look after her at home, thank God. About two months ago now. She is now in late convalescence, but still wearies easily and is under weight.

A dear friend of mind died recently of a brain tumour. In her early forties. It appeared five or six years ago. It was in the left hemisphere. Fortunately Pammy was one of those rare people whose functions are all controlled by both hemispheres, so that they were able to operate. Unfortunately, they couldn't get it all. I ran into Pammy three months ago. We kept on meeting when shopping. We arranged, but hadn't seen much of one another for years (*sic*). We arranged to have coffee, or lunch next time. There wasn't one. But she worked right up to the end, then went into a coma for several weeks. She spoke only once to say, "I've got to get up. I've got work to do." She was an artist. She had a ten year old son Tim. The coma was a good thing for Tim, because he hadn't acknowledged the fact that Pammy was going to die—neither had Pammy. Tim is the son of Peter Hicks who wrote that poem addressed to me in the Flinders Anthology. There is a new mural in the city to be dedicated to Pammy tomorrow night. Annie Newmarch (Jake and Bruno's mum) will make the dedication speech.

Pammy was a Broken Hillite—a special breed. She and I once did a trip the Hill on my BMW. She wore Christine's gear and I'll always remember that she could hardly move it was so tight. It was on that trip that the young (bus ticket) woman told me that she was really into philosophy. I was playing my flute in the back yard and she rushed down the lane and came in, as they do in The Hill. Pammy had won a prize with a beaut picture in an exhibition in the BH gallery and she bought us all champagne in one of the many pubs—one that hadn't been tarted up. It was on that trip too that we set the Silverton pub alight—not Pammy—but a Silvertonite bloke and myself, playing music and singing. (Can't do that sort of thing now.) Silverton is an old mining town out from The Hill. Population of two or three thousand during the first world war. Now perhaps twenty. During that stoush, a couple of local Turks had their own little war and opened up with rifles on a train on the BH–Silverton line. Wonderful old cemetery. Amongst all the correct and proper inscriptions, one stands out. A young man records the bare details of his young wife's life and death. Then no religious cant. Just, *Blighted Hopes.* The family we stayed with on that occasion, much loved friends of Pammy's, husband, wife, two young kids, were wiped out by a semi-trailer shortly afterwards. Pammy felt the urge from then on to ring them up and tell them about this terrible thing that had happened to her wonderful friends.

I hope this isn't too full of terrible typos. It's late and I'm pretty tired, so I've probably read over a bundle. Enjoy Moscow, Spain. Travel well, safely. Lots of love. Love to John. I hope he enjoys his retirement.

Iris Murdoch to Brian Medlin
[Letter 5]

30 Charlbury Road
OX 2

Dearest Brian,

I have been on your fine spirited text for a time now (having returned from (a) Russia (b) Spain). I love it because it is very you. However there is a difficulty, which is that I disagree with some of your main tenets—the root of which is your sort of Marxism-Leninism and your anti-bourgeois arguments. I can't go into this in detail now, & I haven't yet finished my close study. I just wonder, considering this disagreement, whether you would want me to write some (short) counter piece, or not?

The other deep stream of your thought, as I see it, is your excellent ecological argument. It will anyway take me some time to write a worthy reply.[i] Have you any dead-line, I mean must the piece be sent along very soon? <u>Please forgive</u> this fussy letter! Much love and to Chris.

I.

I am so sorry Chris is ill—I hope she is better. I hope you are well and <u>writing poetry.</u> I like your references to cricket.

---

[i] Marginal note here: "Something fairly short I think."

Iris Murdoch to Brian Medlin
[Letter 4]

30 Charlbury Road
OX 2

Brian, PS to last (recent) letter. I did not want to imply that the ecology theme was the only thing I wanted to discuss apart from the "bourgeois" (& neo-Marxist, if I may put it so) problem! For instance I like your argument about "rationalism" and "irrationalism"—and there is much to say on the meaning of "bourgeois"—And of course the survival question connects absolutely with the rationality question.[i] I think to do it all some proper degree of justice would/will take me a long time—and then may not be what you want!
    Much love I
    and to Chris

    I mean, must the piece be done in time for the periodical you mentioned? In fact I could produce something shorter & sooner if this is necessary. I am recovered from all the rushing about. Only one more brief visit to Moscow, where John is involved on the jury of the new <u>Russian Booker prize</u>!
    Very sorry for delay—My heart is with you—never mind about the bourgeoisie.

---

[i] Marginal note here: "<u>It</u> is full of passion!"

Iris Murdoch to Brian Medlin
[Letter 3]

PPS

Of course I will and can write it—only it will take me some time I think! Ignore my defeatism in previous letters.

Much love & to Chris

I

Brian Medlin to Iris Murdoch
Letter MDC090

69 Albert Street
Prospect
South Australia
5082
Ph: (08) 269 2483

December 2, 1992

Dearest Iris

Thanks for your notes. I hope that your concerns are now cleared up. I still haven't been able to contact Louise Carbines of *The Age*, but I'm sure that there'll be no problem about time. An appearance before Christmas would be better than one after Christmas—when everybody stops reading reviews, I suspect. But the main thing is that you should be happy about it. I must say that I hadn't realised when I asked you to do this how much work it would demand of you.

{3 hours later: I now have your third note bearing unnecessary reassurance. Much of my life in the meantime has been consumed trading scripture and trying to trade reason with a born again Christian who got into this house in the innocent guise of a cabinet maker. He used to be a Papist till he began speaking in tongues. Amongst the many pleasantries he treated us to was a bland assertion that no Papist (he said "Catholic") can be a Christian. I asked him whether that means that they are all damned—and of course it does. Then he had the nerve to tell us that only through God can love and peace and harmony be brought into the world. It slipped my mind to give him the old Ken Tucker. Fucking Christianity! Our friend Tony Moore, an ex-Mick, not yet born again, was here to do some work on the house. So was Christine, who in her very young womanhood was b. a., but has long been unborn. Christine told him that if God was like that she wanted no part of him; and (after an hour) that she hoped the cupboards would be finished in time for the Second Coming— which this bloke expects in his life-time with the same confidence as did St. Paul and with less excuse. Tony was physically sickened—in the head after the English-Australian manner rather than to the stomach after the American. I did remember to sing after he'd left:

I don't care if it rains or freezes
For I'm safe in the arms of Jesus.
I am Jesus little lamb.
Yes by Jesus Christ I am.

However well you know it, you always forget what a detestably evil doctrine Christianity is. What's more I'm convinced that it can only be rescued from its moral vileness by a transformation into something that should no longer be called by the same name. I distinguish between the doctrine(s) and the indoctrinated, of course, as any sensible person should. You may be interested in reading a reference I wrote recently for my dear friend and good mate, Alison Gent. (I have her permission to send it to you.) Alison is a white man, as we used to be allowed to say.}

(I'm sending you a heap of stuff. Don't be dismayed. Most of it is bed-time reading.)

Your reference to my "sort of Marxism-Leninism" reminds me of a story that used to be told of Jock Silverblade, an Adelaide copper in the Moratorium days. Jock, it is said, had a young demonstrator down a side-street and was punching his head into the wall, saying what time, "I hate you bloody communist bastards." Thump! Thump! "All you bloody commos are the same." Thump! Thump! "But I'm an anti-communist!" "I don't care what kind of fucking communist you are!" Thump! Thump![i]

---

[i] [Medlin's note] Let's have a foot-note. I'm afraid I don't believe this of Jock. Not because of the thumping, of which I'm sure he was capable, but because he was neither stupid enough nor witty enough to have replied thus. Further, he was a religious unswearing man. And I knew him fairly well. I was once subjected to a citizen's arrest by the manager of a large shopping arcade when I took small an anti-war demo onto his sacred site. We refused to move on, the grounds being that we were causing no obstruction and were in fact providing some useful entertainment. He took me up into his office and locked it. I pulled out a book, put my feet up on his desk and started reading. I always carried a book in my pocket in those days. Three-quarters of an hour later Jock arrived with a colleague (who later perjured himself blind when I was on trial on a different matter). "Hullo, Brian. How's the Mum? How's the Dad?" Then they sat down and we had an hour-long philosophical discussion about civil disobedience. The manager kept on trying to get back into his office to work, but Sergeant Silverblade kept waving him away with "We haven't finished our interrogation yet." Eventually, Jock let him back in, refused to take me into "lawful custody," gave the poor bastard a 15-minute lecture on the perils of citizen's arrest. The whole thing got a lot of press, because the manager was silly enough to mouth off about it. But in the end we stuffed it up. We made a much publicised return to the arcade two weeks later. This turned out

I'm an *anti*-Marxist-Leninist. I think the monograph proves it. The essence of Leninism is the doctrine of the Vanguard Party which is explicitly rejected on p. 65. I'm sending you as well a copy of a little talk I gave to the Friends of the Waite Institute here. The W.I. is an agricultural/pastoral (but not tragical or comical or historical) research unit, attached to the University of Adelaide. Section X is especially relevant. I don't think I have sent you *The Faculty of Unreason* before. I'd have sent you this second piece anyhow because it is a serious philosophical essay. But it too is relevant to this matter.

And on the matter of the bourgeoisie, bourgeois values, the need for a new social order, I'm sending you an interesting paper by David Nerlich. (I'm assuming that he won't mind.) David is the son of my excellent friend Graham Nerlich, the philosopher of science. I've never met David, but he'd read *HNHS* and asked Graham to send it to me for comment.

As you said about *Metaphysics as a Guide to Morals* (hereafter forever *MGM*), you don't have to read any of this stuff. But it's there if you want it.

It's not often, I suppose, that an author gets the chance of discussion with a reviewer before the event. (Though in the small amount of reviewing I've done I have sometimes sought out the author for discussion.) But as we used to say at school, "You arst for it." I'm astonished at the amount of labour you are putting into this. Jack Smart did a review that was genial enough but very perfunctory.

With respect to *MGM*, I *am* reading it and I'll eventually write to you about it. I have many unwelcome preoccupations at present, so I'm not getting along with anything as well as I'd like. Your book isn't "difficult," but I'm finding it hard to handle. You'll know the feeling. It is a very complex book, at any rate in detail: so far I'm still seeing mainly trees. And you start from so many places different from my beginnings. I mean "beginnings" in many different ways too. Socially, culturally, intellectually. You revere people I abhor—Kant, Schopenhauer especially. David Stove, my wonderful indispensable enemy—the bloke I mention in the Waite Inst. talk who accused me of being on the side of Pol Pot— Stove describes Chopping-Ha-ha—as we used childishly to describe him when a couple of us tried to read him at school—Stove, as I was saying, describes Schopenhauer as a pathological windbag. I sympathise. I do revere Plato, not because I think he got it right about Goodness, but because he came early, he was the "first" theoretician, he *worked*, he had

---

to be a disaster, partly because of poor organisation on my part, largely because of the unreliability of a street theatre group.

the rare gift of intellectual infanticide. But I'm finding *MGM* a marvellously exciting book and sooner or later I'll try to say some sensible things about it. I read that rather unkind review by Eagleton. (I read bloody everything—except Schopenhauer—even Paul bloody Davies the new nobodaddy-monger.) I don't have Eagleton's piece with me. But two things.—I think that it's outrageous to say that Derrida has shot his bolt. Even if it's true, nobody can know it yet. And supposing it to be true, I fear there will a worse come in his place. Especially if the place is left vacant. I can't be bothered talking particularly about the particular doctrines of any of those waffling, pretentious French fuckwits. But their influence permeates modern thought, especially amongst the unthinking lumpen intelligentsia and if Eagleton doesn't know it then either the Poms are luckier than we are or he hasn't walked abroad or had a cup of coffee for a long time. You might as well say that Popper and Kuhn have shot their bolt. Or Wittgenstein. Would that it were so!

I think his remarks about goodness and selfishness were misconceived. What the oppressed and deprived need isn't selfishness, but solidarity, the very opposite. Selfishness *divides* the oppressed; it unites the *oppressors*. Which is why their ideologists, of whom Eagleton is not one, preach it. This is so on the liberal bourgeois scene at any rate. Totalitarian oppression invokes a community of interest, though a false one. These are oversimplifications, of course. Community of interest, nationhood, etc. also place a large part in the ideology of liberal bourgeois societies.

But I do think that Eagleton's onto something. I've been reading *in* the book so far, not reading it through. So far, as well as I can tell, it is written as though there is just Goodness and one need only to pass through the refiner's fire of Art(?) Philosophy(?) Vision(?) and Bob's your uncle. You will protest, of course, and rightly so, because I haven't captured what I really want to say. I'm just sounding off with some first impressions. There is stacks of stuff that shows me to be literally wrong. But even if there were not, though I *do* mind about the bourgeoisie—mind very much too—and though you are doubtless culturally and ideologically deprived in not being a child of the working class, and though you are certainly culturally intimidating to a child of the working class, my heart is with you. So there!

The material in "Morals and Politics," especially, shows the above description to be inadequate. By the way my paper, "The Faculty of Unreason" has some stuff which contains part of the reason why utilitarianism (by which I mean only the doctrine that actions are to be assessed *only* by their consequences—differing values would give different utilitarian moralities) why utilitarianism cannot constitute a complete moral theory, a complete guide to conduct—why there must be "barriers of principle which are not reducible to system." (What awful sentences I'm writing!) If there weren't, we wouldn't need morality at all. If utilitarianism *worked* we wouldn't need to speak of it. Dunno whether that makes sense to you: I'll write a paper on it next year. I think you may be provoking me to write a book called, *Morality as the basis of Metaphysics.*

Sorry for all this gnomic stuff. I'm just thinking aloud, not playing at profundity. The reason it's obscure is that so far it's confused.

December 3, 1992

There are pelicans flying overhead today. All afternoon. And this reminds me that I once promised you an account of the birds in our yard. Not now. You have enough to cope with and I too.

I'm glad to have news of John. Please give him my love. I hope to see him when you emigrate-immigrate.

Much love

I have by now managed to contact Louise. There is no problem about time. She is delighted to hear that you are in disagreement on some matters. (Well, bugger *her*!) She is very happy for you to do it in your own time. I've given you her address before, but it is:

Louise Carbines
The Age
250 Spenser Street
Melbourne, 3000

Iris Murdoch to Brian Medlin
[Letter 31]

30 Charlbury Rd
OX2

Brian, dear, I am extremely sorry, I just cannot deliver the piece before Christmas, as I hoped I could. I am trying to get the last part right. I do apologise! I have been away, and now Christmas doings are going to take up time (Very jolly but time-consuming, all arranged by John's two elder brothers. He still feels he is the young fellow.) I see the card is marked "May," but it is at least sunny and merry and more in tune with your lovely hot weather, not a snowy scene. We haven't had any snow yet actually but it is forecast. I am sorry to be so tardy, I will do my best. Much love, dear mate, and to Chris,

    ever
    I

[With card "The Month of May," inscribed "With all best Christmas and New Year wishes to Brian and Chris from Iris with much love"]

Brian Medlin to Iris Murdoch
Letter MDC100

69 Albert Street
Prospect
South Australia
5082
Ph: (08) 269 2483

January 5, 1993

Dearest Iris

I fear you are in for a bit of a shock.

Thank you for your review and for the great amount of work you have put into it. But, alas, it was supposed to be about 800 words long! I remember that you knew this at one time, because you remarked over the phone that you didn't find 800 words easy. But I can't find it in any of my letters to you. Sorry, mate. Your paper is over 4000 words long.

Since I would be the only person in Australia who can read your handwriting, I made a typescript—though leaving out about 300 words. Your accompanying note says please "alter or delete." I would not presume to "alter," but I did delete. (That entailed some alteration.) It took me four days, preserving whatever I could, to get it down to 1387 words. Many things dear to your heart (and mine) had to go—Aboriginal painting, for one example. Lenin for another! But I think I preserved all your topics and especially all your criticisms. Not all your arguments unfortunately: much detail went, of course.[87]

I thought that I could not get further without cutting into topics. So at that point I rang Louise Carbines in Melbourne and tried her out on 1400 words. She was adamant, I'm afraid, that 1000 was the absolute limit. I have to concede that this is generous—your big philosophy book is currently being reviewed in 1000 words.

So I spent another day laboriously cutting. This time it was much deeper into the flesh. Schopenhauer had to go, for example—and the praise of Medlin associated with it. But I think I have retained all your topics, though you'll hardly recognise them in their condensed form. I have been particularly careful to retain your criticisms, though again highly condensed.

I'm returning this for your perusal. The deletions being so great—and made by the author reviewed, it would be improper to send it to press without your approval.

I've highlighted one or two things for your special consideration. Mostly things I've added, but one deletion changes your sense slightly. "Bourgeois," I've put in quotes because I've heavily cut your objections to the word—without deleting them entirely. As I've been forced to treat it in the penultimate paragraph, "bourgeois" gets added to the *terms* of line 3. This isn't what you intended, but I can't see any objection to it. We must try to understand the complex realities that lie behind *that* term too.

It is not impossible that you won't want to put your name to the result. One thing that I'm conscious of is that I've lost the Iris Murdoch flavour. There was no way I could retain it while cutting so savagely—especially since a large ingredient of this flavour is a certain leisureliness.

If you are prepared to let this go ahead, please return the copy with your amendments.

I've faxed this draft today to Louise. I'm sure that it'll be OK with her. But she is quite clear on the situation and won't publish anything until we get your approval.

And if you are prepared to let it go ahead, then I have something to ask you. Given the intended audience of the book and of the review, perhaps you might find yourself able to comment explicitly on the readability of the book. It is meant to be readable by a general audience and I believe that it is. Which is not what people would expect of a philosophical text. But: *We have at most one thousand words.* It occurs to me that the job could be done merely by inserting a few words into the first line between "monograph," and "*Human Nature ...*" But that's as you wish and see fit. Of course it is: what a bloody daft thing to say.

Dear Iris, I'm sorry about this kerfuffle. I hope you aren't too disappointed or displeased. I know you put a lot of energy into it at a time when you were very tired. I assure you that I've also put a lot of energy into it. I've agonised over every word and comma trying to preserve as much as possible what you had said. And I've tried to make as little trouble for you as possible.

I found your review most interesting and hated to cut it so savagely. It won't surprise you to learn that I disagree with much of it. I'll write about that later. I don't think it proper to do so now.

Thanks for all you best wishes. Our Christmas was quiet, hooray. I hope 1993 is a good year for you and John.

I'll write about real things later

With much love

Iris Murdoch to Brian Medlin
Letter 11

30 Charlbury Rd
OX2

Brian dear, thanks very much, I think it's splendid, much better than the rambling original version! Could put, first sentence, "B M's passionate, very readable, monograph …" Also: "Here Medlin takes an important stand, with which I personally would disagree." (Comma, or if you prefer dash—) All the rest absolutely OK[i]—I'm so sorry you had to work on the thing—it is now greatly improved! Well done, cobber,
    lots of love
    Iris

---

[i] Marginal note here: "Perhaps add: technological amusement, and to …"

Iris Murdoch to Brian Medlin
[Letter 39]

30 Charlbury Rd
OX2 6UU

[13.3.1993]

Dearest mate Brian, thanks very much for sending the piece. I think it looks jolly good, at least it make sense, and sends forth some important signals! I like the dramatic picture too. I trust B. Matthews will get in touch. His name sounds familiar. I hope you are OK and life untangling. I am rather tired and our (European) politics are so awful, I hate the Maastricht Treaty (I think I am one of the very few people in Britain who have even tried to read it—actually is non-readable). But I fear we shall be forced to sign it. Our leaders (Major & Co) are nice and well-intentioned but confused & weak. (The other lot are worse.) I gather that the left wing are winning the Oz election, so you will be pleased (March 13 as I write.)[88]

Meanwhile (here) the IRA continue their activities (in London etc.).[i]

Write soon, <u>be well</u>, much love to you my dear

I

---

[i] Marginal note here: "Terrible news from Bombay. What a world. I think you have no terrorists?" [On 12 March 1993 13 bombs were exploded in Bombay, India, killing about 250 people.]

Iris Murdoch to Brian Medlin
[Letter 43]

30 Charlbury Rd
Oxford OX2

[No date]

Dearest Brian, please forgive my not writing for a while—various pressures including just exhaustion. Better now. I hope you and Christine are well. I wish you lived a bit nearer. Anyway three cheers for South Africa. I am trying to write another novel with not much success. Anyway there is a lovely English spring & our garden full of all sorts of flowers and birds.

Well, your birds fancier than ours. Oxford is quiet and proceeds in its dignified scholarly manner. I think of you singing in New College.

How is old Oz getting on? (Are things better for the Abos?) Europe— lovely <u>dear</u> Europe—is in perpetual muddle. It is difficult to see who is governing England. And there is Bosnia. I feel I would like to go for a cruise, but somehow I can't at present. Please write to me, my dear—I miss your far-off presence. I hope you and Christine have discovered new kinds of birds and plants—give my love to Christine—

Love to you, my dear old friend—
Yours
Iris.

Iris Murdoch to Brian Medlin
[Letter 40]

30 Charlbury Rd
OX2

[No date][i]

Brian dear, many thanks for <u>long</u> letter and for Christine's lovely and interesting account of plants and birds and beasts.[ii] I still can't quite picture mallee, and assumed that a billabong was a pond (when apparently it is something more complex). You certainly live in a paradise and <u>enjoy</u> it. Brian Matthews yes I recall I think. Dinkum Oz. I much like Christine's <u>Wirra</u> piece, and her care for "resident creatures."[89] All this is much wilder than anything one comes across in England—and much nearer to the <u>original</u> garden put there by God. Our front garden is full of wild flowers, commented on not always pleasantly by neighbours. But our "wild" is recognizable order, things which are familiar, & prettily drawn in books. I am touched by your TRUTH statuette man, how a very touching (*sic*) tribute, and a reminder.[90] I am also delighted, to return, by Christine's little black spot that turned out to have a body and a head. Thanks also for Peter Hicks's poem, I hope your poems continue. Jack Smart and your garden … do you see him much now?[iii] Returning to the start, our politics are just as awful as yours, only in a different way.[iv] Did I tell you I have a dinkum Oz man in my next novel. He is the nicest (though secondary) character.[v] Forgive short letter. I am about to go to JAPAN for two weeks to give talks etc. to the Japs, and view Fujiyama etc. It's not far from Australia. Be well.

> Much love to Christine
> Much love to you
> ever I

---

[i] Note in Medlin's writing reads: "*Rcd. 24(?).v.93*'
[ii] Inserted above line: "+ caterpillar & wasp days."
[iii] Marginal note here: "I love your garden with billies on fires & super butterflies."
[iv] Marginal note here: "The Maastricht Treaty is deadly, but we shall be forced to accept it.'
[v] Marginal note here: "We are <u>short</u> of butterflies."

Billabongs

Extract from a letter to Iris[i]

And yes, you're right. A billabong isn't just a pond. I don't know what "pond" means to you, but I take it to be something quite small. I suppose there's no reason why a billabong shouldn't be small. In fact the billabong in Duck paddock at *Tolka* is fairly small, though I wouldn't call it a pond. Usually, however, it will be sizable, because it's got to be semi-permanent to qualify, or at least long-lasting.

The other qualification is that it should be associated with a river. There has to be *some* association. An isolated water-hole, miles from a channel is a lake, a spring or just a water-hole, a small one a gilgai, especially if ephemeral. A pool on top of Uluru is a rock-hole. Classically the association occurs in one of two ways.

Either as a cut off ox-bow bend whose entrance and exit have silted up. *Meath* billabong and the homestead billabong at *Tolka* are of this kind. You may remember me talking about Retail Bend and Retail Island in the Murray. Retail Island was formed quite recently by the cutting off of a large ox-bow bend. This bend doesn't yet qualify as a billabong. The island is still an island, the original ox-bow channel is still continuous with the main stream. The process of silting up has begun. I have found the upstream mouth of the bend cut off by silt once when the river was low. Probably the downstream mouth was cut off too at this time—I'm sure it is shallower, which makes sense—but I didn't have the wit to investigate at the time.

Or as a water-hole in an alternative channel parallel to the main channel. Many Australian rivers, perhaps most, stop flowing during the dry season or in droughts. And many are multi-channeled, over some of their lengths, because of the flatness of the country. (The Murray is one such river, The Cooper in the spectacular channel country another. There the channels reach from horizon to horizon across the river as you fly over them at 5000 feet.) Many of these carry water-holes, some permanent,

---

[i] This is transcribed from a printed document in the Medlin Collection. The remainder of the letter does not survive.

some semi-permanent, some ephemeral. A waterhole in the main channel of the river isn't a billabong—except by a barbarism. It's a waterhole.

The Glenelg, by the way, flows through a single channel
You can call waters billabongs without attracting local derision that are somewhat loosely associated with rivers. The billabong I have just mentioned in Duck on *Tolka* is pretty close to the river (100 metres?) but, so to speak, naked on the river flat. It will occasionally get overflow from the river but only when the river breaks banks. At other times it is fed by seepage. So is the larger billabong in the Kangaroo on *Tolka*. This is further from the river channel (half a kilometre?). And right under the old river dunes, now stringy-bark forests rich in springs seeping out onto the chocolate loam flats.

As a matter of fact, both the homestead billabong and *Meath* are spring-fed. They would hardly be so nearly permanent otherwise. Both now lie high about the present channel of the river and receive water from the river only when it overflows. Both lie immediately against the old dunes. *Meath* billabong is mainly fed from what must have been an old creed running into the river in its original course. The channel of this creek is still quite noticeable, its bed is often very damp, but I have never seen it running with surface water.

An artefact isn't a billabong either even though it may seem indistinguishable from, say, the billabong in Kangaroo. Bob and Ivy have created such an artefact, a permanent surface water, as a wildlife haven. They scooped out an area just under the dunes and just where some strong springs seep out. They've strung a top-wire electric fence around it. This keeps out stock but allows passage to native animals. You can call this a dam, even a lake. Nobody's likely to call it a billabong. Its official proper name is "The Folly."

Iris Murdoch to Brian Medlin
[Letter 33]

30 Charlbury Road
OX2

[July 1993][i]

Brian dear, thank you very much for your letter. I have been away in Japan, then in north of England with John & John's brothers (usual annual holiday) and now have to go to Ireland (Coleraine, Ulster) to receive hon. degree and <u>make</u> <u>speech</u> to hundreds students, dons, relatives, etc. I <u>detest</u> such things but must do them!

Thank you ever so much for the Billabong information—you are wonderfully close to nature, wild things & green things—this is very Australian. Nothing like this in the Cotswolds. I'm sorry that Australia is being given away to Japan. The Japanese are indeed voracious, and so clever and busy, taking tops off mountains & making them into islands. They are brilliantly ingenious, their trains are beautiful & very long & fast and accurate. They were very nice to us. Position of women not so good however. Still, we have Japanese friends, and they <u>love</u> trees. [ii]

I don't look forward to the visit to Ireland—the Irish problem and the sorrows of Ireland go on and on. Much love to you & Chris ever

I

---

[i] "July [1993]: Having just returned from Japan, IM has to go immediately to Ireland to give a talk and to receive an honorary degree." Valerie Purton, *An Iris Murdoch Chronology* (Basingstoke: Palgrave Macmillan, 2007) 207.
[ii] Marginal note here: "I am very tired, but <u>will</u> recover!"

Iris Murdoch to Brian Medlin
[Letter 34]

30 Charlbury Rd OX2

[no date]

Dearest Brian, hope you and Christine are well. I have been a little under weather but better now. Lucky lovely sunshine down under! All very very best for <u>1994</u>! Do send news—much much love

    I

Will write. Thinking of you. Parrot brings love.

Iris Murdoch to Christine Vick
[Letter 36]

Following

Dearest Christine, I am <u>so</u> <u>sorry</u> to write so late—I love your card of beautiful flowers and your kind words. Thank you to tell me of the flowers that last only a day or two and are much loved by tiny native bees. And the strong stems make fishing nets for Aborigines. I wish I had come <u>then</u>—I wish both of you very well, and with much love
   Iris

Iris Murdoch to Brian Medlin
[Letter 35]

Following

Dearest Brian, I wish I had written to you long ago now—how was this? I cannot feel the <u>time.</u> The Kookaburra, the mallee, a spider 1cm long, a pretty little bloke, and you let him free. And Crimson Rosellas.

Christine's wasp story, How much time has passed. Please pardon my slippage of time. I have written a novel and may try to write another.

Much love, dearest Brian, do write—
Iris.

Also; love, mortality and the meaning of life.

IRIS MURDOCH'S REVIEW
OF *HUMAN NATURE, HUMAN SURVIVAL*
BY BRIAN MEDLIN

[Full text of review by Iris Murdoch published in the *Age*, 27 February 1993.]

Brian Medlin's passionate monograph, *Human Nature, Human Survival*, tells us to take seriously, to believe in, the possible destruction of the human race in the not too distant future. He reminds us of our wanton destruction in the recent past, and in the present, of flora and fauna and humans, the treatment of the Australian Aborigines is an instance, there are many instances. This has been a terrible century. At the end of the last century, when good people were getting rid of slavery, there was a kind of general optimism, a feeling that civilisation was now everywhere and that there would be mutual understanding between states and peoples, even that there would be no more war. After all war was senseless. In this century there have been two World Wars, made increasingly hideous by advances in technology, and continual local nationalistic wars. A celestial spectator might well conclude that the planet was not possessed of reason and was swarming with evil and should be quietly exterminated. Medlin is suggesting to us that extermination may be nearer than we imagine, brought about by our selfish ways and lack of rationality. We have to change. We have to think. We must at least try. He concludes (p. 43) that "the unexamined life is no longer an option. (It never really was.) For us, henceforth, the examined life is the only life on offer."

Medlin is a philosopher and an ardent defender of philosophy. Philosophy needs defending. In an increasing number of universities it is now regarded as otiose, since the genuine questions which it asked have now (we are told) been answered by science—by psychology, biology, sociology, economics—and the old useless questions are to fade away, as God fades away. The great metaphysical systems are over. What is left of philosophy consists of idle arguments about sense data or perception or will which are resolved or obliterated elsewhere. Philosophy is no longer revered as a unique and necessary form of thinking. Medlin wants to change this; "if we are to save our civilisation and our planet we must get our philosophy right." What is philosophy?

> Philosophy is the commitment to thinking about the whole of life … All this (and more) together with the commitment to uncompromising rationality. This latter commitment being to rationality in action as well as in thought, the two being not rationally separable, the commitment extending further to the rational ordering of desire and feeling, for the philosophical life is not cold, unemotional, dehumanised, only a passionate, compassionate person could hope to achieve it … Philosophy is a way of life, a passion, an obsession—for those in its grasp, a duty and a right. (p. 5-6)

Philosophy is <u>difficult</u>. Good philosophical writing must be <u>lucid</u> and <u>patient</u>, a philosopher must be ready to explain exactly what he means at length. Great problems which concern the whole human race are still a proper object of philosophy. To rescue ourselves from the results of our follies and vices we require the ability to think clearly, something other than purely scientific thought. Medlin tells us that the possibility of human science

> was not a foregone conclusion. Two large related assumptions were needed. The first was that for all the complexity of phenomena, the universe had an underlying simplicity. The second, an assumption about human nature, was that human beings were capable of the kind of intelligence and rationality needed to perceive this simplicity. Both assumptions were contentious. Yet each was the rational assumption to act upon.

This claim is justified, Medlin tells us, not by hindsight, but by what he has called elsewhere

> A Main Principle of Rational Action: we must act with regard not only to relative probabilities, but, along with these, with regard to the magnitude and value (whether good or bad) of the possible consequences of our own assumptions. (p. 9)

What is reason, what is rationality? This question has indeed, in various forms, troubled philosophers. Medlin himself gives us an example of how to think about reasoning, rationality and irrationality, and rationalists and irrationalists. He startles us by quotations from Keats. "Do not all charms fly At the mere touch of cold philosophy?" Also "I am certain of nothing but the holiness of the heart's affections and the truth of the Imagination—

what imagination seizes as beauty must be truth—whether it existed before or not." Also "I have never yet been able to perceive how anything can be known for truth by consequitive reasoning …" Here is a good case of what Plato called "the old quarrel between philosophy and poetry." Medlin (himself a poet) opens a path for intuition. "The usefulness of literature depends largely upon the large fact that intuition is often the better road to truth. A basic confusion (Medlin tells us) shared by rationalists and irrationalists is that both tend to identify rationality with mere ratiocination (like Keats's "consecutive reasoning"). On the rationalist side this leads to "arid pretentious intellectualism," an inability to be agnostic, which may alternate with wholesale scepticism. On the irrationalist side the identification involves a total rejection of rationality, especially ratiocination, a lack of agnosticism, again alternative with self-destructive scepticism.

> Ratiocination doesn't constitute rationality, not even where the reasoning involved is correct. For ratiocination too is action and, hence like any other action subject to assessment as to its own reasonableness. Clearly, there are times when it is irrational to engage in explicit verbal reasoning, even with oneself. (Driving a car, to take a trivial example.) Supposing that the rationality or a performance resides in the discourse that monitors it is stark egomania. Gilbert Ryle called it more tolerantly the intellectualist legend. Some rational actions and amongst them some intellectual performances, will be executed without being explicitly monitored by rational discourse—and will be nonetheless rational for it. Nothing prevents us then from acknowledging that some tasks, even intellectual tasks, may be better performed intuitively. (pp. 39-42)

The reference to Ryle is good. Ryle's enlightening book (its first chapter is called "Descartes' Myth") is now less read by philosophers. *The Concept of Mind* was published in 1949, Wittgenstein's *Philosophical Investigations*, eclipsing all else, in 1953. Medlin's careful discussion of rationality is fundamental to his argument for the importance of intelligent philosophy in our attempt to survive. "We see now the urgent practical importance of philosophy. Unless enough of us get our philosophy right enough and quickly enough we are all dead" (p. 43).

We have to stop destroying our planet: this is not a task to be left only to clever scientists. There must be the force of the will of peoples behind them, and that will must be both clear and ardent. We have a terrible past, we must improve ourselves, and we must <u>look at the time</u>. Philosophy is of radical value for the clear thinking which is necessary. Here we must work as human individuals. We look back at the destruction of civilisations and the destruction of the individual. The concept of the individual is still fairly recent, and we must preserve and cherish it. At this moment innumerable particular humans are being crushed by poverty, famine, cruelty. Here Medlin looks critically at philosophy. What has it done in the past, what good, and what damage? What has rationality and rationalism done? The conscience of Marx and Engels stirred bourgeois thought. But "thinking" also embraces the Irrationalism of Rousseau and Nietzsche, and even within the rationalist scientific tradition the individual could be lost. "The principles of Cartesian epistemology led smartly to a self-stultifying solipsism. So, less rapidly, did those of British Empiricism" (p. 14). Medlin castigates Locke and Berkeley (no real tables and chairs), also Hume (no real selves, only bundles of perceptions). Even more recent thinkers (he cites Susan Blackmore) tell us that "What we perceive is a mental construction" (not the real world) and that "the self we value so much is [merely] a mental model." It is certainly surprising to see how long that philosophical tradition has worried itself with how we can connect inner perceptions with outer realities and make real things out of atoms. I think however that Brian has been a bit unfair to Locke (On Tolerance), and Hume (elsewhere named as vice-captain of Brian's team: "Nature has not left it to our choice whether there be body or no:" that is, it's all just there!), and (not mentioned by Brian) J.S. Mill (On Liberty). And I think he is unkind to Kant, who was also a great liberator, but let us leave that aside. Medlin is right to emphasise the various intellectual forces, previous and modern, which tend toward the destruction of the individual, the dissolution of the self. He mentions as a destructive agent Nietzsche; and I would add the later work of Heidegger. Jacques Derrida is also a destroyer. So is television, as a substitute for reading, and a purveyor of sleepy junk and violence and pornography. What threatens our modern technological civilisation is a form of determinism, of lassitude, a sense of "there's nothing more we can do," bringing a feeling of idle relief. Derrida's archi-ecriture, the sea of language which we cannot master. (Unless we are clever intellectuals who can invent language and play with it!) Derrida's "metaphysic" is also of course an attack upon philosophy, philosophy as clarity and truth. Philosophy, according to Derrida and late Heidegger, ought now to be poeticised! That is by the way.

Medlin has mixed feelings concerning the philosophical tradition of British Empiricism. On the one hand, the dissolution of the individual. On the other hand however the liberation of the individual, the doctrines of freedom and truthfulness (objectivity), scientific truth and with it individual truth-telling—and also, to be recognised as a general human characteristic, altruism (p. 30), "Cooperativeness and altruism are—of the very essence [of society]. Those of us who have encountered utter selfishness will know what a socially disabling affliction that can be. ... Even the most intensely competitive and uncooperative human activity, warfare, demands for its prosecution the most intense cooperation and altruism." I would refer here to the similar wisdom of a philosopher, not particularly one of Brian's friends, Schopenhauer. He speaks of

> the everyday phenomenon of compassion, of immediate participation, independent of all ulterior considerations, primarily in the suffering of another, and thus in the prevention of it; for all satisfaction and well-being and happiness consist in this. It is simply and solely this compassion that is the real basis of all voluntary justice and genuine loving-kindness. (On the Basis of Morality, the Foundation of Ethics, section 16.)

Compassion: not love, since love can be mingled with egoism. About Schopenhauer: his philosophy is somewhat confused and incoherent, he is best known for his famous concept of Will, a superhuman force postulating a total egoistic determinism, from which we cannot escape except by a mystical denial of self available to few humans; while elsewhere, with cheerful inconsistence, he speaks wisely of the profoundly various nature of human being, its undeniable egoism, but also its capacity for unselfish, even self-sacrificial, concern for others. This is also very well expressed by Medlin. A degree of selfishness is required for human survival, and this may go with a measure of unselfishness. A regard for one's own interest does not constitute selfishness, and a regard for the interest of others is a pervasive feature of human life. But while such qualities are common they are not of the very essence of society, whereas altruism is of the very essence. As an instance, Medlin movingly mentions his father, who fought in the first world war.

> To my knowledge he fought believing that he was serving human civilisation, and fought reconciled to death in that service ... I can imagine no merely selfish motive strong enough, misguided enough, to have enlisted him into the horrors of Flanders. (p. 31)

> The bourgeois philosophers proposed the systematic manipulation of non-human nature "for the relief of man's estate"—in Francis Bacon's phrase. ... This has required the development of technology and science, both of which they envisaged. (p. 9).

Here we must pause to consider the important concept of "the bourgeois": the bourgeoisie, bourgeois values, bourgeois philosophers, the bourgeois view of human life. Medlin points out various senses of the word: a mode of production, a social class, a kind of society, a historical era, a system of ideas, an ideology (p. 44). Not every feature of bourgeois ideology is bad, Medlin says, for instance the development of technology involved "objectivity," that is accuracy and truth. The bourgeois philosophers were concerned to change the world, they believed human nature could be improved. "Remove the old tyrannies, basic human nature would emerge. Rational self interest would do the rest." After Marx and Darwin, we can see that this view of human nature is wrong. Against the bourgeois philosophers, Marx had maintained that to achieve the New Earth it was necessary to change human nature. "It was going to be necessary once again to rationalise social organisation, and especially the social means of production." Capitalism is institutionalised selfishness. "The overthrow of capitalism is a necessary condition of human survival." So "shall we side with the philosophers or the bourgeoisie, with reason or authority?" (pp. 11-13). Further on (p. 25) Medlin makes an important statement. Tolerable social order cannot be achieved without repression. "Successful revolution has to deal with both internal subversion and hostility from without. The fundamental problem for the next kind of revolution will be to find, for the first time, ways of defeating that original force, and subsequently those internal and external dangers, with a revolutionary repression; and defeating them while yet establishing and preserving freedoms even more extensive than those of the most liberal capitalist democracies. Solving this problem will include preventing those who exercise the repression from constituting themselves as a new exploiting class." Medlin calls this problem "the fundamental political paradox of the age." He adds,

> I don't know how to solve it and neither do you. This shouldn't surprise us, since Lenin couldn't solve it either. Don't say it can't be solved, because the solution to this fundamental paradox is a necessary condition for human survival.

Brian ends his argument (p. 43) upon a somewhat less exacting note.

> Finally I hope I haven't given you the impression that we are likely to achieve a human life without aggression, selfishness, greed, stupidity, irrationality. That would not <u>be</u> a human life. We live by standards, moral, aesthetic and intellectual. This is not a casual matter. Standards are <u>needed</u> because we frequently fall short of them. That is what it is to be moral rational animals. … The enterprise before us is not to achieve heaven on earth. Yet it would be daft indeed to let the unattainability of heaven condemn us to our present hell. The question is not whether we can eliminate our vices. The question is whether our virtues will allow us to survive by carrying us into a better world.

Medlin's outcry concerns something of the greatest importance, the most profound and important problem which confronts the planet: a problem wherein we are to find ourselves together, all in danger together, upon this absolutely lovely island. The matter is indeed "cosmic," and many of those who are aware of it may turn away dazed and in a quiet despair: "Not in our time, thank heavens!" Here we must bless those brilliant scientists who are visibly and passionately and actively concerned. But, as Medlin points out, these scientists should have behind them the <u>force</u> of an immense informed and concerned laity. There are, in this miserable world, innumerable good causes which citizens, salving their consciousness, support financially at intervals. There are Green Parties and special anxieties about flora and fauna. All this is good. We are awakening. But perhaps too late? What is particular in this "appeal" is its generalised urgency and the hugeness of its theme. Also, let not the unattainability of heaven condemn us to hell, and let us not mope over our vices but cultivate our virtues and make them flourishing and strong! How this is to happen involves individuals and their governments, political science as well as cosmic science, understanding, expertise and <u>will</u>.

Brian links these urgent necessities with radical (revolutionary) reforms of our "modes of production," our modes of government, our modes of being. No doubt "radical reforms" are always necessary and of first importance, and provide the subject matter of political activity. However Brian envisages some more complete removal. Do the "advanced countries," Europe, America, Australia etc., possess the <u>best available</u> forms of government? Is the answer a reluctant yes, or an angry no? Medlin has indeed clearly pointed out the extreme difficulties of this "next kind of revolution" which is to be discovered "for the first time." Indeed his description may also serve as a warning against promoting <u>any</u> revolution. Surely we are fortunate to have reached the (imperfect) stage of the liberal democracy. Medlin admits that his dilemma (the creation of a successful revolution, overcoming the difficulties mentioned and preserving freedoms "more extensive than those of the liberal capitalist democracies') is "the fundamental paradox of the age"—and that neither he nor we can solve it, even Lenin couldn't. (Indeed the case of Lenin is edifying: the "ideal state" that turns rapidly into a tyranny.)

Though Brian denies that it is "old-fashioned," I would think that the word "bourgeois" is not helpful here, it is too ambiguous and over-loaded. The pejorative term "capitalist" might be similarly accused. These words in these senses suggest a Marxist terminology. Of course there are good "neo-Marxists," Adorno was one, perhaps Brian would not mind the term, and possibly early Marx was one too. The virtues of Marxism were born when Marx and Engels surveyed the poor of Manchester. The nature of society and the concept of a state have changed too since Dickens attacked the class system. We still have with us the horrors of poverty, the rich and the poor. Our liberal elected governments <u>try</u> to remove unemployment and poverty, they tax the rich and aid the poor, they tinker with "modes of production," assisted by the newly powerful science of economics, and all this is <u>imperfect</u>, and a <u>muddle</u>. There cannot be ideal Utopian states, the diversity of mankind forbids it, but there can be decent states where there is freedom and justice and tolerance and continuous <u>attempts</u> to look after the citizens and give them happy lives! In spite of all urgency, and all disappointment, I think that the "advanced countries" should keep their improvements inside their given structures and not dream of a virtuous revolution. Apart from anything else, we have no time to try out extreme solutions. A consideration among others is that we must keep our confused and defective machinery going in order to able to help people in other parts of the planet! If we think about the political and social problems of India, we may decide that we are better employed improving our present arrangements rather than experimenting with profoundly radical change.

Brian spoke of an eventual liberation of bourgeois society from all forms of religious dogma. This seems unlikely to occur and is not necessarily to be desired. Religion appears everywhere in various forms, many of which we may view with horror. (Religious wars, religious intolerance.) On the other hand in the <u>nineteenth</u> century and later many forms of enlightenment have been supported by a religious background. Religion constantly changes in its long relationship to mankind. Theologians can now speak of a Christianity without <u>literal</u> beliefs in God or a divine Christ. We are increasingly aware of Buddhism and forms of meditation. This isn't crazy stuff, not every form of religious faith is to be <u>censured</u> as irrational and dangerous, we must find our way: perhaps dogma can be separated from religion! Here we come back to the individual whose fate is not only a political one. More dangerous, in the west, is a surrender of the mind to innumerable available forms of inane and depraved technological amusement, and to an idle hedonistic determinism which goes with it. Plato spoke of an old quarrel between philosophy and poetry. Today we have a quarrel between philosophy and "poeticised thinking" (late Heidegger, Derrida), and also between philosophy and mis-used technology.

Also, reading Medlin, we must keep in mind the early idealistic Marx, and the vision which moved him. We have to care on a large scale, there is so much to do, we have to see <u>a bad</u> society, we have to picture a good society. Returning to Schopenhauer, surely this passionate and charitable writer, with his concern for animals, should not have set love aside. Of course there are many kinds of "love," whereas "compassion" has a clearer and less ambiguous sense. But surely we are able (usually, often) to discriminate between selfish and unselfish love. Love is passion, love is intelligence. Brian tells us that

> the racists were wrong about the intelligence of materially primitive peoples such as the Australian aboriginals (*sic*). It required just as much intelligence to live the life of a tribal Australian before white settlement as it did to live that of an English gentleman. ... Just sit down on an old aboriginal campsite in the Strzelecki Desert, surrounded only by those artefacts to be found there, and work out where your next feed is coming from. The result ought to be an enormous respect, even reverence, for the people who could make a living in that area so equipped. (p. 37)

Respect and reverence are also being given now, late in the day, to the great talents of Aboriginal painters, whose brilliantly beautiful and movingly spiritual paintings now adorn the homes and galleries of "civilised" and "advanced" countries. "Marxism" sounds out-of-date, perhaps "religion" and "God" may begin to sound out of date; but one must try to understand the complex realities which these terms stand for. Many people who now cannot "take" a literal Christ and God, may passionately desire to "keep" what these huge icons mean and stand for. Many believers, including clergy, are taking this, often difficult, path. The case of Marxism is difficult too since "Marxist states" have, in intelligible ways, proved so unforgivably tyrannical in practice, and people will not return to the dreams of early Marxism. Yet a portion of that idealism may be preserved and retained as some piece of precious truth. Help the poor, attempt to remove poverty, forget self, understand the ills of the world and tend them. Surely this has a familiar ring. Are there not dedicated left-wing priests and not only in South America, are there not men and women of all religions or none, and not only in India, who choose poverty themselves to be a support to others? Poverty must be fought with, and this too depends upon the fight to preserve the whole planet. We should not imagine Utopian states, existing democratic states cannot be perfect, and should not try to be. What is valuable is an omnipresence of sympathy and caring, an attention to those who constantly remind us of the grief and evil which haunt all human societies, including our half-way "decent" ones. We can change these things, we can change ourselves—this admonition and this hope was what led many young people into Marxism when I was young. We thought then in terms of extremes, and in this respect we were mistaken. Revolutions will not improve liberal states. The cause of democracy in undemocratic states should be pursued peacefully if possible: we must hope that the United Nations, or whatever something like it will (if it exists) be called in the next century, may increase in wisdom as well as in power. Of this the twentieth century has produced the merest (yet hopeful) beginnings. What will our poor ailing planet be like in the next century?

Brian Medlin is a poet as well as a philosopher. He is also a prophet crying out to his people. Prophets are needed. We have to change ourselves if we are to change the world. Time passes and we must think about the ecological disaster which is by now increasingly visible.

Iris Murdoch

ENDNOTES

[1] *The Fire and the Sun: Why Plato Banished the Artists* was published in July 1977 by Oxford University Press. This book was based on the Romanes lecture given at Oxford University on 13 February 1976.

[2] Murdoch's mother Irene's health started to decline in summer 1975, and she died on 30 August 1985.

[3] Medlin published about 50 poems in various magazines, mainly between the 1940s and the 1970s, and wrote stories under the pen name of Timothy Tregonning which appear never to have been published. Some of these stories are held in the Medlin Collection at Flinders University Library.

[4] Tom Collins is the pseudonym of Australian author Joseph Furphy (1843-1912), author of the novel *Such is Life*.

[5] This may be a response to an account by Medlin of the 1974 occupation of the Flinders University Registry in protest at assessment methods in the History Department. The protesters wanted to abolish exams and replace them with continuous assessment, including peer and self-assessment. See David Hilliard, *Flinders University: The First 25 Years 1966-1991* (Adelaide: Flinders University, 1991) for a summary of Medlin's time at Flinders University and an account of the occupation.

[6] *The Fire and the Sun: Why Plato Banished the Artists* was published in July 1977 by Oxford University Press.

[7] In fact Murdoch had written two political plays, *The Servants and the Snow*, produced in 1970 at the Greenwich Theatre, and *The Three Arrows* in Cambridge in 1972. Neither was a success. See Conradi's biography for a discussion of Murdoch's relationship with the theatre.

[8] *The Book and the Brotherhood* was written between March 1985 and September 1986, and published in September 1987. The philosoph may have been *Metaphysics as a Guide to Morals*, published in October 1992, based on the Gifford Lectures she gave at Edinburgh in 1982.

[9] Joh Bjelke-Petersen was the Premier of Queensland from 1968-1987. His National Party government was famous for its extreme right conservatism and corruption.

[10] Timothy Tregonning was the pen name used by Brian Medlin when writing fiction.

[11] Medlin was Professor of Philosophy at Flinders University from 1967 to 1988.

[12] i.e. Thomas Aquinas.

[13] A stobie pole is a power line pole made of two steel joists held apart by a slab of concrete in the middle.

---

[14] Steven P. Rose (born 1938) is a Professor of Biology and Neurobiology; Hilary Rose (born 1935) is a prominent British feminist sociologist of science and social policy.

[15] Geoffrey Ernest Maurice de Ste. Croix (1910-2000) was the author of *The Class Struggle in the Ancient Greek World: From the Archaic Age to the Arab Conquests* (London, Duckworth, 1981).

[16] Medlin's brother was Harry Medlin (1920-2013), a lecturer in physics at Adelaide University.

[17] *The Book and the Brotherhood* was published in September 1987. Murdoch's next novel was *The Message to the Planet*, published in October 1989.

[18] Albert Facey (1894-1982) was author of a memoir, *A Fortunate Life* (1982).

[19] The Matthews article appeared in the *Adelaide Review* February 1989 and is reproduced by permission of the current publisher of the magazine. Correspondence regarding the Barnett article is in Box 2 of the Medlin Collection.

[20] John Bray (1912-95), Adelaide poet and lawyer, Chief Justice of the South Australian Supreme Court 1967-78.

[21] "Warrigal" is an Aboriginal word for the dingo or wild dog in the Dharug language of the Aboriginal people of the region around Sydney, New South Wales. Warrigal Alf is a character in Furphy's *Such is Life*.

[22] Christopher Hill (1912-2003) was an English Marxist historian. Many of his most notable studies focused on 17th century English history.

[23] i.e. Australian Labor Party.

[24] Charles B. Martin (1924-2008), Professor of Philosophy at Calgary University, had been at the University of Adelaide from 1954-66 and University of Sydney 1966-1971 (*Independent* 2 December 2008).

[25] The cricketer Ian Chappell attended Prince Alfred College, a Methodist private school in Adelaide. St Peter's College is an Anglican private school in Adelaide.

[26] In 1860-61 Robert O'Hara Burke and William John Wills led an expedition of 19 men with the intention of crossing Australia from Melbourne in the south to the Gulf of Carpentaria in the north, a distance of around 3,250 kilometres (≈2,000 miles). At that time most of the inland of Australia had not been explored by non-indigenous people and was completely unknown to the European settlers. The south-north leg was successfully completed (except they were stopped by swampland 5 kilometres (3 miles) from the northern coastline) but owing to poor leadership and bad luck, both of the expedition's leaders died on the return journey. Altogether, seven men lost their lives, and only one man, John King, travelled the entire expedition and returned alive to Melbourne.

[27] Jacques Cousteau (1910-1997) was a famous French undersea explorer.

[28] A reference to the famous case of Azaria Chamberlain, a baby who disappeared near Uluru (formerly know as Ayers Rock) in 1980.

[29] Hugh Proby was the son of the Earl of Carysfort. He arrived from Ireland in 1851, took up and stocked Kanyaka Station, but drowned in Willochra Creek the following year. Proby's grave is a well-known landmark in the Flinders Ranges.

[30] Charles Warren Bonython (1916-2012) was a conservationist, explorer, author and chemical engineer.

[31] Edward John Eyre (1815–1901), English explorer of inland Australia, led the expedition to Mount Hopeless in 1840.

[32] The song "Four Little Johnny Cakes," which appears on a website of Australian folksongs at http://folkstream.com/index.html, includes the reference to "whalin' in the bend." On the website it claims that this song is in A.B. Paterson's *Old Bush Songs*. The Flash Sydney Shearers (see http://www.rowethmusic.com.au/Site/BTL_Six.html) contains the verse

> And when all the shearing is over,
> And the mince-balls have come to an end.
> It's then you will find those flash shearers,
> Cooking Johnnycakes down at the bend.

[33] The editors have been unable to trace this quotation.

[34] Wilfred Frank Flexmore Hudson (1913-88), Australian poet and senior English master at Scotch College for many years.

[35] Robert Green Ingersoll (1833-1899), American political leader noted for his defence of agnosticism.

[36] David Hollands, *Eagles, Hawks and Falcons of Australia* (Melbourne: Nelson, 1984).

[37] Hans Mincham wrote *The Story of the Flinders Ranges* (Adelaide: Rigby, 1964).

[38] "A Bush Christening" by A.B. "Banjo" Paterson (1964-1941) begins:

> On the outer Barcoo where the churches are few,
> And men of religion are scanty,
> On a road never cross'd 'cept by folk that are lost,
> One Michael Magee had a shanty.

[39] See Chapter 1 of Peter Conradi's biography for a more detailed account of Murdoch's family history.

[40] Presumably *The Green Knight*, published 1993 (her previous novel, *The Message to the Planet*, was published October 1989), and *Metaphysics as a Guide to Morals*, published in October 1992.

[41] Murdoch used the expression "too difficult for humans" of philosophy in her letter of 12 May 1986. It is a recurring theme in the letters.

[42] In *The Green Knight* there is a minor character, Kenneth Rathbone, an Australian who runs a pub in London.

[43] John Donne, Satire III.

[44] G.A. Wilkes wrote several books on Australian English, including *A Dictionary of Australian Colloquialisms*, which was first published in 1978 and went through 4 editions.

[45] This limerick is mentioned in a footnote Peter Conradi's *Iris Murdoch: A Life*. He quotes from her journal, 28 May 1990 [actually 1991, confirmed by Conradi by email, 18 May 2010]: "Offering from Brian Medlin: [the limerick quoted in full]. (Very cheering.)" (316n)

[46] Brian Matthews, Joost Daalder and Syd Harrex were all academics in the English Department at Flinders University at this time. Daalder was born in the Netherlands.

[47] Ben Jonson, "A Farewell to the World."

[48] d'Arenberg is a winery in McLaren Vale, South Australia.

[49] The Sheffield Shield competition is the first-class interstate cricket competition in Australia.

[50] Friedrich Ludwig Gottlob Frege (1848-1925) was a German mathematician, logician, and philosopher.

[51] i.e. Ludwig Wittgenstein. Murdoch met Wittgenstein at Cambridge in October 1947.

[52] Medlin mentions this book again in his letter of 11 November 1991 with the title "Love, Mortality and the Meaning of Life." A paper of that title was presented at a conference and a seminar in Adelaide in 1993, and a copy is in the Medlin Collection.

[53] Henry Salter (1944-2006), theatre director and actor, was a lecturer in the Drama Department at Flinders University.

[54] The editors have only been able to trace the published version of one of these six articles, "Objectivity and Ideology in the Physical and Social Sciences" (listed in the Bibliography). Typescripts of all the others except "Rationality and Ratiocination" are held in the Medlin Collection.

[55] Felix Dzerzhinsky (1877-1926) established and developed the Cheka (1917–26), the Soviet State Security force.

[56] "Thus when God forsakes us, Satan also leaves us." Thomas Browne, *Christian Morals* Section XX.

[57] From "My Mate Bill" by A.B. Paterson.

[58] Emeritus Professor J.J.C. (Jack) Smart (1920-2012), AC, Emeritus Professor of Philosophy, Monash University; Professor of Philosophy, University of Adelaide 1950-72. Medlin's (and Nerlich's) first teacher in philosophy and Hughes Professor of Philosophy, University of Adelaide. Most of Smart's very distinguished work was done in Australia. The paper discussed in the text is probably a draft and may not have been published.

[59] C.D. Broad (1887-1971), Knightsbridge Professor of Moral Philosophy at University of Cambridge. His main interests lay in epistemology, philosophy of science and ethics. The books most likely relevant to this letter are *Scientific Thought* (London: Kegan Paul, Trench Trubner & Co, 1923) and *Examination of McTaggart's Philosophy* (Cambridge: Cambridge University Press, 1933).

[60] *The Philosophy of C.D.* Broad, edited by P. A. Schilpp. The Library of Living Philosophers (New York, Tudor Publishing Company, 1959). Each volume in this

series has an autobiography and a collection of essays on the subject's work followed by a reply to critics.

[61] Peter T. Geach, (born 1916), British philosopher. His main interests were history of philosophy, philosophical logic and personal identity. Medlin cites no text but the argument he attacks probably comes from Geach's *Reason and Argument* (Blackwell, 1976).

[62] The Australian physicist Paul Davies' celebrated book *The Mind of God: The Scientific Basis for a Rational World* (Simon and Schuster) was published in 1992.

[63] These comments owe something (not everything) to the Socratic attitude to philosophy.

[64] *The Flinders Jubilee Anthology* edited by Annie Greet & Syd Harrex (Bedford Park, S.A.: Centre for Research in New Literatures in English, 1991).

[65] Prof Peter Sutton FASSA, School of Earth & Environmental Sciences, University of Adelaide & Division of Anthropology, South Australian Museum (SAM), curated the exhibition "Dreamings." It opened at the Asia Society in New York in 1988, went to Chicago, Los Angeles, Melbourne, then Adelaide (SAM) for the 1990 Festival, which is where Brian Medlin would have seen it. The accompanying book had US, Australian and UK editions but the exhibition never went to London. It must be another exhibition that Iris Murdoch saw.

[66] The Braithwaite Murdoch would have been referring to is R. [Richard] B. Braithwaite, Sidgwick Lecturer in Moral Science in the University of Cambridge from 1934 to 1953, and the Knightbridge Professor of Moral Philosophy in the University of Cambridge from 1953 to 1967. Philosopher of science and of religion. Medlin quotes John Braithwaite, "Dangerous Simplification" (*Australian Society* March 1991) in his article "The Critique of Reason Pure and Practical," in *On the Same Premises: Proceedings of the Second National Conference on Reasoning* (Adelaide: 1991) ed. P.D. Jewell (Bedford Park: Philosophy Department, Flinders University, 1992: 203-219).

[67] Verse and chorus from "The Springtime It Brings on the Shearing."

[68] "On February 19, 2010 Pope Benedict XVI announced that Mary MacKillop will become Australia's first saint and her canonisation will take place in Rome on Sunday 17 October, 2010." www.marymackillop.org.au

[69] Charles Sturt discovered the Darling River in February 1829.

[70] Presumably Murdoch means Roy Lichtenstein (1923–1997).

[71] Paul Keating replaced Bob Hawke as Australian Labor Party Prime Minister in December 1991.

[72] Rodney Allen, philosopher at Flinders University.

[73] i.e. the name given to this strait by Matthew Flinders, maritime explorer, when he explored the region in 1802.

[74] Flinders Ranges, South Australia.

[75] This is taken from letters written by Medlin to Graham Nerlich.

[76] Philosopher at Flinders University

[77] From Satire 3, by John Donne.

[78] Ashley Mallett, *Trumper* (London: Pan Macmillan, 1985).

[79] Extract of correspondence to Graham Nerlich ends here.

[80] Although it is true that they have suffered many tragic losses, the Kaurna People of the Adelaide Plains do in fact survive and their dreamings, culture and language have not been lost.

[81] The song "Travelling Down the Castlereagh" by A.B. (Banjo) Paterson has a chorus beginning "So it's shift, boys, shift."

[82] Murdoch's *Metaphysics as a Guide to Morals*, based on the 1982 Gifford Lectures, was published in 1992.

[83] Alan Bullock, *Hitler and Stalin: Parallel Lives* (HarperCollins, 1991).

[84] Adrian Desmond and James Moore, *Darwin* (London: Michael Joseph, 1991).

[85] Steele Rudd (1868-1935), satirical Australian author famous for *On Our Selection.*

[86] Harold Nicolson, *Tennyson: Aspects of His Life, Character and Poetry* (Constable, 1925).

[87] The full text of Murdoch's review is included at the end of this book.

[88] On 13 March 1993, the Australian Labor Party, who had been in government since 1983, won the federal election.

[89] Christine Vick published a short essay on her Wirra in *Treasure* (Prospect, S. Aust.: Prospect Gallery, 1993).

[90] In *Treasure*, published by the Prospect Gallery, Medlin included an account of an admirer who visited him at Flinders University and presented him with a statuette symbolising Truth.

SELECT BIBLIOGRAPHY

Brian Medlin

Published works by Medlin

"The Contingency Argument," *Sophia* 5, no. 3 (1966): pp. 17-34.

Human Nature, Human Survival (Adelaide: Flinders University, 1992).

"Objectivity and Ideology in the Physical and Social Sciences". In *Cause, Mind, and Reality: Essays Honoring C.B. Martin*, edited by John Heil, 201-220. Norwell: Kluwer, 1989.

"The Origin of Motion", *Mind* 72, no. 286 (1963): pp. 155-175.

"The Theory of Truth-Functions," [2-part article] *Australasian Journal of Philosophy* 42, no. 1 (1964): pp. 1-21; 42, no. 2, pp. 183-198.

"Ultimate Principles and Ethical Egoism." *Australasian Journal of Philosophy* 35, no. 2 (1957): pp. 111-118.

"The Unexpected Examination." *American Philosophical Quarterly* 1 (January 1964): pp. 66-72.

Medlin, B.H. and Smart, J.J.C. "Moore's Paradox: Synonymous Expressions and Defining." Analysis 17 (June 1957): pp. 125-134.

Two essays by Christine Vick and Brian Medlin appear in *Treasure* (Prospect, S. Aust.: Prospect Gallery, 1993).

Poems published in Meanjin 11, no. 4 (1952); 12, no. 1 (1953); 13, no. 1 (1954); 13, no. 3 (1954); 13, no. 4 (1954); 13, no. 3 (1954); 15, no. 1 (1956); 15, no. 4 (1956); 16, no. 1 (1957); 16, no. 3 (1957); 28, no. 1 (1969).

Biographical

Schumann, John. "Brian Herbert Medlin BA (Adel): BPhil MA (Oxon), Professor of Philosophy, Flinders University 1967-1988 (Emeritus 1988). 10/12/1927 to 28/10/2004." [Obituary] Online. http://www.schumann.com.au/john/articles/brian_medlin_obit.pdf

—. "Inaugural Brian Medlin Memorial Lecture July 8th, 2006." Online. http://www.schumann.com.au/john/articles/brian_medlin_memorial.pdf

Archives

Brian Medlin Collection, Special Collections, Flinders University Library. http://library.flinders.edu.au/resources/collection/special/medlin/

Iris Murdoch

Novels (in chronological order)

Under the Net. London: Chatto & Windus, 1954.
The Flight from the Enchanter. London: Chatto & Windus, 1956.
The Sandcastle. London: Chatto & Windus, 1957.
The Bell. Harmondsworth: Penguin Books in association with Chatto & Windus, 1986. (First published London: Chatto & Windus, 1958.)
A Severed Head. London: Chatto & Windus, 1961.
An Unofficial Rose. London: Chatto & Windus, 1962.
The Unicorn. London: Chatto & Windus, 1963.
The Italian Girl. London: Chatto & Windus, 1964.
The Red and The Green. London: Chatto & Windus, 1965.
The Time of the Angels. London: Chatto & Windus, 1966.
The Nice and The Good. London: Chatto & Windus, 1968.
Bruno's Dream. London: Chatto & Windus, 1969.
A Fairly Honourable Defeat. London: Chatto & Windus, 1970.
An Accidental Man. London: Chatto & Windus, 1971.
The Black Prince. London: Chatto & Windus, 1973.
The Sacred and Profane Love Machine. London: Chatto & Windus, 1974.
A Word Child. London: Chatto & Windus, 1975.
Henry and Cato. London: Chatto & Windus, 1976.
The Sea, The Sea. London: Chatto & Windus, 1978.
Nuns and Soldiers. London: Chatto & Windus, 1980.
The Philosopher's Pupil. London: Chatto & Windus 1983.
The Good Apprentice. London: Chatto & Windus, 1985.
The Book and The Brotherhood. London: Chatto & Windus, 1987.
The Message to the Planet. London: Chatto & Windus, 1989.
The Green Knight. London: Chatto & Windus, 1993.
Jackson's Dilemma. London: Chatto & Windus, 1995.

Poetry and Plays

A Severed Head (with JB Priestly). London: Samuel French, 1964.

The Three Arrows with *The Servants and the Snow*. London: Chatto & Windus, 1973.

A Year of Birds with wood engravings by Reynolds Stone. London: Chatto & Windus, 1984.

Joanna, Joanna. London: Colophon Press with Old Town Books, 1994.

The One Alone. London: Colophon Press with Old Town Books, 1995.

Poems by Iris Murdoch. Ed. Yozo Muroya and Paul Hullah. Japan: University Education Press, 1997.

Philosophical and non-fiction works

Acastos: Two Platonic Dialogues. London: Chatto & Windus, 1986.

The Fire and The Sun: Why Plato Banished the Artists. London: Oxford University Press, 1977.

Existentialists and Mystics: Writings on Philosophy and Literature edited by Peter Conradi. London: Chatto & Windus, 1997.

Sartre: Romantic Rationalist. London: Bowes & Bowes, 1953.

The Sovereignty of Good. London: Chatto & Windus, 1970.

Letters and interviews

Conradi, Peter J. ed. *Iris Murdoch: A Writer at War - Letters & Diaries 1939-1945*. London: Short Books, 2010.

Dooley, Gillian, ed. *From a Tiny Corner in the House of Fiction: Conversations with Iris Murdoch*. Columbia: University of South Carolina Press, 2003.

Morgan, David. *With Love and Rage: A Friendship with Iris Murdoch*. Kingston: Kingston University Press, 2010.

Biographical and bibliographical

Bayley, John. *Iris: A Memoir of Iris Murdoch*. London: Duckworth, 1998.

—. *Iris and the Friends: A Year of Memories*. London: Duckworth, 1999.

Conradi, Peter. *Iris Murdoch: A Life - The Authorized Biography*. London: Harper Collins, 2001.

Fletcher, John and Cheryl Bove. *A Descriptive Primary and Annotated Secondary Bibliography*. New York and London: Garland, 1994.

Martin, Priscilla and Anne Rowe. *Iris Murdoch: A Literary Life*. Basingstoke: Palgrave Macmillan, 2010.

Purton, Valerie. *An Iris Murdoch Chronology*. Basingstoke: Palgrave Macmillan, 2007.

Archives

The Iris Murdoch Collection, Kingston University, London.
    http://fass.kingston.ac.uk/research/iris-murdoch/collections/
Iris Murdoch Papers, Special Collections, University of Iowa Library.
    http://collguides.lib.uiowa.edu/?MSC0212

INDEX